Understanding
Personal, Social, Health *and*
Economic Education *in* **Secondary Schools**

SAGE was founded in 1965 by Sara Miller McCune to support the dissemination of usable knowledge by publishing innovative and high-quality research and teaching content. Today, we publish over 900 journals, including those of more than 400 learned societies, more than 800 new books per year, and a growing range of library products including archives, data, case studies, reports, and video. SAGE remains majority-owned by our founder, and after Sara's lifetime will become owned by a charitable trust that secures our continued independence.

Los Angeles | London | New Delhi | Singapore | Washington DC | Melbourne

Understanding
Personal, Social, Health *and* Economic Education *in* Secondary Schools

Jenny McWhirter | Nick Boddington | Jenny Barksfield

Los Angeles | London | New Delhi
Singapore | Washington DC | Melbourne

Los Angeles | London | New Delhi
Singapore | Washington DC | Melbourne

SAGE Publications Ltd
1 Oliver's Yard
55 City Road
London EC1Y 1SP

SAGE Publications Inc.
2455 Teller Road
Thousand Oaks, California 91320

SAGE Publications India Pvt Ltd
B 1/I 1 Mohan Cooperative Industrial Area
Mathura Road
New Delhi 110 044

SAGE Publications Asia-Pacific Pte Ltd
3 Church Street
#10-04 Samsung Hub
Singapore 049483

Editor: James Clark
Editorial assistant: Robert Patterson
Production editor: Tom Bedford
Copyeditor: Solveig Gardner Servian
Indexer: Silvia Benvenuto
Marketing manager: Lorna Patkai
Cover design: Naomi Robinson
Typeset by: C&M Digitals (P) Ltd, Chennai, India
Printed and bound by CPI Group (UK) Ltd,
Croydon, CR0 4YY

Library of Congress Control Number: 2016933252

British Library Cataloguing in Publication data

A catalogue record for this book is available from
the British Library

ISBN 978-1-4739-1362-2
ISBN 978-1-4739-1363-9 (pbk)

At SAGE we take sustainability seriously. Most of our products are printed in the UK using FSC papers and boards.
When we print overseas we ensure sustainable papers are used as measured by the PREPS grading system.
We undertake an annual audit to monitor our sustainability.

This book is dedicated to all the young people with
whom we have worked over the years, and especially to those
with whom we have shared our lives: Alison, Andrew, Sammie,
Tom, Charlotte, Laura, Conrad, Séamus, Greg and Kieran.

It is also dedicated to Alastair McWhirter, Karen Boddington and
Gerry Czerniawski, with our love and thanks for their unfailing support.

Contents

About the Authors

Jenny McWhirter is a freelance researcher and writer who became interested in young people's health and wellbeing when working as a part time youth worker in the 1980s. As a lecturer at Southampton University and then as education adviser for drug education and accident prevention charities she has developed curriculum resources and evaluated the effectiveness of PSHE education in primary and secondary schools. Recently Jenny has turned her interests to effective interventions for families where parental drug and alcohol misuse causes harm to children and young people.

Nick Boddington started his career as an art and mathematics teacher working in both primary and secondary schools in north London, then joined the Advisory Service where he specialised in the teaching of sensitive issues including SRE, HIV, anti-bullying and drug education. One of the first Ofsted Inspectors to be trained, he left the Advisory Service as Lead Senior Adviser for Children's Wellbeing for Essex Local Authority before taking up his current position as Subject Adviser with the national PSHE Association. Nick is committed to a model of PSHE education that places young people's individual and unique understanding of their world and their own enquiry at the centre of learning. He is co-author of a number of government documents, academic texts and teaching resources committed to improving the quality of PSHE education. Nick has spent nearly 30 years championing the importance of placing high-quality PSHE education at the centre of the school curriculum.

Jenny Barksfield started her working life as a nurse before deciding on a different path and qualifying as a teacher of modern foreign languages. A defining career moment came when she was asked to cover a PSHE education lesson at the end of which a student remarked, 'You make a much better PSHE teacher than French teacher, Miss'. He was right: Jenny had found her passion and from that moment she dedicated her teaching career to developing high-quality PSHE education in the schools where she worked, including ten years as Head of PSHE education in a large state secondary school, and since 2009 through her roles as Training and Development Lead and now Senior Subject Specialist and Deputy CEO at The PSHE Association.

Acknowledgements

Our thanks to: Andrew Brown, Public Health England; Mark Bowles, The Training Effect; Dr Pooky Knightsmith; Anne Clare; Parama Chakravorty; Robert Bickers; Katie Gurney; Adrian King; staff and students of St Martin's School, Essex; Newent Community School and Sixth Form Centre, Gloucester; Hurworth School, Darlington.

Also, our thanks to the following organisations: The Association for Young People's Health; The PSHE Association and The Royal Society for the Prevention of Accidents.

Finally, we would like to thank the editorial staff at SAGE Publications for their advice, guidance and support.

1

Introduction

Aim

To introduce personal, social, health and economic (PSHE) education.

Learning objectives

Through reading and reflecting on the content of this chapter you will begin to:

- understand PSHE education and how it relates to the other aspects of secondary education
- recognise the contribution PSHE education makes to young people's personal development
- have an opportunity to reflect on your personal experience of PSHE education to date and consider how you can develop as an effective practitioner

Introduction

This book has been written for beginning teachers in secondary schools; that is, student teachers and those who qualified recently and are embarking on their career as teachers of 11–18 year olds.

It aims to give you a general grounding in the theory underpinning Personal, Social, Health and Economic (PSHE) education, some practical approaches, and the evidence which supports these approaches drawn from a wide range of disciplines such as developmental psychology, anthropology, sociology and neuroscience. As well as learning about adolescent development (Chapter 2), you will find some chapters that deal specifically with effective approaches to teaching, learning and assessment in PSHE education (Chapter 3–6), and other chapters that deal with specific topics for which you may not feel adequately prepared – and which are sometimes called 'sensitive issues', such as mental and emotional health (Chapter 8) drug education (Chapter 9) and relationships and sex education (Chapter 10), but also risk education (Chapter 7) and economic education (Chapter 11). Each chapter will encourage you to think about the evidence in terms of effective practice in the classroom and provide examples from schools and classrooms to help you to reflect on what you observe and do in *your* classroom.

As you embark on your professional career as a secondary school teacher you will have good knowledge in your chosen subject(s). You will have completed degree level study and may have postgraduate qualifications and be working towards or have recently completed teaching qualifications. You may also have relevant professional or vocational experience acquired before or after qualification which you bring to your specific subject. In addition you may be a parent with children of your own or be part of a family where there are younger siblings still at school. You will draw on all of this as you become an effective teacher of PSHE education.

Alongside your formal teaching role, you will also find yourself with responsibility for the welfare and safety of young people both as a subject teacher and probably also as a form tutor. Both will provide you with a great deal of fulfilment and satisfaction, as well as a range of challenges! With more senior colleagues, you will also share the responsibility for the pastoral care of students. We will explore the overlap between this and PSHE education in Chapters 12 and 13.

Through your teacher education you will already have some understanding of how young people develop, and some of the different ways they learn. You will develop teaching skills and strategies to maximise the learning for young people. Importantly you will learn how to assess their learning needs and plan for their next steps. This book will help you understand how PSHE education fits into all this. It will help you to see the vital role PSHE education plays in the personal and social development of the young people you teach.

Getting started

We believe PSHE education is an exciting and challenging part of the curriculum in secondary schools. It may be that your training has not included a great deal about PSHE education so far and your own experience at school will colour your expectations. Try to keep an open mind and use this book to hold up a mirror to the wide range of practice you will encounter in the different schools with which you will be involved in your first years as a teacher.

A word about terminology

In this book we refer to 11–18 year olds as 'young people' or as 'adolescents'. Chapter 2 will explore what it is to be an adolescent – and what that means for PSHE education. By referring to 'young people' rather than pupils or students, we hope to emphasise that while we have responsibility for their learning, young people are entitled to expect us to respect their rights and needs as individuals.

You will also find that PSHE education has different titles in different schools and even sometimes different titles in different year groups in the same school. So you may be teaching 'Lifeskills' or PSD (Personal and Social Development) or PESHE (Personal, Economic, Social and Health Education) or PSHCE education (combining PSHE education and citizenship within the same programme) or recently 'character education'.

It is increasingly common to refer to sex and relationships education (SRE) as relationships and sex education (RSE), to reflect the emphasis on relationships rather than purely the biological process of sex. We prefer and have used RSE in this book unless referring to another source.

Character education

At the time of writing 'character education' (or education for the development of personal 'characteristics' or 'traits') is receiving a great deal of attention, led by the Department for Education (DfE) and some academy chain and independent school leaders and academics. While being clear that there should be no one single definition of character and encouraging schools to take their own approaches, the DfE has described character as a set of traits, attributes and behaviours such as: perseverance, resilience and grit; confidence and optimism; motivation, drive and ambition; neighbourliness and community spirit; tolerance and respect; honesty, integrity and dignity; conscientiousness, curiosity and focus (Department for Education, 2015).

There are clearly some overlaps between the aims of character education and those of PSHE education, but currently there is a great deal of evidence for what works in PSHE education and very little clarity about what character education is or does. Just as with PSHE education, it is not just what young people are taught in the classroom but the sum of their experiences at school that contributes to the development of traits such as resilience, critical thinking, autonomy and perseverance. However, where PSHE education differs from many character education programmes is that PSHE education does not seek to define how young people should feel, what choices young people should make or even what they 'need to decide'.

We would argue that PSHE education, taught in line with the evidence for effective practice, focussing on the development of skills and personal attributes through different contexts of knowledge and understanding, is all 'character education' – and a lot more.

So what is PSHE education?

PSHE education is a planned programme of learning through which children and young people acquire the knowledge, understanding and skills they need to manage their lives now and in the future. As part of a whole school approach, PSHE education develops the qualities and attributes pupils need to thrive as individuals, family members and members of society.' (PSHE Association, 2016)

Taking a closer look at these statements we can see that the PSHE Association sees young people as learners but that their education is – and should be – *personal*. For a beginning teacher this can seem one of the most daunting aspects of the subject. You may wonder if this means you are expected to take on the personal issues for every young person in the class. How do you keep your own personal views about such issues as drugs or sexual relationships separate from your responsibility as a teacher?

What do parents expect of a curriculum that is intended to develop personal understanding, attitudes and skills?

What 'personal' means in the context of PSHE education is 'relevance to the *person*'. Starting from where young people are (see Chapter 5), you can make the most sensitive issues appropriate and relevant to the young people you are teaching this year – who will, of course, be different from the young people you will teach next year and every year hereafter! 'Personal' also emphasises the importance of identity to young people and their health and wellbeing. Learning to know oneself is an important psychological task, beginning in childhood and continuing throughout adolescence and on into adult life (see Chapter 2). Young people of secondary school age will undergo one of the most amazing physical, intellectual and social transformations of their lives – and you will have the privilege of helping to guide and shape that transformation, alongside many other influences, not all of which are benign.

PSHE education also supports young people in developing *intrapersonal* skills and attributes so that they are resilient in the face of adversity, can manage change and develop a realistic sense of their own worth and capability.

Key intrapersonal skills developed through PSHE education include:

1. Critical, constructive self-reflection (including being aware of own needs, motivations and learning, strengths and next steps for development, how we are influenced by our perception of peers' behaviour).
2. Learning from experience to seek out and make use of constructive feedback.
3. Setting challenging personal goals (including developing strategies to achieve them and knowing when to change them).
4. Making decisions (including knowing when to be flexible).
5. Recognising some of the common ways our brains can 'trick us' or 'trap us' in unhelpful thinking (including generalisation, distortion of events, deletion of information, misconceptions or misperceptions about the behaviour of peers).
6. The skills that contribute to resilience (including self-motivation, adaptability, constructively managing change including reframing setbacks and managing stress).
7. Self-regulation (including managing strong emotions, e.g. negativity and impulse).
8. Recognising and managing the need for peer approval.
9. Self-organisation (including time management).

And finally, 'personal' means drawing on the young people's existing knowledge and experience so that they can relate what they are learning in the classroom to their real lives, real families and real communities. One of the most important parts of any PSHE education lesson is that space, usually towards the end, where young people have the opportunity to reflect on what they have learned to do or say, perhaps as part of a group activity, and to think about what it means to them 'personally', as individuals.

PSHE education is also *social*. This means it is fundamentally about relationships, whether with friends and staff at school or with family members. Relationships between people underpin every aspect of our lives, for good and bad. Some relationships can always be relied upon to be strong and nurturing, some may be fun but brief, and others, sadly, may have the potential to damage a young person's health and wellbeing. Peer relationships are hugely important in adolescence, but not to the exclusion of all others, as we shall see in Chapter 2. The relationships young people develop with their peers during secondary school may last a lifetime; they may get young people into trouble through excessive risk taking or be a real source of support and encouragement in difficult circumstances. The attitudes, understanding and *inter-personal* skills young people can develop through effective PSHE education will help them to enjoy the best and deal with the worst of life's challenges and include:

1. Active listening.
2. Empathy.
3. Communication (non-verbal and verbal including assertiveness and recognising how this differs from aggressive and passive behaviour; being able to present and communicate ideas, arguments and thoughts effectively).
4. Team working (including agreeing clear and challenging outcomes, facilitation, co-operation, networking and the ability to provide, receive and respond to, constructive feedback and take on different roles; the ability to recognise and learn from others' experience).
5. Negotiation (including flexibility, self-advocacy and compromise).
6. Recognising and utilising strategies for managing pressure, persuasion and coercion.
7. Responding to the need for positive affirmation for self and others.

The skills young people develop in PSHE education can also prepare them for the relationships they will make in the adult world, including the workplace. Where else in the curriculum do young people learn to negotiate, cooperate and take responsibility for their own decisions? These so-called 'soft skills' are as much sought after by employers as the academic qualifications required for the job.

Walmsley (2011) stated in her support for statutory PSHE education:

> There are many young people who do not get from their home environment communication skills, problem-solving, punctuality, perseverance, conscientiousness, the ability to work in a team, social and emotional maturity, drive and energy, initiative, ability to adapt to change, the skills needed to learn new things et cetera – all the things that make a successful employee. It is important for those young people that schools and colleges provide opportunities to develop all those.

The 'soft skills' or those that are uniquely human are among the least likely to be replaced by the rise of 'artificial intelligence' in the workplace. The UK Commission for Employment and Skills (2014) identified the key skills and attributes that will be at a premium in future, including:

> resilience, adaptability, resourcefulness, enterprise, cognitive skills (such as problem solving), and the core business skills for project based employment.

Health provides some of the most complex and interesting content for PSHE education. Of course, there are strong cross-curricular links here with the biological aspects of physical education (PE) and the science curriculum. There are also strong associations with wellbeing, so we find that in PSHE education *health* is about much more than biology. What can be more relevant to a young person than how their body and sense of identity are growing and changing (or not growing and changing as fast as their friend's body), what is happening on the inside that no one can see and why that growth and change affects how they feel about themself and their relationships?

This is a good moment to ask 'What is health?'. For some young people, health is simply the absence of disease, for others it is about achieving their full potential, whatever their physical, mental, social and emotional capabilities and limitations might be. There are clearly many factors that contribute to a person being healthy: biological, environmental, mental and emotional, as well as social and financial.

Life expectancy in the UK

Young people in secondary schools in the UK in 2016 have an average life expectancy of around 80 years, depending on their gender and where they were born. This is an increase of approximately 10 years when compared with children born in the 1950s and life expectancy in the UK continues to increase (ONS, 2013a, 2015a). It is predicted that one-third of babies born in 2013 will live until they are 100 years old (ONS, 2013b). The reasons behind this are threefold: a lower prevalence of smoking; better medical interventions; a healthier lifestyle than previous generations enjoyed. However, recent data has shown that in the UK where you are born can make a big difference, not only to life expectancy but also to the number of years people can expect to be healthy (ONS, 2015a). Across society as a whole factors such as: poverty, disability, social class and access to the best of health care all contribute to real health inequalities.

Together, these are some of the many challenges which PSHE education should help young people to explore and, perhaps, overcome.

Economic education is a relative newcomer to PSHE practitioners and has clear links with the maths curriculum among others. A separate programme of study for 'Economic wellbeing and financial capability' was incorporated into the National Curriculum non-statutory programmes of study for PSHE education in 2007. The revised National Curriculum of 2013 saw personal finance education included in elements of both the maths and citizenship programmes of study, despite PSHE education retaining the final 'E' for 'Economic wellbeing'.

You may ask why 'economic education' is still included in PSHE education and not just in maths and citizenship. If you think about it, the link with wellbeing is just as great as it is with relationships and sex education. How do you feel just before you check your bank account balance online? Or when you get an unexpected gift of money? PSHE education can help young people to understand that the decisions we make about our personal finances are linked to our feelings – and our identities as risk takers – as well as (perhaps more than!) our capability in arithmetic.

A 'joined up' approach in which PSHE education, citizenship and mathematics departments work together to plan a comprehensive programme for personal finance education and economic wellbeing can harness young people's enthusiasm for learning about money and what money means in their lives which goes beyond arithmetical knowledge and understanding.

And finally – *education*. The word 'educate' comes from the Latin *educo*, meaning 'I lead forth' or 'I raise up'. From this you can see that while education is the means by which knowledge, skills, culture and values are passed from one generation to another, it is not a passive process. It has often been said that young people do not come to school 'tabula rasa' or as empty vessels to be filled with knowledge. Just as young people are not empty vessels, they are also not sponges – they do not simply absorb information, but make sense of it in relation to what they already know and understand – and by the age of 11 they are more than ready to challenge what adults tell them.

After all, what do we know? They have always known the internet, are familiar with Google and social media apps on phones and tablets, while some of their teachers were born before the mobile phone was invented. By the time young people arrive at secondary school they have 11 (or more) years of experience on which to base their understanding of the world.

The good news is that everything you are learning about education, about young people's cognitive and emotional development, everything you discover about how young people learn and how to teach and assess their learning applies to PSHE education. However, there are some approaches to teaching and learning that are particularly important in PSHE education, which you may not use as frequently in other aspects of the curriculum. This will be explored in more depth, especially in Chapters 3, 5 and 6.

It is also important to recognise that *education* is happening all the time, not just in lessons, but in assemblies, on the playing fields, in the corridor waiting to go into a lesson – and on the way to and from school. Neither do schools have the privileged status with regard to education in its broadest sense. Young people are being educated informally in the family, through the media – especially social media – and in the wider community. As the definition of PSHE education above tells us, PSHE education may simply be the only *planned* part of school life where young people can, with your help, make sense of the many influences and experiences they are living through.

Are schools in England required to teach PSHE education?

PSHE education (apart from some aspects of sex and relationships education) is not a statutory subject in the national curriculum for English schools. However, at the time of writing, the National Curriculum for England states that 'All schools should make provision for personal, social, health and economic education (PSHE), drawing on good practice' (Department for Education, 2014). There has been a longstanding debate about the status of PSHE education in schools in England. In 2015 the House of Commons Education Committee's report 'Life lessons: PSHE and SRE in schools' called for PSHE education to be compulsory in all primary and secondary schools. Responding to the report in February 2016, the Education Secretary Nicky Morgan stated that 'PSHE is a crucial part of preparing young people for life' but rejected the recommendation to make it a statutory subject in England. PSHE education (or its equivalent) is required in schools in Northern Ireland, Scotland and Wales.

In addition, all schools in England are statutorily required to publish details of their curriculum, including their PSHE education provision, on their school website, regardless of their status as maintained schools, free schools or academies.

Why do most schools include PSHE education in their curriculum?

PSHE education makes a major contribution to schools' statutory responsibilities to provide a curriculum that is broadly based, balanced and meets the needs of all pupils. Under section 78 of the Education Act 2002 and the Academies Act 2010 such a curriculum must:

> promote the spiritual, moral, cultural, mental and physical development of pupils at the school and of society, and prepare pupils at the school for the opportunities, responsibilities and experiences of later life.

Maintained schools also have statutory duties to:

> promote children and young people's wellbeing (Wellbeing is defined in the Children Act 2004 as the promotion of physical and mental health; emotional wellbeing; social and economic wellbeing; education, training and recreation; recognition of the contribution made by children to society; and protection from harm and neglect.)

> And promote community cohesion (Education and Inspections Act 2006; Education Act 2002)

Furthermore, the Ofsted inspection framework for whole-school section 5 inspections (at the time of writing) requires inspectors to make judgements on, amongst other things, the personal development, behaviour and welfare of pupils; the arrangements for safeguarding, including how pupils are taught to keep themselves and others safe; the breadth and balance of the curriculum; and the spiritual, moral, social and cultural development of pupils. This inevitably means that whilst there is no explicit requirement to inspect PSHE education provision, an effective PSHE education programme will provide invaluable evidence for each of these judgements. In 2013 Ofsted produced a descriptor to help inspectors recognise outstanding teaching in PSHE education:

> Teachers demonstrate very high levels of confidence and expertise in their specialist knowledge and in their understanding of effective learning in PSHE. Clear learning objectives are complemented by explicit and appropriate learning outcomes. Teachers use a very wide range of imaginative resources and strategies to stimulate pupils' interest and active participation and, as a result, secure rapid and sustained progress. Highly effective and responsive teaching ensures the needs of all pupils, including the most able are met. Teachers are confident and skilled in discussing sensitive and/or controversial issues. Effective discussion is a very strong feature; pupils are encouraged to investigate, express opinions and listen to others. Consequently they develop excellent critical skills, can evaluate information well and make informed judgments. Teachers communicate very high expectations, enthusiasm and passion for PSHE. They know how well their pupils are achieving, build on their previous knowledge and provide effective feedback to help them to improve further. They ensure that pupils have their attainment and progress recognised across all aspects of knowledge and skills development in PSHE.

Statutory duties and school inspection aside, schools recognise a number of other benefits from providing PSHE education. PSHE education is not only the easiest and most effective way to support their young people's physical, emotional and social health (as well as the development of essential employability skills), but there are benefits also in terms of academic success. PSHE education has the potential to reduce or remove barriers to learning, such as bullying, low self-esteem, and unhealthy or risky behaviours, whilst also developing attributes that equip young people to succeed academically, as well as in other aspects of their lives. In recent years a number of different outcomes associated with PSHE education have been linked to academic success. In its 2012 report for the Department for Education, the Childhood Wellbeing Research Centre found that 'children who have higher levels of emotional, behavioural, social, and school wellbeing tend to have higher levels of academic achievement and school engagement both concurrently and at a later point in time'. In 2014 Public

Health England stated that 'pupils with better health and wellbeing are likely to achieve better academically' and 'effective social and emotional competencies are associated with greater health and wellbeing, and better achievement'. It concluded that 'promoting the health and wellbeing of pupils and students within schools and colleges has the potential to improve their educational outcomes and their health and wellbeing outcomes'. In his editorial for the *British Medical Journal* in 2014, Bonell stressed that 'programmes to promote students' broader wellbeing and development also benefit their academic learning'.

Sadly, despite the huge benefits for both young people and schools that an effective PSHE education programme offers, Department for Education (2015) data suggests the amount of time schools give the subject has dropped by 21 per cent between 2011 and 2014.

The place of PSHE education in the secondary curriculum

While there is currently no National Curriculum programme for study for PSHE education, this leaves schools free to organise and prioritise their PSHE education provision to meet the needs of their young people and their school. The PSHE Association (2014) has developed a national programme of study to support schools to develop their own programme and schemes of work.

One of the key problems teachers face is that with so many critical issues that young people need to learn about, how do we avoid trying to squeeze them all into limited curriculum time and creating a 'patchwork' of unrelated topic-based lessons? These inevitably focus only on 'factual content' and were described by one secondary school student as:

> like episodes from Buffy the Vampire Slayer – each week in PSHE education they tell us about a different monster!

We do not approach subjects such as history or geography in this way. PSHE education is no different. We select appropriate topics to provide a context through which pupils gradually expand key concepts, develop positive personal attributes and develop and rehearse key transferable strategies and skills.

The national programme of study, divided into three core themes ('Health and wellbeing', 'Relationships' and 'Living in the wider world'), is based on key concepts through which to develop relevant knowledge, attributes, skills and understanding. You will find each of the concepts outlined in the box below are explored in varying depth throughout this book.

1. Identity (their personal qualities, attitudes, skills, attributes and achievements and what influences these).
2. Relationships (including different types and in different settings)
3. A healthy (including physically, emotionally and socially), balanced lifestyle (including within relationships, work-life, exercise and rest, spending and saving and diet).
4. Risk (identification, assessment and how to manage risk rather than simply the avoidance of risk for self and others) and safety (including behaviour and strategies to employ in different settings).
5. Diversity and equality (in all its forms).
6. Rights (including the notion of universal human rights), responsibilities (including fairness and justice) and consent (in different contexts).
7. Change (as something to be managed) and resilience (the skills, strategies and 'inner resources' we can draw on when faced with challenging change or circumstance).
8. Power (how it is used and encountered in a variety of contexts including persuasion, bullying, negotiation and 'win-win' outcomes).
9. Careers (including enterprise, employability and economic understanding).

What can young people be expected to achieve through PSHE education?

The aims of PSHE education are to help children and young people to develop the knowledge, understanding, attributes, attitudes and skills to keep themselves healthy and well, to manage the opportunities and challenges they face now and in the future, and to contribute to the health and wellbeing of others. Effective PSHE education facilitates learning so that young people can draw on their talents and skills, and on the resources provided by their families and communities, to achieve their full potential.

So what do we mean by effective PSHE education? We mean teaching and learning that is based on sound evidence, which has been subject to critical peer review and published in reputable journals and other academic publications. Since PSHE education aims to have health benefits then we should expect it to stand up to similar scrutiny as medical interventions.

In Chapter 3 we will review the evidence for effective practice in PSHE education, which suggests that PSHE education contributes to greater academic attainment, better mental health, increased fruit and vegetable intake, greater use of contraceptives (with no overall increase in sexual activity). It can also contribute to decreased bullying and reports of being bullied, and of drug use. These outcomes, as well as being linked to higher economic wellbeing, are also linked with reduced crime.

It is important to remember, however, that PSHE education is not the only aspect of school which impacts on these important outcomes. While PSHE education contributes to young people's personal development it is not a form of inoculation against all the excitements and difficulties of life.

What can PSHE education *not* be expected to achieve?

Despite what some demand of the subject, and the evidence summarised in the last sections, it's important to point out that the aim of PSHE education is not to determine how young people should behave or what lifestyle, career or financial choices they should make in the future. PSHE education is about the provision of knowledge and the development of skills, attitudes and attributes which enable children and young people to make effective choices and take opportunities which will help them to live happy, healthy, successful lives, now and in the future. PSHE education helps young people to develop their decision making skills; it does not set out to predetermine what those decisions should be.

Making effective choices includes enabling young people to recognise and assess the benefits and risks of their actions, and to act on their best intentions, whatever the pressures to do otherwise. This means that PSHE education is about influencing young people's attitudes and developing their skills to manage different influences and pressures, as part of their personal development.

What does PSHE education have in common with other school subjects?

As you will see, PSHE education has a body of knowledge, and is based on well known and understood theories and models for which there is good evidence. It includes a clear set of skills and competences. Like other subjects in the curriculum, PSHE education can be differentiated according to a young person's needs and abilities. It can also be assessed in a range of ways, depending on what is being taught.

How does PSHE education relate to other school subjects?

PSHE education provides the opportunity for pupils to reflect on the personal and social elements of some topics which are learned in other areas of the curriculum. For example, the effects of exercise on the body may be part of physical education, but what adolescents think and feel about the appearance of their bodies may have a bigger influence on whether they decide to take part in physical activity or not.

Similarly, the science curriculum provides opportunities to discuss the effects of tobacco on the lungs or alcohol on the liver and heart, but it is in PSHE education where young people can reflect on what this information means in their lives, what influences people to start smoking or to drink too much and how substances affect them, their friends and families and their communities. Through PSHE education, young people can also be encouraged to think about the personal, financial aspects of smoking and alcohol misuse and the alternative uses to which they can put their money.

While knowledge of health and wellbeing are essential, they are not sufficient to enable us to act on our knowledge. PSHE education also enables young people to use skills they have developed elsewhere in the curriculum, which are transferable to other aspects of their learning. For example, planning a healthy meal on a budget will draw on their arithmetical skills as much as their knowledge of healthy eating and will be strongly mediated by a range of social influences.

Importantly, PSHE education can provide an opportunity for young people to reflect on issues which do not arise as part of the formal curriculum, for example understanding themselves, their interests and needs, managing challenging relationships in and out of school, understanding their personal response to risk, and recognising the contribution they make to the wider community.

However, none of this cross-curricular enrichment happens automatically. Chapter 4 describes how some schools structure their PSHE education programmes to maximise this potential, while considering the risks of relying on other subjects to deliver PSHE education.

How is PSHE education different from the other school subjects?

PSHE education deals with real life issues which affect young people, their families and their teachers on a day-to-day basis. If taught well it engages with the social and economic realities of young people's lives, and draws on the values, experience, attitudes and emotions they bring to their education as well as their knowledge and understanding. Because of this, it is often said that PSHE education starts where young people are. (This does not mean, however, that the teacher does not need to plan where they may go from this starting point!) Chapter 5 goes into more depth about this important aspect of effective practice in PSHE education.

Some of the traditional topics within PSHE education (such as relationships and sex education, drugs and safety education) may have a moral, social or political context which is much more apparent than in other subjects such as maths or French. However, as teachers of other subjects such as English, religious education, science, geography and history, you will also have to deal with important and complex moral and political issues. What is different about PSHE education is that the moral and political is also *personal*; personal for teachers, parents and carers and also for the young people in your classes. This means that what is learnt in PSHE education can and will have an immediate application in the lives of young people. It also means that some aspects of PSHE education can be challenging as well as potentially exciting for teachers.

Importantly, PSHE also draws on a body of knowledge about behaviour (particularly health behaviour) which is not a common element of a teacher's training or professional development. We offer you some of that knowledge and understanding in Chapter 3.

Whole school approach

This may seem obvious, but PSHE education is most effective when it is part of a whole school approach. We will examine the rationale and evidence for this in Chapter 4. We will also take a closer look at the link with pastoral care and how schools offer and support therapeutic interventions in Chapter 12.

The best example of a whole school approach is the healthy schools movement. In England, the National Healthy Schools Programme enjoyed cross-government support for many years. While the national programme no longer exists, some local authorities continue to provide support for schools to become 'healthy schools' through local programmes usually funded through public health budgets.

You may find yourself on teaching practice or teaching in a school which has 'healthy school' status in one form or another. If so it will be part of a huge movement across Europe and other parts of the world to help schools focus some of their precious time and effort on creating a physical and policy environment in which healthy choices are the easy choices, for students and staff. This means that the school staff work together with students, parents and community partners to identify priorities for action which will create a healthy, safe place to work and learn. Ideally, these priorities will complement those in the local community so that those healthy choices are also easier to implement outside of school.

The alternative to a whole school approach, where what is taught about health, safety and wellbeing are in conflict with school and community policy, makes it more difficult for young people to act on what they are learning in PSHE education.

Is PSHE education *too* personal?

Some teachers who are new to PSHE education fear that they may get in 'too deep' with this subject. You might be concerned about questions young people may ask which are about your personal behaviour, or find yourself using examples from your own life. You might wonder if you have to be the perfect role model, who does not drink, smoke or spend more than your income. You may be teaching about healthy eating while vaguely aware that young people in your class have an eating disorder, or you may have experienced an eating disorder yourself.

The answer is that this is all about finding the balance between the personal and professional that works for you. Some teachers are comfortable with questions about their family and things they like to do out of school. Some 'disclosure' helps the young people to see you as a real person, not just as someone who exists only to teach them but as someone who has a real life beyond the school gates. On the other hand, while you may be happy to reveal you have a Friday afternoon doughnut habit, it would not be appropriate to disclose drug taking or other risky behaviour you may have been involved in as a student. And while experiences such as eating disorders may help you to empathise with young people going through similar experiences, PSHE education is not the place to work through your own problems and concerns. Indeed, sharing details of unhealthy coping strategies such as eating disorders and self-harm can have the opposite effect to that which we intend. Pupils experiencing or vulnerable to such behaviours can find personal stories inspirational and instructional (see Chapters 3 and 8).

Setting the boundaries between what it is OK to ask or say in the classroom and what is not OK is an important part of PSHE education in itself and something the young people and you need to agree at an early stage, in the form of ground rules, a learning agreement or contract. This creates a safe environment for learners and teachers alike. Ultimately you, and the young people, should always have the right to 'pass' or not answer a question – something else which makes PSHE education unique. We will go into this in more depth in Chapter 3 and again in Chapter 7.

The other concern expressed by teachers is whether the content of PSHE education might provoke strong emotions, which might be difficult (or inappropriate) to manage in the classroom. A PSHE education lesson might prompt a young person to disclose that they are being harmed by a peer or a member of their family or the community. This is a matter for you and the staff of your school to consider carefully. Good planning for PSHE education along with good pastoral knowledge of the young people in your classes should mean you are prepared to minimise the emotional impact of these rare events, while maintaining the young people's entitlement to know and understand what is happening to them and to be able to ask for your help when it is needed.

If you think this is too much to ask of you as a teacher, consider the alternative: a curriculum and pedagogy designed to *prevent* young people from seeking adult help. This would be morally and educationally inadequate in every sense.

Consider

Now you have read this chapter, ask yourself, what kind of school did you go to? Was PSHE education part of your curriculum? How did your school encourage you to make healthy choices? Were you aware of efforts to consult pupils or parents about being and staying healthy? Did you notice conflict between what you were taught about being healthy (e.g. healthy eating) and the overall approach to this issue in school (the range of food and drinks available in the school)?

What were the relationships like in the schools you attended? Were you treated with respect, as capable of fulfilling your potential as an individual? Were you encouraged to treat others with respect?

How were you taught to keep yourself and others safe? Was this limited to a set of 'health and safety' rules for how to conduct yourself around the school and when out on school trips? Were you taught about keeping safe off and online? Did any online safety education you received go beyond the technical aspects of applying privacy settings and so on?

How did you learn the skills you now use as an employee and member of a team of teachers, working for the good of the young people in your school?

Now ask yourself about schools where you have developed as a teacher, whether on observation or as a teacher in training. Was PSHE education valued by senior staff as part of the overall contribution a school can make to the personal development of the young people? Was it well structured and resourced, or were there times when you were unsure how PSHE education fitted into the curriculum and policies of the school? There is so much to do and see when you enter school as a professional that you can be forgiven if these questions have never occurred to you until now. Make time to consider these questions in the school where you are working, and the possible implications of your reflections for the young people attending the school.

Chapter overview

Secondary school is a very special time in a person's life. Young people arrive on the cusp of adolescence. During their time at secondary school they may encounter some of life's major challenges, possibly for the first time: bereavement, family breakdown, moving house, financial worries or serious illness. They will almost certainly make new friendships, experience the excitement of achievement in acquiring new knowledge and skills, enjoy new forms of sport and exercise and spend nights away from home on school visits or with friends. They may have their first sexual experience, be challenged by public examinations and perhaps develop physical, mental or emotional problems which need professional care. Good PSHE education will help you and the young people in your care to prepare for and manage all these many and varied challenges.

Further reading

Ofsted (2013) 'Personal, Social, Health and Economic (PSHE) Education Survey Visits: Generic grade descriptors and supplementary subject-specific guidance for inspectors on making judgements during visits to schools'. https://www.pshe-association.org.uk/curriculum-and-resources/resources/ofsted-grade-descriptors-pshe-education (accessed 18.4.16).
A clear description of what Ofsted is looking for in PSHE education when inspecting schools.

Ofsted (2013) 'Not yet good enough: personal, social health and economic education in schools'. Available at www.ofsted.gov.uk/resources/not-yet-good-enough-personal-social-health-and-economic-education-schools (accessed 15.3.16).
Part A focuses on the key inspection and survey findings. Part B describes the characteristics of PSHE education that are outstanding and those aspects that require improvement or are inadequate. Part B can be used to evaluate the quality of PSHE education in a school.

Whilst there is no National Curriculum programme of study for PSHE education, the Department for Education signposts the PSHE Association Programme of Study (2014) for key stages 1 to 4, available at https://pshe-association.org.uk/resources_search_details.aspx?ResourceId=495&Keyword=&SubjectID=0&LevelID=0&ResourceTypeID=3&SuggestedUseID=0 (accessed 15.3.16).

References

Bonell, C. (2014) 'Why schools should promote students' health and wellbeing?', *BMJ*, 348: g3078.

Department for Education (2012) *The Impact of Pupil Behaviour and Wellbeing on Educational Outcomes*. London: DfE.

Department for Education (2014) *National Curriculum in England: Framework for Key Stages 1 to 4*. London: DfE.

Department for Education (2015) *Personal, Social, Health and Economic (PSHE) Education: A Review of Impact and Effective Practice*. London: DfE.

Morgan, N. (2016) Letter to Neil Carmichael, Chair of Education Select Committee. Available at www.parliament.uk/documents/commons-committees/Education/Letter-from-the-Secretary-of-State-to-the-Committee-on-statutory-status-for-PSHE.pdf (accessed 26.4.2016).

Office for National Statistics (2013a) 'National Population Projections: 2012-based Statistical Bulletin'. Available at www.ons.gov.uk/ons/dcp171778_334975.pdf (accessed 22.1.16).

Office for National Statistics (2013b) 'One-third of babies born in 2013 are expected to live to 100'. Available at www.ons.gov.uk/ons/rel/lifetables/historic-and-projected-data-from-the-period-and-cohort-life-tables/2012-based/sty-babies-living-to-100.html (accessed 22.1.16).

Office for National Statistics (2015a) 'National Population Projections: 2014-based Statistical Bulletin'. Available at www.ons.gov.uk/ons/dcp171778_420462.pdf (accessed 22.1.16).

Ofsted (2013) 'Personal, Social, Health and Economic (PSHE) Education Survey Visits: Generic grade descriptors and supplementary subject-specific guidance for inspectors on making judgements during visits to schools'. Available at www.pshe-association.org.uk/uploads/media/17/7604.pdf (accessed 19.1.16).

PSHE Association (2014) PSHE education Programme of Study. Available at www.pshe-association.org.uk/sites/default/files/PSHE%20Association%20Programme%20of%20Study%20October%202014%20FINAL_0.pdf (accessed 18.4.16).

PSHE Association (2016) Why PSHE education matters. Available at www.pshe-association.org.uk/what-we-do/why-pshe-matters (accessed 23.4.2016).

Public Health England (2014) 'The link between pupil health and wellbeing and attainment: A briefing for head teachers, governors and staff in education settings'. London: PSHE Association. Available at www.gov.uk/government/publications/the-link-between-pupil-health-and-wellbeing-and-attainment (accessed 14.7.16).

UK Commission for Employment and Skills (2014) *The Future of Work: Jobs and Skills, in Evidence Report 84*. London: UK CES.

UK Parliament (2015) 'Life lessons: PSHE and SRE in schools'. Available at www.publications.parliament.uk/pa/cm201415/cmselect/cmeduc/145/14502.htm (accessed 25.1.16).

Walmsley, J. (2011) Education: 16–18 year-olds: Grand committees. Available at www.publications.parliament.uk/pa/ld201011/ldhansrd/text/110404-gc0002.htm (accessed 19.1.16).

Part One

In this Part we offer advice to students and newly qualified teachers about the theory, evidence and underlying principles that apply to all PSHE education no matter what the content. We consider how adolescent development informs practice in PSHE education, how PSHE education is organised in the curriculum and how we can assess young people's learning. A critical element of assessment is understanding the prior learning young people bring to our lessons and we explore the importance of 'starting where young people are' to provide a baseline for lesson planning and to ensure that our teaching is relevant.

2

Understanding Adolescent Development

Aim

To review what is understood about adolescent physical, social, emotional and cognitive development, including major changes in brain structure and function and the implications of this knowledge for PSHE education.

Learning objectives

Through reading and reflecting on the content of this chapter you will begin to:

- recognise how different definitions of adolescence shape our response to adolescents
- know the principle theories of adolescence and how they have shaped our understanding
- relate these theories to our emerging understanding of brain development
- have an opportunity to reflect on how these theories help inform PSHE education.

Before we start

An experienced colleague in a large secondary school told me recently that he was facing one of the most difficult challenges of his career. Having advanced through the school as Head of Year from Year 7 to Year 11, he was starting again with a new Year 7 – and he was not looking forward to it:

> 'It's such a huge difference. Year 11s have some real problems, but in Year 7 everything is a problem.'

Try to put yourself back in the mind of your Year 7 and Year 11 selves. Make two lists – one of the problems you had when you were in Year 7, and one of the problems you had in Year 11. Were your Year 7 problems any less real than those in Year 11, or just different? What did you learn about dealing with your problems between Year 7 and Year 11, and how did school help?

What happens between Year 7 and Year 11 (and beyond) that transforms us so much that even experienced teachers find supporting young people through that process daunting?

Introduction

It is common for adolescents to be characterised as troubled and troublesome. Adolescence is widely associated with emotional turmoil, when it appears to young people that no one understands them. It is a time when some young people can be simultaneously a source of annoyance and anguish to their families and communities as a result of their apparent recklessness or deliberate risk taking behaviour. It is also a time when some young people can harm themselves in ways that adults can find incomprehensible.

What is adolescence – is it a distinct phase of human development? What marks the beginning and the end of this phase of our lives? What is 'normal' and 'abnormal' in terms of adolescent development? Are adolescents 'sad' or 'bad' or 'mad' or perhaps misunderstood? This chapter hopes to help you answer some of these questions by summarising the work of researchers past and present, examining various theories of adolescent development and asking you to reflect on your own experience of adolescence and the young people you work with.

In this chapter we will focus on normal adolescent development. Later chapters will look at why some young people are more at risk or more likely to take risks than others (see in particular Chapters 7, 9, 10 and 13), and where PSHE education can contribute to their overall development.

For more about adolescent lives, health and wellbeing see Hagell et al., 'Key data on adolescence' in Appendix IV.

What is adolescence?

Definitions of adolescence can be problematic.

The World Health Organization (WHO) defines the age boundaries of adolescence which appear to fit neatly with the duration of secondary and tertiary education in many countries:

> Adolescence is the period in human growth and development that occurs after childhood and before adulthood, from ages 10 to 19. (WHO, 2009)

Other definitions take account of gender differences, recognising that the onset of puberty differs for boys and girls, for example:

> Adolescence: Between childhood and manhood (14–25) or womanhood (12–21). (Pocket Oxford Dictionary, 1967)

Recently health analysts have divided the transition to adulthood into three age groups: 10–14 years (early adolescence); 15–19 years (late adolescence); and 20–24 years (early adulthood) (Sawyer et al., 2012).

What is puberty?

Puberty is a recognisable physical stage which is associated with the appearance of both primary and secondary sexual characteristics and the capacity for reproduction. The beginning of adolescence coincides with the onset of puberty and varies from one individual to another but usually occurs between 8 and 14 years of age in girls and 9 and 14 years of age in boys.

During the 20th century, improvements in nutrition and public health in high-income countries contributed to earlier menarche (first

(Continued)

(Continued)

period in girls), and regular ovulation follows in the next two years. Since the 1960s menarche has stabilised at around 12–13 years. In a recent British cohort study the average age of girls' first period was 12.9 years and the average duration of puberty was 2.7 years (Christensen et al., 2010). On average in the UK, puberty for girls begins during Year 6/7. The onset and end of puberty in boys are harder to identify, but a recent study in Spain found that puberty for boys begins around age 12 and ends around 16 years, similar to studies in the USA (Garcia et al., 2010).

In both sexes, the first half of puberty is associated with a noticeable growth spurt, the timing of which is different for girls and boys, with the striking result that 11-year-old girls can be taller than boys one or even two years their senior.

Some descriptions of adolescence imply a deficit model of young people, defining it in terms of what it is not, and as a lack of capacity:

> Adolescents are different both from young children and from adults. Specifically, adolescents are not fully capable of understanding complex concepts, or the relationship between behavior [sic] and consequences, or the degree of control they have or can have over health decision making including that related to sexual behaviour. [This] inability may make them particularly vulnerable to sexual exploitation and high-risk behaviours. (WHO, 2016)

Other definitions avoid issues of gender and age and define adolescence simply in terms of change:

> [A]dolescence is the transitional period between childhood and adulthood. (Goossens, 2006)

According to Goossens, adolescence is a kind of 'waiting room' with a blend of biological and social boundaries, beginning with the biological changes of puberty and ending with various social markers of autonomy, such as leaving home; completing education or training; getting married; having children; and financial independence.

Consider

Does it matter how we define adolescence?

We think definitions matter because even subtle differences can affect our response to young people. The two WHO definitions illustrate this dilemma. Definitions which rely too heavily on biological change can have unforeseen social consequences. For example, do we expect more of girls in educational settings, perhaps in terms of behaviour, because physically they mature earlier than boys?

Meanwhile, deficit models can result in laws, customs and practices that affect adolescents differently when compared with adults. Focussing on young people's incapacities may have the unintended consequence of stigmatising young people's normal behaviour as deviant. This can make it more difficult for them to access sexual health information and advice and services (e.g. contraception) rather than empowering them with information, skills and confidence to seek advice and help.

By combining biological with social boundaries, Goossen takes account of sexual and social maturation but this leads to an unexpected result: in the early 21st century in the UK, full financial independence from parents may not occur before our late twenties. This means adolescence could extend from age 8–9 years to 28–30 years. This is equivalent to a quarter of one's expected lifespan and with the result that recently qualified teachers and the young people they are teaching are all defined as adolescents!

However, all these definitions have one thing in common: they see adolescence as a stage we have to pass through, not a period in our lives to be celebrated and enjoyed, with choices, rights (and responsibilities) in common with other humans.

Consider

The framework document for the National Curriculum for England and Wales (2016) states that:

(Continued)

(Continued)

Every state-funded school must offer a curriculum which is balanced and broadly based and which:

- promotes the spiritual, moral, cultural, mental and physical development of pupils at the school and of society
- prepares pupils at the school for the opportunities, responsibilities and experiences of *later* life (author's emphasis).

These aims are often quoted as a rationale for a planned, progressive curriculum in PSHE education. What kind of definition of adolescence do you think underpins the National Curriculum aims? Does it make a difference to how we plan PSHE education? (Chapter 5 looks at planning in detail.)

Just like the National Curriculum, PSHE education also often focuses on the future health and wellbeing of young people. Many of the outcomes of the choices we make when we are young have few obvious short-term consequences, but epidemiology tells us that the longer-term consequences can be harmful. The definition of PSHE education we have adopted in this book helpfully reminds us that this subject is also about

> the knowledge, understanding and skills [young people] need to manage their lives *now* and in the future. (author's emphasis: PSHE Association, 2013)

So in thinking about PSHE education in secondary schools we should take care not to overlook all the pleasures and excitements of adolescence. These help to shape our future health and wellbeing, but also bear fruit in the present as positive relationships with family and peers and in creative, intellectual and physical accomplishments, valued in their own right. Adolescence is so much more than an apprenticeship for adult life.

Is adolescence a distinct phase in human development?

There have been various theories of adolescent development over the years, reflecting the state of scientific and psychological knowledge of the time. Common threads run between them; after all, they are all trying to describe the same phenomenon. The theories can be divided into biological, psychoanalytic, socio-cultural, cognitive, integrative and developmental contextualism. As well as thinking about each theory in turn, try to reflect on how each theory fits your own experience of growing up in the late 20th and early 21st century.

Early biological theories

Although 'youth' has always been associated with particular behaviours which philosophers and scientists have sought to understand, the first biological theory of psychological development in adolescence was proposed in the early 20th century (Hall, 1904). Granville Stanley Hall's views emerged from the experience of western industrialised societies and were influenced by Lamarck and Darwin and their respective theories of evolution. Hall hypothesised that as each person develops they recapitulate (or repeat) the social evolution of the species as a whole, from what he described as 'animal' through 'anthropoid' or ape-like and 'barbarian', to 'civilised' behaviour. This theory paralleled the now disproven theory that the developing human recapitulates human physical evolution from a unicellular organism or embryo to a fish-like creature with gills, before developing human characteristics. The idea of recapitulation in psychological development is a powerful one and also influenced other, later, developmental psychologists such as Freud and Piaget. As we will see later in this chapter, evolution (but not recapitulation) remains key to our current understanding of brain development.

Hall's (1904) ideas continue to be influential because he pioneered the hypothesis that adolescence is characterised by 'storm and stress'. According to Hall, 'storm and stress' is the result of the 'civilised emotions' such as reasoning, morality, religion, sympathy, love and aesthetic pleasure, battling more 'primitive' emotions during adolescence.

Hall's theories had practical applications in education since he believed civilisation advanced through the full expression every stage of development through play and learning activities. This has much in common with other educationalists whose ideas were popular at the time, including Dewey and Montessori, and to the philosophy of Jean-Jacques Rousseau who first espoused developmentally appropriate education (Muijs and Reynolds, 2011) (see Chapter 3). In particular, Hall recommended that parents and educators of 13–20 year olds should actively nurture and encourage the full expression of adolescents' emotions. At the same time he emphasised the importance of both external and internal or 'self' control to the maintenance of order in society.

Hall believed that the human species would continue to evolve through the full development and transmission of the social characteristics developed during adolescence to the next generation and beyond. This was Hall's 'task of adolescence'. Our understanding of genetics and of brain development has advanced considerably since the early 20th century, yet some of Hall's insights continue to influence the public's understanding of young people's behaviour, particularly the ideas of adolescence being a time of 'storm and stress': of conflict with parents, emotional turmoil and of heightened risk taking and impulsiveness, all of which need to be controlled.

Psychoanalytic theories

The psychoanalysts also recognise adolescence as a distinct phase of development and their theories include elements of recapitulation (Freud, S., 1953; Freud, A., 1966; Blos, 1979). In this case the changes in adolescence recapitulate earlier oral, anal, phallic, latent and genital stages of individual development, leading to the idea that heterosexual sexual intercourse is the only healthy outlet for sexual energy (see Jackson and Goossens (2006) for more on psychoanalytic theory of adolescence).

The psychoanalysts accepted Hall's notion of 'storm and stress' as a normal part of relationships between adolescents and parents. However, Sigmund Freud described these relationships in sexual terms: a longing for affection and approval from the parent of the opposite sex and aggressive impulses towards the same sex parent. To a psychoanalyst the task of the adolescent is to mount a defence to these impulses. Young people must overcome their dependence on their parents and incorporate their sexual identity into their adult personality.

Social-cultural theories

In the 1920s and 1930s, social-cultural theories of adolescence began to emerge and were highly influenced by the findings of anthropologists, including Margaret Mead. The argument became not whether adolescence exists as a distinct phase of development, but whether it is shaped by the competing forces of nature or nurture.

Mead (1928) challenged the idea that 'storm and stress' is a universal feature of adolescence, citing evidence from an immersive anthropological study on one island in Samoa revealed that young people appeared to navigate adolescence without conflict with their parents or authority figures. In interviews with Samoan teenagers Mead recorded a casual, relaxed attitude to growing up, including to pre-marital sex, which was taboo in the USA at the time.

Although she did not do a similar in-depth study of US teenagers, Mead argued that 'storm and stress' was not normal for adolescents and that western culture was to blame for American teenagers being both troubled and troublesome.

These conclusions were challenged after Mead's death when evidence emerged that the Samoan teenagers she interviewed may have been teasing her about their customs and culture. Freeman (1999) also argued that her contemporaries working on other islands in Samoa found no evidence to support her views but their work was not as well known. Nevertheless, later studies within the USA have supported Mead's view that extreme 'storm and stress' during adolescence is not universal (Offer and Sabshin, 1974). It is now more widely accepted that most teenagers have positive relationships with their parents (and other authority figures such as teachers) (Arnett, 1999). Similarly, most young people do not experience severe stress or emotional crises and our image of all teenagers as risk takers may be exaggerated (see Chapter 7).

Cognitive theories

Most teachers will be familiar with the ideas put forward by Piaget that the way we think changes during adolescence in distinct stages, as our capacity to reason develops from 'concrete' to 'formal' operations. According to Inhelder and Piaget (1958) the implications of the stages of cognitive development are not confined to the kind of reasoning needed in maths or science.

For example, concrete operations are associated with a stage of moral development where right and wrong are absolutes. This results in an apparently naïve and idealistic view of the world and how to solve its problems, which is characteristic of many young adolescents. Becoming older and wiser (or being able to see a situation from different perspectives and evaluate possible outcomes) accompanies the development of abstract reasoning.

Another cognitive psychologist, Elkind (1967) explored what Piaget described as adolescent egocentrism and identified two cognitive traps which adolescents can fall into during the transition to abstract reasoning, known as the 'imaginary audience' and the 'personal fable'.

As adolescents become more self-aware, how they appear to others becomes a dominant part of their thinking. According to Elkind, this is because they assume that others are equally attentive to them as they are to themselves. This gives rise to the idea of the 'imaginary audience' to which the adolescent continuously performs. This audience can be highly critical: adolescents can be very critical of themselves and think that others, especially peers, are equally, if not more critical, with the result that self-awareness becomes self-consciousness, accompanied by feelings of shame and embarrassment.

Consider

Anyone who has tried to tell a teenager that no one else will notice an outbreak of spots knows it is pointless, since the spots 'must' be obvious to everyone. Not only that, but a quick browse on social media sites encourages the idea that spots are caused by 'bad behaviour' such as poor hygiene or excessive fat or chocolate consumption (neither of these theories is based on reliable evidence) and can be cured with expensive products and/or hours spent on personal hygiene.

However, when the imaginary audience becomes extremely critical it can lead to distorted body image and contribute to eating disorders.

How could you use your understanding of the 'imaginary audience' when planning PSHE lessons? Is information alone likely to influence how a young person sees themselves? A critical review of magazines and internet sites that focus on appearance for teenage girls and boys could help students to develop an understanding of how marketing contributes to young people's misperception of their 'flaws'. In PSHE education, reflection is key to helping young people to see things from different perspectives and fine tune their perception of themselves and their own behaviour in the light of the work you are doing. Reflection is usually built into a PSHE lesson at the end, but it can be encouraged at different points throughout a lesson to help students process the information you are sharing.

Adolescents also over-differentiate their own feelings from those of others, giving rise to the 'personal fable'. In this story of themselves, which is inevitably unrealistic, Elkind (1967) suggests that adolescents can feel unique, omnipotent and invulnerable, or conversely, powerless, stupid and incapable. Since their feelings are unique to them, what they are experiencing must also be incomprehensible to others. These two constructs of the imaginary audience and the personal fable are often used to explain adolescents' apparently reckless risk taking behaviour as well as their feelings that 'no one understands' them.

Consider

Health campaigns targeting young people's health risk behaviour (such as drug taking or speeding while driving) often seek to make young people feel guilty or more aware of their vulnerability using shock tactics. (Take a look at Chapter 3 and the health action model, Figure 3.1, to see how this approach can be challenged).

Cognitive theories of adolescent development suggest that young people who feel invulnerable will find it difficult to accept that what happens to others might also happen to them. Conversely, young people whose personal fable is one of helplessness may feel they have nothing to lose by adopting risky behaviours. This resistance to health messages can lead well-meaning campaigners to exaggerate the harms, which sets up denial. A better understanding of adolescent development can help to explain why shock-horror approaches are memorable, but not very effective, in helping young people's adopt safer, healthier behaviour.

Integrative approaches

The theories of adolescent development described above have more in common with one another than might at first appear and this has led to the so-called integrative approaches which recognise biological, cultural and cognitive perspectives. The best known of these theories is Erikson's Lifespan theory. According to Erikson (1968) there are eight life stages, each of which is characterised by specific 'crises' and associated tasks. Successful completion of these tasks results in specific 'virtues'.

Completion of the tasks is influenced by cultural and other factors, and the virtues or strengths developed at each stage are thought to be crucial to resolving the crises of the next stage. Unlike other 'stage' theories, however, there is an expectation that some stages may need to be revisited so that past crises can be resolved. According to Erikson, the specific task of adolescence is 'identity formation' and the resulting virtue is 'fidelity'.

Erikson recognised that the task of adolescence is not completed until the late teens. Marcia (1993) extended Erikson's model, based on semi-structured interviews with older (initially all male) adolescents, which examined the development of two dimensions of identity status: exploration and commitment (see Figure 2.1).

The strength of Marcia's model is that while Erikson's original work was derived mainly from psychoanalytic perspectives, the identity states described by Marcia correlate reasonably well with other psychological constructs such as self-esteem and authoritarianism, which derive from different theoretical perspectives (Kroger and Marcia, 2011).

Marcia's work built on Erikson's original ideas about the adolescent identity crisis, known as 'identity diffusion'. In this status a young person has not made or taken much interest in, or is avoiding choices or commitments to any particular personal identity. Young people in this status are often described as easy going but also easily swayed by others.

Another identity status described by Marcia is 'foreclosure'. According to the model a foreclosed individual has a 'bequeathed' commitment to an

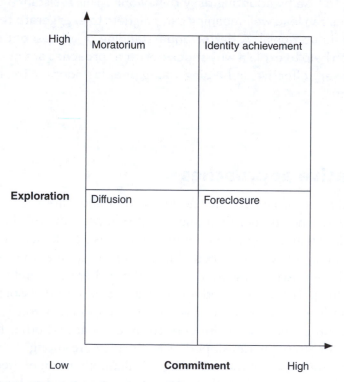

Figure 2.1 Model of exploration and commitment (based on Marcia, 1993)

identity which is similar to that of their parents (or an alternative authority figure) and is strongly influenced by the associated customs and culture, without any exploration of possible alternatives. This identity is associated with low levels of anxiety, but also with greater authoritarianism and defensiveness in response to challenges to the received norm.

A developmentally more healthy status (although associated with higher measures of anxiety) is 'moratorium'. This status describes an individual who is 'struggling' but also actively exploring identity choices. Although Marcia's model of identity is not itself a stage theory, moratorium must occur before identity achievement is reached, possibly after several cycles between diffusion and moratorium, after a period of exploration.

'Identity achieved' individuals have a strong sense of who they are and have made a commitment to the kind of life they would like to lead professionally and ideologically.

This status is associated with higher self-esteem and a more internal locus of control, where an individual feels they can influence what happens to them, for example by working hard to prepare for exams or sporting events. In experimental studies these individuals cope better than others when presented with stressful cognitive challenges.

Identity achievement is also associated with the 'post conventional' stage of moral development (Kohlberg, 1984) where individuals can judge moral issues on the basis of broad ethical principles, such as human rights, rather than conventional rules of 'right and wrong'. Interestingly in these correlates of identity achievement we can, perhaps, detect echoes of Hall's 'civilised' state.

Developmental contextualism

While all the theories we have considered are based on empirical findings (i.e. on observation of young people), they are all somewhat partial. The psychoanalysts, for example, based their studies on observation of patients who were seeking help for anxiety or depression. The anthropologists were looking for the exceptions which might prove whether nurture or nature was the key to understanding adolescents. Many of the studies, like those of Piaget, were based on very small samples of young people from high-income countries. In the USA, college students were a convenient cohort for academics to study, who are not necessarily typical of the population as a whole.

More recent theorists have stepped back from debates about 'storm and stress', 'nature versus nurture' and developmental 'crises'. Developmental contextualism recognises that the whole environment in which a young

Table 2.1   A summary of the main elements of developmental contextualism (adapted from Coleman, 2011)

The context or ecology of development is essential to its understanding	This includes not only the family but also structural factors such as geographical, political, social and historical context of the young person.
Timing is critical	The developmental impact of any transition for a young person depends on when it occurs in their life.
Human development is continuous	Adolescence is in some senses a continuation of childhood and should not be treated as though it is disconnected from earlier (or later) phases. Adolescence is not the only transition we experience throughout life. For example, the transition from being single to living as a couple.
Parents and children influence one another reciprocally	The young person is part of a system: their development impacts on parents' behaviour, and changes in how the family functions as a whole will impact on young people.
Individuals are agents of their own development	Young people's development is not completely at the mercy of their hormones, their culture or education. They are also actively engaged in understanding themselves and shaping their own development.
Outcomes for young people depend on how well matched the characteristics of the young person are with their physical and social environment	If we seek to understand adolescent outcomes we need to take account of both individual and environmental factors and how they interact in the social and political context.

person is growing up contributes to their overall development. Leading thinkers in this approach include social constructivists such as Vygotsky, Bronfenbrenner and also Richard Lerner whose book, *The Good Teen* (2007) sets out the case against 'storm and stress'. Developmental contextualists draw on evidence from large, community based samples of young people from different cultures and ethnic groups. Their studies have found that most young people negotiate their adolescence relatively successfully (see Table 2.1), without experiencing either extreme emotional crises or extreme risk taking behaviour (Coleman, 2011)

Further evidence comes from the Health Behaviour in School Aged Children survey (Currie et al., 2012) which asks 11, 13 and 15 year olds in Great Britain to report on levels of 'life satisfaction'. In 2010 around 4 in 5 young people reported high levels of life satisfaction, despite living through one of the biggest financial crises for a generation (Currie et al., 2012)

The idea that young people are active agents in their own development is, for some, the most radical theory of adolescence thus far.

According to John Coleman, of Oxford University:

> It is no longer acceptable to consider only one side of the picture; the person and the context are inseparable. In addition, it is no longer possible to ignore the fact that the individual adolescent shapes his or her own world. (2011:17)

For Coleman it is essential that any theory of adolescence must be able to take account of individual differences in development. You will know young people who have grown up in the same town, attended the same school and lived in similar social and economic circumstances but who have quite different social and educational outcomes. Equally you will know young people who have experienced very different circumstances and yet whose educational and social achievements are similar to their peers. An important question for PSHE education is this: Why are some young people more resilient in the face of adversity than others?

Coleman (1974) set out to answer this question with a large scale survey of 11–17 year olds. He sought their attitudes and opinions on a wide range of topics including self-image, being alone, sexual relationships, family relationships, friendships and large group situations. The data was examined for positive and negative elements and he explored the common themes expressed by the young people in the sample. He found that attitudes to all relationships varied with age, but crucially their concerns about different issues also peaked at different ages. This study has since been replicated in several different countries (see Goossens, 2006).

This led Coleman to formulate one of the more interesting theories of adolescence, known as the 'focal theory'. According to Coleman, most young people adapt to the changes which happen during adolescence because the focus is on one developmental issue at a time. This happens in part because the process of adaptation is spread over a number of years, and because our social structures (families, schools and communities) are set up to offer support at crucial times, but also because young people actively manage these transitions, drawing on their individual strengths and capacities. What is striking about Coleman's focal model is that it highlights what young people can do, rather than what they can't.

The focal theory also helps to explain why some young people are more vulnerable than others; how bereavement or other life event at a key point in their development can cause more problems than at other times.

The focal theory also differs from previous stage theories in that the resolution of one stage is not critical to the resolution of the next; there are no fixed boundaries between stages and, crucially, culture and environment impact on the order in which the different issues come into focus (Goossens and Marcoen, 1999). At first glance this model seems complicated, and yet its value is that it can explain how most adolescents cope with a wide range of transitions in a relatively short period without extreme stress or difficulty, while others find it more difficult to cope.

Consider

All the change of adolescence can be overwhelming for some young people. Add to this the likelihood that during this time a young person will experience the death of a grandparent or other close relative, have their first romantic attachment and almost inevitably their first heartbreak, sit exams that everyone tells them are crucial to their future success. Remarkably, most adolescents manage all this change very well, or at least well enough to emerge as capable, responsible, caring adults.

Case study – Tom's story

Tom is an intelligent young person from a stable family who has moved house – and school – three times during his secondary education. After the first move, at the beginning of Year 8, Tom experienced considerable distress at leaving behind his close friends, most of whom he had known since primary school. At first he found it hard to fit in at his new school, but eventually he found acceptance among a group of young people, most of whom were less able than him, some of whom were experiencing turbulent family relationships. Tom started smoking, of which he was ashamed; he knew it was bad for his health and that his parents disapproved. However, he enjoyed the status of 'rebel' that smoking conferred on him with his new friends. He constructed a series of complex lies to cover up his behaviour, but continued to smoke. Tom's progress at school was disappointing, given his abilities.

When Tom was just about to start Year 10, the family had to move house again because of his father's work. Tom's parents were concerned about the disruptive effect of the last move and talked about this with his new Year Head. The Year Head arranged to meet with Tom every two weeks for the first half term and kept in touch with his parents by e-mail to let them know how he was settling in.

At first Tom lacked confidence but gradually he began to do better at school. He made friends with young people of similar interests and abilities to himself, none of whom were smokers. Tom joined an after-school drama group where he excelled. He stopped smoking. Aged 17, and with some good GCSEs behind him, he made the decision to move to a sixth form college which had good facilities for drama. He formed positive relationships with other students, remaining friends with several young people from his previous school.

It took Tom some time to settle on a university course and at 18 didn't have a clear idea of what he wanted to do as a career. During a gap year he worked in a hotel restaurant and as a farm labourer, then went travelling, volunteering for three months in a school in India. On his return to the UK he decided to work towards a career in International Development.

Think about this case study in relation to the different theories of adolescence in this chapter. Is there evidence here for Murcia's model of identity formation, or Coleman's focal model? Why did the impact of his second move differ from the first? Do any of the theories help to explain why Tom started and subsequently stopped smoking or his eventual career choice? In Chapter 7 we look at risk taking behaviour and what factors make some young people more vulnerable than others to multiple risk taking.

Adolescence and brain development

Compared with the approaches to understanding adolescence described above, our understanding of brain development is relatively new. Until the 1990s much of what we understood about the brain and human development was based either on animal experiments or post-mortem studies where parts of the animal or human brain could be dissected, or on observations of the effects of brain injury or abnormality on development in individuals or invasive techniques which involved the use of radioisotopes to monitor the metabolism of the brain (positron emission tomography or PET scanning).

Our current understanding has been assisted by the use of non-invasive techniques for studying the brains of living people such as: functional magnetic resonance imaging (fMRI), magneto-encephalography (MEG) and optical tomography (OT) (Koizumi, 2008). Each technique has its strengths and weaknesses and the results are often combined. While fMRI and MEG reveal a great deal about the structure and activity of the brain when a person remains still, optical tomography enables neuroscientists to study the brains of people while they are going about their normal activities. This has recently been used in breakthrough investigations which have demonstrated that adults with 'locked in syndrome' (where the person is unable to move or communicate in any way) are conscious.

Together these studies have contributed to a remarkable new understanding of adolescence which shows that the brain continues to develop into adulthood (Giedd, 2004; Patton and Viner, 2007).

The human brain

The human brain consists of approximately 10^{11} neurones and 10^{14} connections. This means that in every cubic millimetre of brain tissue there are 60,000 neurones. Each individual neurone connects with 10–20,000 other neurones and receives inputs from a similar number of other neurones, mostly in the same vicinity, but some in other, more remote areas of the brain.

Thanks to evolution most of these connections are determined genetically. Because of this the human baby is born with a brain whose architecture 'knows' or anticipates many of the properties of the world in which she will develop, endowing her with innate abilities; for example, to recognise human faces and speech, to interpret certain wavelengths of electromagnetic radiation as visual experiences and to store and retrieve past events in the form of memory. However, at birth many of these complex abilities are incomplete, so that a newborn baby is highly dependent on its environment and experience for the brain to develop normally. Some functions, such as sight and language development, are located in specific regions of the brain and there are critical periods of development (Singer, 2011) after which these structures (and their function) cannot develop normally.

During normal development, exposure to sensory stimuli and experience shapes the connections between neurones so that some pathways are consolidated while others are lost. As the neuroscientist Wolf Singer puts it, 'Neurones that fire together, wire together' (in Battro et al., 2011: 101).

Previously it was thought that neurological development was more or less complete in early childhood, when the number of connections between neurones increases rapidly. Now it is clear that the number of connections between neurones peaks in early adolescence and this is followed by a gradual loss of connections (known as synaptic pruning) which occurs throughout adulthood. At the same time there is a gradual process of myelination of neurones, which increases the speed with which neurones transmit signals to one another. We now know that the human brain retains considerable 'plasticity' throughout adult life.

The rate at which these processes happen varies across different brain structures and particularly with the onset of puberty (see Blakemore and Choudhury, 2006) so that chronological age is less important than pubertal stage to brain development.

One of the most interesting features of adolescent brain development to emerge from recent research is the lack of uniformity in brain development during adolescence. The limbic system, which is responsible for reward systems, appetite and pleasure seeking, develops earlier in adolescence than does the prefrontal cortex. The prefrontal cortex is the site of 'executive control', including planning, emotional regulation or impulse control, decision making, multitasking and self-awareness. Indeed, the difference between the development of these two regions of the brain is greatest in early to mid-adolescence and coincides with an increase in social cognition and self-awareness (Blakemore, 2010) and in social and physical risk taking (Blakemore and Choudhury, 2006). We shall return to this in Chapter 7 when we take a closer look at brain development, risk taking and decision making in adolescence.

Our emerging understanding of brain development sheds light on past theories of adolescence, which in turn have sought to explain some of the characteristic behaviours we observe among young people. Sarah Jayne Blakemore, a leading neuroscientist, believes that there may be critical periods during adolescence when we can more effectively intervene to promote healthy development and learning (Blakemore, 2010). Blakemore is concerned about the impact of social media on young people's social skills and makes a strong case for PSHE education, including an understanding of how the adolescent brain develops:

> If early childhood is seen as a major opportunity – or a 'sensitive period' – for teaching, so too should the teenage years. During both periods, particularly dramatic brain reorganization is taking place. [....] the research on brain development suggests that education during the teenage years is vital. The brain is still developing during this period, is adaptable, and needs to be moulded and shaped. Perhaps the aims of education for adolescents might

change to include abilities that are controlled by the parts of the brain that undergo most change during adolescence. These abilities include internal control, multitasking, and planning – but also self-awareness and social cognitive skills such as the perspective-taking and the understanding of social emotions. Finally, it might be fruitful to include in the curriculum some teaching on the changes occurring in the brain during adolescence. Adolescents might be interested in, and could benefit from, learning about the changes that are going on in their own brains. (2010: 4)

There is no doubt that a better understanding of brain development in adolescence will help us to develop better responses to the challenges adolescents face, but we need to be aware of the possibility of a return to the biological determinism of Granville Stanley Hall and his contemporaries, where young people are deemed incapable because their brains are still 'under construction'. Other researchers have urged caution in leaping to conclusions about education and curriculum development, based on our as yet imperfect understanding of the relationships between brain development and learning (Battro et al., 2011). Steinberg (2008) points out that most of the studies of adolescent brains are not longitudinal; that is, they don't follow the development of individuals, but take measurements of neurotypical adolescent brains of different ages. Without an insight into the social and cultural environment of the young people concerned it is difficult to know the role of the environment in shaping brain structures.

What does this mean for PSHE education?

For PSHE education the important question is not just about how the brain develops or how this advances our understanding of adolescence, but whether this knowledge helps us to plan and deliver more effective approaches to PSHE education which are more in tune with the social, emotional and physical needs of young people.

Consider

If puberty, brain development and social context, not chronological age, are driving some of the key changes for young people, how can you plan PSHE education lessons to meet the needs of a class of young people who will all be at different stages of physical, social, emotional and cognitive development?

In Chapter 3 we will explore the key principles of effective PSHE education, one of which is 'starting where young people are' (see also

Chapter 5) which helps to plan bespoke PSHE lessons and schemes of work. Whole school planning will help to ensure that topics are revisited in different ways so that the needs of most young people can be met as they develop. One way to achieve this is to have horizontal themes through which a vertical spiral curriculum is expressed. For example, in Year 7 the theme may be 'Healthy Lifestyles' and in Year 8 the theme may be 'Managing Change'. The Year 9 theme may be 'Finding a Balance', Year 10 'Risk and Reward' and Year 11 'Healthy Futures'. These themes give teachers an opportunity to look at familiar topics such as sex and relationships, drugs, healthy eating and safety education from a fresh perspective with each year group. (See Chapter 4 for the pros and cons of different approaches to planning in PSHE education.) From time to time some young people may also need a more targeted approach (see Chapters 7 and 12).

Chapter overview

In the past, developmental psychologists may have been guilty of treating adolescents like a kind of 'black box' about whom they could observe inputs and outputs but not what happens within. This has resulted in some rather negative expectations of young people. However, some recent theories and a greater understanding of brain development offer a more positive view of young people as they develop and engage actively in constructing their present and future selves.

It is important that we use what we are learning about adolescent development to inform PSHE education in secondary schools.

Try this

Draw a mind map of a young person in Year 9. Try to include all the different influences that may impact on their feeling of wellbeing. Now try to identify which of these influences a school might contribute to. Are those contributions positive, negative, or neutral? Where does PSHE education fit in? To what extent can PSHE education help young people to promote their own health and wellbeing? We hope what follows will help you to answer this question.

Further reading

A. Freud ([1935] 1979) *Psycho-analysis for Teachers and Parents: Introductory Lectures*. London: Norton.
Anna Freud, daughter of Sigmund Freud, emigrated from Austria to England and became a British citizen in 1938. She was very interested in the problems of children, particularly those affected by homelessness and war. Her lectures are still regarded as one of the most lucid introductions to child psychoanalysis.

J. Kroger (2007) *Identity Development: Adolescence Through Adulthood*. London: Sage.
This book explores adolescence in the context of the lifelong process of identity development. It includes discussion of identity formation for young people who for reasons such as adoption or immigration may face particular challenges during adolescence.

J. Roche, S. Tucker, R. Thomson and R. Flynn (2004) *Youth in Society* (2nd edition). London: Sage.
This text offers the whole children's workforce, including teachers, youth workers and social workers, an introduction to a wide range of topics relevant to our understanding of young people including youth cultures and subcultures, how young people are portrayed in the media, social exclusion and youth policy.

D. A. Sousa (2011) *How the Brain Learns* (4th edition). Thousand Oaks, CA: Sage.
A good general and practical guide to the brain and how a teacher might use this knowledge to facilitate learning across a range of subjects, all of which is relevant to PSHE education.

References

Arnett, J.J. (1999) 'Adolescent storm and stress reconsidered', *American Psychologist*, 54(5): 317–26.
Battro, A.M., Fischer, K.W. and Léna, P.J. (eds) (2011) *The Educated Brain: Essays in Neuroeducation*. Cambridge: Cambridge University Press.
Blakemore, S.J. (2010) 'The developing social brain: implications for education', *Neuron*, 65(6): 744–7.

Blakemore, S.J. and Choudhury, S. (2006) 'Development of the adolescent brain: implications for executive function and social cognition', *Journal of Child Psychology and Psychiatry*, 47(3): 296–312.

Blos, P. (1979) *The Adolescent Passage*. New York: Free Press.

Christensen, K.Y., Maisonet, M., Rubin, C., Holmes, A., Flanders, W.D., Heron, J., Ness, A., Drews-Botsch, C., Dominguez, C., McGeehin, M.A. and Marcus, M. (2010) 'Progression through puberty in girls enrolled in a contemporary British cohort', *Journal of Adolescent Health*, 47(3): 282–9.

Coleman, J.C. (1974) *Relationships in Adolescence*. London: Routledge.

Coleman, J.C. (2011) *The Nature of Adolescence*, 4th edn. London: Routledge.

Currie, C., Zanotti, A.M., Currie, D., de Looze, M., Roberts, C., Samdal. O., Smith, R.F. and Barnekow, V. (eds) (2012) *Social Determinants of Health and Well-Being Among Young People. Health Behaviour in School-aged Children (HBSC) Study: International Report from the 2009/2010 Survey*. Copenhagen: WHO Regional Office for Europe (Health Policy for Children and Adolescents, No. 6).

Department for Education (2016) *National Curriculum Framework Document*. London: Department for Education. Available at www.gov.uk/government/uploads/system/uploads/attachment_data/file/335116/Master_final_national_curriculum_220714.pdf (accessed 11.04.16).

Elkind, D. (1967) 'Egocentrism in adolescence', *Child Development*, 38: 1025–34.

Erikson, E.H. (1968) *Identity: Youth and Crisis*. New York: Norton.

Freeman, D. (1999) *The Fateful Hoaxing of Margaret Mead: A Historical Analysis of Samoan Research*. Boulder, CO: Westview Press.

Freud, A. ([1936] 1966) 'The ego and the mechanisms of defence', in *The writings of Anna Freud* (II). New International Universities Press.

Freud, S. ([1905] 1953) 'Three essays on the theory of sexuality', in J. Strachey (ed.), *The Standard Edition of the Complete Psychological Works of Sigmund Freud* (7: 135–243) (trans. by Strachey). London: Hogarth Press.

Garcia, C.B., Gónzalez, V.A., Arana, C.C., Diaz, M.E. and Tolmo, M.D. (2010) 'Assessment of the secular trend in puberty in boys and girls', *Anales Pediatria (Barc)*, 73(6): 320–6 [article in Spanish].

Giedd, J. (2004) 'Structural magnetic resonance imaging of the adolescent brain', *Annals of the New York Academy of Sciences*, 1027: 77–85.

Goossens, L. (2006) 'Theories of adolescence', in Jackson, S. and Goossens, L. (eds), *Handbook of Adolescent Development*, pp. 11–29. Hove: Psychology Press.

Goossens, L. and Marcoen, A. (1999) 'Relationships during adolescence: constructive vs negative themes and relational dissatisfaction', *Journal of Adolescence*, 22: 65–79.

Hagell, A., Coleman, J. and Brooks, F. (2013) *Key Data on Adolescence 2013*. London: Association for Young People's Health. Available at www.ayph.org.uk/publications/480_KeyData2013_WebVersion.pdf (accessed 19.05.15).

Hagell, A., Coleman, J. and Brooks, F. (2015) *Key Data on Adolescence 2015*. London: Association for Young People's Health.

Hall, G.S. (1904) *Adolescence: Its Psychology and its Relation to Physiology, Anthropology, Sociology, Sex, Crime, Religion and Education* (2 Vols). New York: Appleton.

Inhelder, B. and Piaget, J. ([1955] 1958) *The Growth of Logical Thinking from Childhood to Adolescence: An Essay on the Construction of Formal Operational Structures* (trans. by A. Parsons and S. Milgram). London: Routledge & Kegan Paul.

Jackson, S. and Goossens, L. (eds) (2006) *Handbook of Adolescent Development*. Hove: Psychology Press.

Kohlberg, L. (1984) *The Psychology of Moral Development: The Nature and Validity of Moral Stages (Essays on Moral Development, Vol. 2)*. New York: Harper & Row.

Koizumi, H. (2008) 'Developing brain: a functional imaging approach to learning and educational sciences', in Battro, M, Fischer, K.W. and Lena, P.J. (eds), *The Educated Brain*, pp. 166–80. Cambridge: Cambridge University Press.

Kroger, J. and Marcia, J.E. (2011) 'The identity statuses: origins, meanings and interpretations', in Schwartz, S.J., Luyckx, K. and Vignoles, V.L. (eds), *Handbook of Identity Theory and Research*, pp. 31–53. New York: Springer.

Lerner, R. (2007) *The Good Teen: Rescuing Adolescence from the Myth of the Storm and Stress* Years. New York: Three Rivers Press.

Marcia, J.E. (1993) 'The relational roots of identity', in Kroger, J. (ed.), *Discussions on Ego Identity*. Hillsdale, NJ: Lawrence Erlbaum.

Mead, M. (1928) *Coming of Age in Samoa: A Psychological Study of Primitive Youth for Western Civilisation*. New York: Norton.

Muijs, D. and Reynolds, D. (2011) *Effective Teaching: Evidence and Practice*. London: Sage.

Offer, D. and Sabshin, M. (1974) *Normality: Theoretical and Clinical Concepts of Mental Health*. New York: Basic Books.

Patton, G. and Viner, R. (2007) 'Pubertal transitions in health', *The Lancet*, 369(9567): 1130–9.

PSHE Association (2013) 'Corporate information'. Available at www.pshe-association.org.uk/content.aspx?CategoryID=1043 (accessed 19.05.15).

Sawyer, S.M. Afifi, R.A., Bearinger, L.H., Blakemore, S., Dick, B., Ezah, A.C. and Patton, G.C. (2012) 'Adolescence: a foundation for future health', *The Lancet*, 379(9826): 1630–40.

Singer, W. (2008) 'Epigenesis and brain plasticity in education', in Battro, M, Fischer, K.W. and Lena, P.J. (eds), *The Educated Brain*, pp. 97–110. Cambridge: Cambridge University Press.

Steinberg, L. (2008) 'A social neuroscience perspective on adolescent risk taking', *Developmental Review*, 28: 78–106.

World Health Organization (2009) *Global Health Risks: Mortality and Burden of Disease Attributable to Selected Major Risks*. Geneva: World Health Organization.

World Health Organization (2016) 'Adolescent Development'. Available at www.who.int/maternal_child_adolescent/topics/adolescence/dev/en/ (accessed 19.05.15).

3

Theory, Evidence and Practical Approaches to Effective Teaching and Learning in PSHE Education

Aim

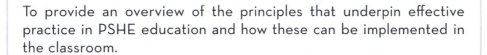

To provide an overview of the principles that underpin effective practice in PSHE education and how these can be implemented in the classroom.

Learning objectives

Through reading and reflecting on the content of this chapter you will begin to:

- understand the principles that underpin effective PSHE education and the evidence for them
- be familiar with one approach to teaching PSHE education
- consider a range of active learning techniques that work well in PSHE lessons.

Before we start

The following words are often used in connection with 'health': education, promotion, protection, prevention, information, improvement. These words all describe activities that are essentially about 'public health'. They are about helping the population to be as healthy as they can be for as long as possible – adding years to life, but also life to years. PSHE education can contribute to public health, alongside improvements in housing, medical treatments and workplace safety. It is a universal intervention for all children and young people; that is, it is aimed to improve outcomes for individuals and the population as a whole. Although the name 'Personal, Social, Health and Economic Education' would seem to imply that 'health education' is only a quarter of the subject, in fact each of the four elements contribute to the physical, emotional and social health of the individual, in its broadest sense, so while much of this chapter draws on our understanding of effective teaching and learning, it also draws on evidence of effective interventions in public health.

Introduction

This chapter is divided into three sections:

• Section 1 will look at the theoretical principles that underpin effective practice in PSHE education.
• Section 2 will ground this by looking at one possible model for structuring classroom learning.
• Section 3 will offer illustrations of interactive teaching and learning in PSHE education.

This chapter will not cover general theories of teaching and learning as these are widely covered elsewhere, including in our previous book *Understanding PSHE in the Primary School* (Boddington et al., 2014: Ch.2).

Instead, Section 1 of this chapter will look specifically at evidence-based principles of effective teaching and learning in PSHE education and relate these to classroom strategies for teaching and learning.

It is important to define 'effective practice' in PSHE education as being concerned primarily with learning, not with future behaviour or wellbeing outcomes, which can be influenced by many factors. PSHE education does not lay down prescriptive 'rules for living' but develops the language, strategies, skills and attributes that, together with an understanding of balanced, factual information, enable young people to make and enact informed choices, in the same way that learning French does not mean you have to go and live in France or even speak French if you don't want to.

In this way PSHE education can be far more effective in supporting a positive outcome in terms of healthier, safer and more economically competent young people who are able to manage their lives than crude 'health or lifestyle propaganda' that seek to shock, withhold, limit or distort learning in order to gain compliance with a desired set of health or economic behaviours. This is not to say, however, that preventing harmful behaviours is not a valid objective of PSHE education. Often prevention education is about supporting young people's intentions to make healthy, safe and prudent choices. So 'prevention education' is a *component* of PSHE education, and good practice in PSHE education is 'preventive'.

'First do no harm' – a word of warning about poor practice in PSHE education

'Do no harm' is one of the key principles underpinning the Hippocratic oath usually associated with the medical profession, but also underpins the ethics of the work of many other professionals such as social workers. Although the boundaries between benefit and harm can be blurred in some extreme examples, it is important to bear in mind that any effort to influence what people think, feel or do about their health and wellbeing can backfire and do more harm than good. This includes PSHE education.

Do no harm

Education to prevent self-harm and eating disorders is a good example of how misguided practice in PSHE education can cause harm. These behaviours are essential aspects of a comprehensive PSHE education programme. However, poorly planned teaching can inadvertently either instruct vulnerable pupils in how to successfully self-harm or starve themselves, or inspire vulnerable pupils to strive to 'do better' in their unhealthy coping behaviour.

Imagine young people listening to someone, perhaps in person or in a video clip, who has suffered from anorexia. The clip details their

(Continued)

(Continued)

weight loss and the apparent benefits of their unhealthy coping strategy: 'My weight dropped to 35kilos and for the first time I truly felt in control of my life'. Might a young person in the class who is in the early stages of anorexia see this as encouragement, something to aim for, or even that they are 'not yet a good enough anorexic' if they weigh more than the speaker? This is sometimes referred to as inadvertently 'inspiring' young people to more extreme behaviours.

Poorly planned PSHE education can also inadvertently provide 'instruction'. For example, imagine a person recounting their own experience of self-harm and explaining in detail different ways in which they harmed themselves and the techniques they employed to hide this from their families. Whilst of genuine academic interest to many young people, there may be those in any class who are already self-harming and are learning new ways to hide their behaviour from their family or peers.

Similarly, it would be unwise to invite young people to undertake their own online enquiry into either of these issues as part of PSHE education as there are websites that actively encourage self-harm and eating disorders and offer mutual support to sufferers. Source material should be carefully managed so that young people are aware of the dangers of such sites, and that those vulnerable or already suffering are not exposed to further unhealthy coping strategies.

What influences our health-related behaviour?

To understand best practice in teaching PSHE education, it is helpful to understand what influences behaviour in relation to physical and mental health.

This question has taxed public health researchers for many years, and there are numerous theories which can be used to design interventions and PSHE education programmes. Some of these theories and models were reviewed by Boddington et al. (2014) in *Understanding PSHE Education in Primary Schools*. Perhaps the most comprehensive and useful model for use with young people in school is the health action model, first developed by Tones (1987) and expanded by Green and Tones in 2010.

Health action model

The health action model (Tones, 1987; Green and Tones, 2010) focuses on the interaction between an individual's beliefs, their environment and the contribution education can make to their intentions to act in a given way. It draws on other well known models and theories of health-related behaviour and behaviour change, including the health belief model (Becker, 1984) and the theory of planned behaviour (Ajzen, 1991) among others (see Green and Tones, 2010).

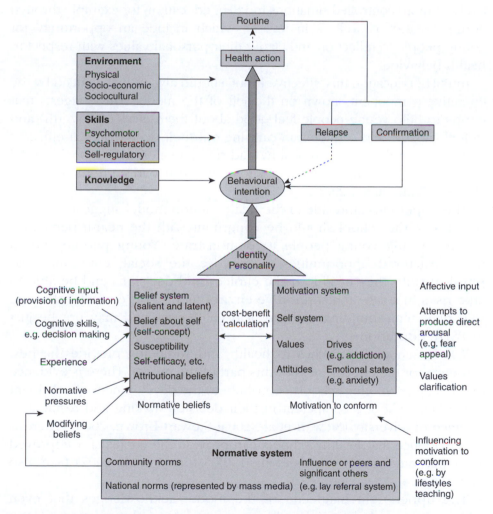

Figure 3.1   Health action model (adapted from Tones, 1987 and Green and Tones, 2010)

The health action model is particularly useful for planning in PSHE education. Figure 3.1 is based on two versions – one older and one more recent. At the base of this model are the norms of our community, family and peers, which have a powerful effect on our motivation and beliefs about health behaviour. The lower right-hand side shows how emotional arousal can influence our intentions. In communities this typically happens through high-profile media campaigns and in schools through visiting road shows or presentations that are intended to make young people fearful of the consequences of unhealthy or unsafe behaviour or can be inadvertently triggered for example by social media. Emotional arousal can be used positively in more controlled situations in PSHE education, for example through 'forum theatre' as well as in lessons which include an opportunity for young people to reflect on and clarify their personal values with respect to health behaviour.

In PSHE education this 'affective input' should always be balanced by the cognitive component shown on the left of the model. This suggests that efforts to help young people feel good about themselves (self-worth) and to feel capable and confident in carrying out their decisions (self-efficacy) will also help them to form healthy and safe intentions. Emotional arousal without this balancing input is likely to be ineffective in supporting healthy choices (Ruiter at al., 2001).

The upper left-hand side of the health action model suggests that the policies of the school should be congruent with the health behaviour we are asking young people to demonstrate. Young people should have structured opportunities to practise the social, emotional and physical skills they need to make choices and decisions and be able to take risks in a safe and supportive environment. This could be through role play, team building and physical challenges and may not be just in PSHE education.

Whole school approaches to health and wellbeing provide the best evidence for the effectiveness of this part of the model. There is evidence that health promoting schools contribute to the development of confident individuals who are competent in their decision making and resilient in the face of adversity (Stewart et al., 2004; Stewart-Brown, 2006). There is also evidence that healthy schools can provide the context for improved academic outcomes (Symons et al., 1997; Murray et al., 2007) (see also Chapter 4).

The upper right hand-side of the model acknowledges that even when we try to behave in healthy ways we don't always succeed, but that what we learn from failure as well as success can help us to do better next time.

Obviously not all of PSHE education is 'health education', but the health action model shows us not to expect a 'magic bullet' effect in PSHE education which will prevent all young people's personal, social, health or economic problems. Knowledge, social norms, some idea of personal susceptibility, our experience, our environment, our skills in decision making and our confidence in carrying out our decisions all matter when it comes to whether or not we make appropriate decisions. This suggests that using a range of approaches to teaching and learning in PSHE education might be more effective than focussing on one or another.

You may find it useful to refer back to this model as you read about the ten principles for effective practice in PSHE education.

Section 1 – Key principles of effective practice

In this section we consider ten key principles that underpin effective practice in PSHE education (PSHE Association, 2014). Evidence for the principles draws on our understanding of teaching and learning and of models of health-related behaviour such as the health action model above.

Principle 1

Start where children and young people are: find out what they already know, understand, are able to do and are able to say. For maximum impact involve them in the planning of your PSHE education programme.

Young people will all bring some prior understanding of most themes covered in PSHE education to their lessons. Whatever prior learning is in place, you need to be aware of it if you are to plan relevant PSHE education lessons. Whilst you may have a more detailed knowledge of the challenges and opportunities young people may experience, you also need to understand how they are making sense of these issues in their lives. Chapters 5 and 6 consider this principle in greater detail and offer some practical classroom techniques relevant to planning and assessing specific aspects of PSHE education.

Principle 2

Plan a 'spiral programme' that introduces new and more challenging learning while building on what has gone before, and which reflects and meets the personal developmental needs of the children and young people.

The spiral curriculum is a well known principle of any education programme and this is equally true in PSHE education, taking into consideration the changing needs of young people as they mature and experience new opportunities or challenges (McWhirter, 2009; Department of Education, 2015). Programmes should be designed to provide progressive, step-by-step learning, with topics covered in a logical order (Kirby et al., 2007), and a planned, sequenced approach to activities (Durlak et al., 2011).

Principle 3

Take a positive approach that does not attempt to induce shock or guilt but focuses on what children and young people can do to keep themselves and others healthy and safe and to lead happy and fulfilling lives.

It seems common sense that people avoid things they fear, so if you frighten young people about the consequences of different lifestyle choices they will avoid them. If only it were that simple. Our reaction to fear is very complex; for example, many people will queue to ride a rollercoaster or watch a frightening film because they enjoy the sensation.

If we are scared in a safe context; for example, in a cinema or a classroom, fear can transform into excitement which makes us want to repeat that experience. Fear arousal can also be unpredictable. For example, imagine you are already doing something risky such as using novel psychoactive substances (NPS) and a lesson makes you genuinely feel afraid. It is the teacher and the lesson that are causing your fear, not your NPS use, so the healthy message may be rejected. Fear can simply generate denial: 'It won't happen to me!' Studies into the effectiveness of drug and alcohol programmes have shown that attempts to scare pupils are found to be ineffective, or worse, to increase the likelihood of substance misuse (UNODC, 2004).

Principle 4

Offer a wide variety of teaching and learning styles within PSHE education, with an emphasis on interactive learning and the teacher as facilitator.

A range of research agrees that 'non-interactive strategies', or more simply those based on providing knowledge alone, are not effective (UNODC, 2004; Jones et al., 2014; Thomas et al., 2015). Opportunities to practise skills are identified as important by a number of reports (UNODC, 2004; Jones, 2010; Thomas et al., 2015). As one of the key aims of PSHE education is to develop skills and strategies such as communication, negotiation, decision making, managing risk and peer influence, it is self-evident that a didactic approach in which young people passively listen is not going to achieve this aim. Herbert and Lohrmann (2011) state that 'General characteristics of active learning include involving students in more than just listening, less emphasis on facts, more emphasis on developing skills, engaging students in activities and focusing their values and attitudes.' They argue that fact-based compared with skills-based curricula fail to incorporate active learning, and are less effective.

Principle 5

Provide information that is realistic and relevant and which reinforces positive social norms.

This principle means the information we share with young people must be grounded in fact and not unintentionally biased towards a particular negative behaviour. If 20 per cent of young people aged 11–15 years have *ever* smoked a cigarette, it means 80 per cent of young people have *never* smoked a cigarette; that is, the norm among young people is not to smoke at all. As every comedian knows, 'It's how you tell them'.

Critically, young people need to recognise either their 'present selves' or their 'future selves' in their PSHE education lessons in order to recognise why learning is relevant to them either now or in their future. Therefore it is also important that PSHE programmes are relevant to the communities in which they are delivered (Department for Education, 2015; Nation et al., 2003; Kirby et al., 2007) as well as to diversity in relation to culture, ethnicity, faith, disability, sexuality and gender identity. Kirby et al. (2007) note the importance of developing programmes that are relevant to youth culture as well.

Principle 6

Encourage young people to reflect on their learning and the progress they have made, and to transfer what they have learned to say and to do from one school subject to another, and from school to their lives in the wider community.

Because PSHE education helps young people learn about themselves, reflection and assessment are very closely linked. Providing young people with a structure to ask themselves 'What do I know, think, believe or feel now that I didn't before' or 'What can I say, do or appreciate now that I couldn't before' is critical. Genuine self-reflection can be one of the most powerful elements of learning in this subject. (This is considered in more depth in Chapter 6). PSHE education can provide a context to draw from across the curriculum (e.g. science may teach about the physiological effects of drugs) and connect this wider learning in a way that is relevant to the young people. (See also 'Understanding' in Section 2 below).

Principle 7

Recognise that the PSHE education programme is just one part of what a school can do to help a child to develop the knowledge, skills, attitudes and understanding they need to fulfil their potential. Link the PSHE education programme to other whole school approaches, to pastoral support, and provide a setting where the responsible choice becomes the easy choice. Encourage staff, families and the wider community to get involved.

Principle 8

Embed PSHE education within other efforts to ensure children and young people have positive relationships with adults, feel valued and where those who are most vulnerable are identified and supported.

This principle is explored in Chapters 8, 12 and 13.

Principle 9

Provide opportunities for children and young people to make real decisions about their lives, to take part in activities that simulate adult choices and where they can demonstrate their ability to take responsibility for their decisions.

No matter how well taught or comprehensive a PSHE education programme is, its effectiveness will be limited if it is not reinforced by the wider school curriculum and culture (see Chapter 4). Reviews of PSHE education (McWhirter, 2008, 2009; Nation et al., 2003; Public Health England, 2014) recommend the use of a 'whole school approach', linking the curriculum to whole school policies and to pastoral support (Mentor-ADEPIS, 2014), integrating preventative approaches within the broader curriculum (Berkowitz & Bier, 2005; Department of Education, 2015) as well as within discrete PSHE education.

Principle 10

Provide a safe and supportive learning environment where children and young people can develop the confidence to ask questions, challenge the information they are offered, draw on their own experience, express their views and opinions and put what they have learned into practice in their own lives.

Principle 10 is expanded in 'A safe classroom climate' on the next page.

Section 2 – One 'way into' structuring learning in PSHE education

We experience life not in 'topics' or 'issues' but in 'moments': some we can clearly foresee, some we expect but the details are unclear and some are completely unexpected. Almost all will require us to make a choice or a decision: some will be mundane with little real consequence of getting it 'right' or 'wrong', some will be critical with more serious consequences and some are the 'crunch moments' when our lives could go on a totally new trajectory depending on our choice.

Making a choice

Think about a few different choices you have made, some trivial (e.g. 'What shall I have for dinner tonight?') and some more significant (e.g. 'Why have I decided on a career in education?).

Have you ever experienced a 'crunch moment' – one where your decision could have altered the course of your life? Think about what you needed to know and understand in order to manage that moment. Next, think about the skills and strategies you needed to use to manage the moment, including what you needed to be able to say as well as do. Finally, think about the personal attributes that helped you manage the moment.

Thinking of those three elements (the knowledge, the skills and the attributes), what role did each play at the precise moment at which you had to make your choice? And what role did they play at the moment when you had to enact your choice? Was one more or less important at that moment than the others?

At crunch moments, we make our choices through a complex combina- tion of our previous experiences, our knowledge and understanding, filtered through our values, our attitudes and our beliefs. The action we take once we have made a choice is dependent upon our personal attrib- utes such as self-confidence, self-esteem and empathy, and our strategies and skills, such as risk management, negotiation, verbal and non-verbal communication. As we have already seen, knowledge alone is not enough and is arguably the least useful of the three elements when facing a crunch moment and enacting a decision.

PSHE education provides the opportunities to develop the skills, strategies and attributes, together with the knowledge and understanding that are so crucial to managing the myriad 'moments' young people encounter. It allows them to draw out what might otherwise have been an 'unconscious' decision, examine it, consider the possible consequences, consider what might 'unconsciously' influence their decision, perhaps compare these with those of their peers, to draw on the experiences of others, imagine the consequences of different choices and actions and explore the alternatives.

Putting pedagogy into practice: The three components of an effective PSHE education lesson

1. A safe classroom climate

Because PSHE education explores young people's day-to-day lives, including potentially sensitive issues, before teaching any PSHE education lesson you must create a safe teaching and learning environment in the classroom. For example, if we are exploring abuse in relationships, some young people in our class may (or more likely will) have experience of an abusive relationship. For this reason one of the most important aspects of teaching PSHE education is establishing 'groundrules' or a 'working agreement'. It is always better to come up with these together as a group, so that young people share 'ownership' of them and see their relevance, rather than imposing a pre-ordained set; however, you may need to steer the process and make suggestions to ensure that important considerations are covered.

The first important consideration is to establish the limits of confidentiality, ensuring that young people understand that if you believe they are vulnerable or at risk you will need to act on their behalf (being honest and clear about what this means). The second is to prohibit personal stories during the lesson – this does not mean that young people are unable to share their concerns with you – and to ensure that opportunities to talk after lessons will be in place and publicised. The third is to encourage questions and allow for anonymous questions.

Table 3.1 presents a useful set of ground rules constructed for lessons exploring discrimination adapted from material produced by Remembering Srebrenica (2015) to raise young people's awareness of the genocide that took place in 1995.

Ground rules alone will not ensure a safe learning environment. Due to the personal nature of the subject and the fact that it is a curriculum subject, not a therapeutic intervention, we need to ensure that the learning

Table 3.1 Ground rules exploring discrimination (adapted from Remembering Srebrenica, 2015)

Ground rule	What this might mean to pupils
Openness	'We will be open and honest but not discuss directly our own or others' personal/private lives. We will discuss general situations as examples but will not use names or descriptions which could identify anyone. We will not put anyone "on the spot" or under pressure to contribute.'
Keep the conversation in the room	'We feel safe discussing general issues relating to discrimination within this lesson and we know that our teacher will not repeat what is said in the classroom unless they are concerned we are at risk, in which case they will follow the school's safeguarding policy.'
Non-judgmental approach	'It is OK for us to disagree with another person's point of view but we will not judge, make fun of or put anybody down. We will "challenge the opinion, not the person".'
Right to pass	'Taking part is important; however, we have the right to pass on answering a question or participating in an activity.'
Make no assumptions	'We will not make assumptions about people's values, attitudes, behaviours, life experiences or feelings.'
Listening to others	'We will listen to other peoples' points of view and expect to be listened to.'
Using language	'We will use the correct terms for the things we will be discussing rather than the slang terms as some people can find them offensive. If we are not sure what the correct term is we will ask our teacher.'
Asking questions	'We know that there are no stupid questions. We do not ask questions to deliberately try to embarrass anyone else. We know we can make use of the question box if we want to ask something anonymously.'*
Seeking help and advice	'If we need further help or advice we know it will be available after the lesson. We also know how and where to seek it confidentially both in school and in the community. We will encourage friends to seek such help if we think they need it and will support them if they wish it'

*Note: Teachers should make sure that a question box is available from the start of the lessons (a large envelope will suffice if necessary) and ensure that it is accessible after the lesson so that students can use it anonymously.

is 'distanced from the learner', at least when approaching a new theme or concept. 'Distancing' creates an 'emotional space' between the young people and the issue that is being explored. For example, asking 'Imagine you are in abusive relationship. What would you say or do?' at best could be difficult for young people who have never experienced this and at worst could reconnect young people who have had such an experience with disturbing or painful memories, potentially re-traumatising them and certainly inhibiting further learning. Instead, using a short video clip, scenario, dialogue or asking 'Imagine a friend of yours had been approached by someone they know. They have told them they are being abused and don't know how to advise them. They ask you for your help. What would you say or do?' enables us to explore strategies objectively in the first instance.

In order to maintain a safe learning environment when encouraging questions, make provision for anonymous questions. Sometimes the 'ask it basket' or anonymous question box only comes out once a year at the start of a module of relationships and sex education. However, we should always encourage young people to ask questions on any of their learning in PSHE education, and they should always have the option of doing this anonymously. The anonymous question box should be available before, during and after PSHE education lessons and therefore it is important to locate it somewhere easily accessible whilst not too public. Sometimes you might want this to be part of the lesson, in which case you could give everyone a slip of paper and ask them all to write either a question or 'no question' to ensure that no-one feels self-conscious about being seen to be writing. An alternative is to ask everyone to write what they had for breakfast or watched on television yesterday and then add any questions they have.

2. Clear learning objectives and intended learning outcomes but a flexible approach

It is important to stress that the apparent contradiction in the heading to this section is deliberate. Lessons in PSHE education are no different from any other lesson in needing clear learning objectives (what the lesson aims to provide for young people) and intended learning outcomes (what they will know, be able to say or do at the end of the lesson). However, there will be times when the young people take the lesson in a different, perhaps more valuable or relevant direction and you need to make a judgement about whether to bring the lesson back to its original objective or allow the young people to lead their own learning. This is when you step back from 'leading the learning' to 'facilitating the learning'. If you start where young people are and involve them in planning their PSHE education, the learning objectives will more closely match the learning outcomes.

3. Learning that balances expanding knowledge, deepening understanding, exploring attitudes, values and beliefs, and developing language, strategies, skills and attributes

Focusing on knowledge

These are the parts of the lesson that provide young people, in a balanced way, with the most up-to-date information that they will need to make an informed choice. It is vital that you provide an accurate picture. Education is not propaganda, and the moment young people believe you are trying to influence their choices by providing false or unbalanced information the learning opportunity is lost.

The role of social norms

It is not simply providing information about the topic. Young people often hold a distorted view, overestimating, sometimes significantly, the risk-taking behaviour of their peers. They may mistakenly believe that all their peers drink alcohol, have sex regularly or use illegal drugs and that those who do not are in the minority. This can create an internal pressure to 'be like everyone else' when in fact their behaviour is in the, often massive, majority. This pressure can be even stronger if the young person believes this behaviour is essential to be accepted by their peers. Normative education is a process that actively promotes 'positive social norms' (McWhirter, 2009) and can reassure young people of the actual extent of different risk taking behaviours of their peers which may be lower – often far lower – than they may have previously believed. Simple activities such as asking young people to estimate the percentages of people their age who have ever smoked cannabis or regularly drink alcohol, for example, then asking them to research the actual percentages can help to redress the balance of their perception.

Focusing on understanding

The critical thing about knowledge is that you need to help young people turn it into understanding. Help them to see its relevance to them and to 'process it' through active learning. It is essential that young people get the chance to explore questions such as:

- So what does this mean to me?
- Why is it important I know this?
- Where can I see myself using this information?
- How does it relate to other things I already know?
- What might I do or say differently now that I know this or can do this?
- What questions do I now have?

We will look at the timing of inputting knowledge and developing understanding in more depth below.

Focusing on attitudes, values and beliefs

Because our attitudes, values and beliefs are so critical in our decision-making, asking the question 'And what do you feel about this?' is probably the single most important question you ask in PSHE education. Without the opportunity to explore and share our values, attitudes and beliefs it is possible for them to affect our decision making in ways we may not recognise. We may be influenced by a belief that when examined more closely is not congruent with the rest of our feelings.

Let's look at a simple way into this. You could identify five positions in the classroom corresponding to 'strongly agree', 'agree', 'not sure', 'disagree' and 'strongly disagree' and invite young people to stand in the position that corresponds to their view as you read to them statements of belief, for example 'Women are better suited to certain jobs than men.':

1. Discuss why they have chosen their different positions and to consider the arguments others have made.
2. Ask those who were 'not sure' if they have heard any argument that has made them less uncertain.
3. Offer the opportunity to move position if they feel they have heard a convincing argument.

This activity is sometimes called an 'attitude continuum' and can demonstrate to young people that even within their class their peers may hold a variety of views about different issues. For some young people this can come as a surprise. For those who feel they are the 'odd one out', it can be encouraging to find they are not alone in their views. It is important in this type of activity to not leave young people vulnerable, so if a single young person is isolated then use your judgement to either invite them to respond, if you feel they would be confident to do so, or if you feel this would be putting them 'on the spot' simply move onto the next statement.

Focusing on language, strategies and skills

We can consider these separately or together. If we are to manage a situation we will need to find the right words, employ them skilfully and do this within the context of a strategy. For example, imagine a young person needs 'to negotiate contraception with a partner'. They will need a language to offer convincing argument and the skills first of negotiation and perhaps if this fails of assertiveness. They may need to pick their time, perhaps recognising when a sexually intimate encounter is likely, so as not to appear 'pushy' but not leaving it so late that they get 'carried away in the moment'.

A PSHE education lesson offers young people a chance to find the words they feel comfortable and confident using and to 'rehearse' their use in a safe environment, where they can 'muck it all up' and try again. They can practise different approaches and through this gain both skills and confidence. Ideally young people faced with a real 'crunch moment' should feel 'I have been here before, I know what to say and do'. Two powerful routes in are through roleplay and forum theatre, which are discussed in Section 3 below.

Developing attributes

In the box below, you are asked to list the personal attributes that helped you manage a particular crunch moment. Perhaps you identified attributes such as confidence, self-esteem, a sense of your own identity, values and 'moral compass', resilience and empathy. The claim that 'effective PSHE education develops personal attributes' trips off the tongue easily but it is this aspect of PSHE education that is perhaps the most challenging for teachers. How do we go about teaching them?

Developing personal attributes

For the personal attributes listed above, make a note of everything a young person might do in a PSHE education lesson that might build or support the development of that particular attribute. For example, using role play to rehearse skills such as managing peer pressure, communicating assertively or being interviewed for a job will build confidence, while being offered opportunities to identify their personal strengths and set targets for development will contribute to self-esteem.

Looking at your notes from the activity above, you may now feel that developing personal attributes is more a by-product of PSHE education teaching and learning; for example, a lesson on managing peer pressure has the additional effect of developing self-confidence. This is true; however, it is also possible to focus specifically on the development of an attribute through our teaching. For example, we may wish to focus explicitly on developing resilience and as part of that might plan a lesson on managing disappointments and setbacks through which our intended outcome is that the young people will be able to describe or demonstrate appropriate techniques to manage disappointments and setbacks in difficult situations and understand how to learn from mistakes and reframe disappointments and setbacks.

Activity

How might you go about providing opportunities within PSHE education lessons for young people to develop a sense of their own identity, values and 'moral compass'? Brainstorm a range of activities and key questions that you might use to facilitate this learning.

Going deeper – using 'story' or 'case studies' as one practical route in

Let's consider one model of constructing learning in PSHE education that draws on the building blocks above. There are many, but this illustrates a useful way into almost any topic.

Lesson material needs to take pupils safely into exploring a 'critical' or 'crunch' moment, so this model makes extensive use of questioning and story. 'Story' (or scenarios and case studies) is one of the most powerful routes into our thinking and one of the best 'distancing techniques'. Stories need not be long: when challenged to write a short story, Hemingway wrote 'For sale, baby shoes, never worn'. Fragments of a story have power to draw us in; they make us curious to know what happened before and what will happen next.

> Sam was sitting by the wall, head in hands. Concerned, Jaz walked up. 'You OK?' Jaz asked. Sam sighed, looking up. 'It's them. It is all starting up again.'

You can build learning around a 'moment' in a 'story' but this needs to be constructed carefully. When we hear a story, we create our own internal 'movie'. So construct stories that do not disrupt the images young people might have, by using 'clean language'[1] to provide stories that are emotionally complex but provide no precise detail. Characters may have names but are never physically described. Each location is 'clean', so the young people never meet 'in the park' but 'where they hang out'. Whatever young people construct in their imagination is theirs and remains valid.

---

[1] The use of 'clean language' in story was influenced by the therapeutic work of David Grove.

Creating emotional zones or 'distancing'

We have already discussed the importance of 'distancing' learning as part of creating a safe learning environment earlier in this chapter. Stories by their nature, distance, taking young people from a cool 'disassociated' zone[2], 'Imagine you were watching this from somewhere safe' to a warmer zone, 'Imagine you were invisible to everyone but the main character. Imagine they asked your advice' to a still warmer zone, 'Imagine you are seeing yourself there as part of what is happening'. This is illustrated in Figure 3.2.

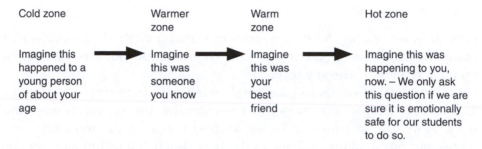

Figure 3.2   Creating zones to help control pupils' emotional exposure

The hot 'associated' zone 'Imagine you are there', or the very hot zone 'Imagine this is happening to you', should only be used when you feel it is safe to do so. Our brains react quite differently when imagining witnessing an event as a 'distant observer' to imagining experiencing the event now, through our own eyes. In this way you can control the 'emotional exposure' the pupils have to any issue.[2]

Using a 'timeline' to deconstruct a case study or scenario

A 'timeline' provides a way to 'deconstruct' and allows young people to engage with the story. They can 'make a movie in their heads' using your story as the 'present'. You can press the 'pause button' then encourage pupils to 'rewind' and explore what could have led to this moment. Explore how the characters could have been better prepared, questions they could have asked and strategies they could have applied.

---

[2] Using 'associated' and 'disassociated' positions to change emotional responses to events is a technique used in supporting individuals managing post-traumatic stress.

Explore whether they might have made a different choice if they had known this was going to happen. Help them create an immediate, short- and long-term future, or multiple alternative futures, exploring the likely consequences of different choices.

You can explore what information they might need in order to advise the characters, or you can add in new characters. For example: 'Imagine someone who really cared about them was watching. Would this change their behaviour or choices? Why?'

This can help young people understand that they themselves may have more than one position on an issue. You can now add new information, asking how this might change the story, influence advice they offer others or their own decisions.

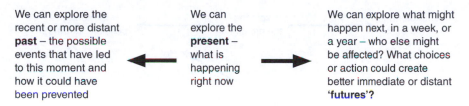

Figure 3.3   Exploring the past, present and futures

You now have two 'dimensions' that you and your students can explore (see Figure 3.3). To our left and right we had the past, present and future of the timeline. Forwards and backwards we had the emotional temperature from cold to hot. Now you can add a third vertical dimension.[3] At the lowest level teachers can ask questions about the environment in which this 'moment' is taking place. For example, is where you experiment with alcohol important? Is meeting someone for the first time, whom you have only previously spoken to online, safer in public or in private?

Moving up a level, we can explore what is influencing characters' behaviour and language and the consequences of their behaviour and language. Above that are questions about the knowledge, understanding and skills people might need in order to achieve a better outcome. You could ask students if they also need to acquire this knowledge and understanding or develop these skills. Still higher, students can explore values, beliefs and feelings that the characters and they might hold. You can offer the opportunity

---

[3] This model of deconstructing story makes use of the 'logical levels' described by Robert Dilts as a framework for structuring questioning. The 'logical levels' is a central model within neuro-linguistic programming.

to reflect on their values, attitudes and beliefs, share them if appropriate and if necessary challenge them. At the next level, you can explore how 'who we are' influences our choices and finally how others' expectations of them – perhaps family, 'significant others', faith or belief – might influence their own or others' choices. Figure 3.4 illustrates putting this all together.

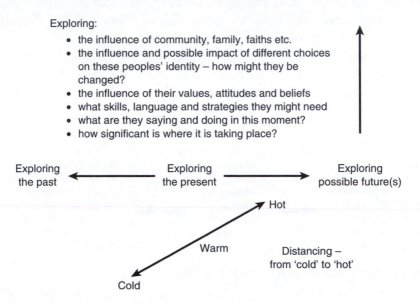

Exploring:

- the influence of community, family, faiths etc.
- the influence and possible impact of different choices on these peoples' identity – how might they be changed?
- the influence of their values, attitudes and beliefs
- what skills, language and strategies they might need
- what are they saying and doing in this moment?
- how significant is where it is taking place?

Exploring the past   Exploring the present   Exploring possible future(s)

Hot

Warm   Distancing – from 'cold' to 'hot'

Cold

Figure 3.4   The three-dimensional space of exploration

Now you have a 'three-dimensional space' within which you can structure and direct young people's learning. You do not have to do all this in one single lesson; you can choose the route you take within these three dimensions. (See Appendix I for example questions).

Because this model encourages dialogue, lesson evaluation is a natural extension of the learning. Because it starts from where pupils are and encourages critical self-reflection on the learning, assessment becomes a natural element of the learning process. It is not 'assessment for learning', it is 'assessment as learning' (see Chapter 6, which explores assessment in greater detail).

Section 3 – Active learning techniques in PSHE education lessons

There are literally thousands of techniques for enabling individuals and groups to learn actively. These are some that we recommend.

'First thoughts' activities

For 'first thoughts' activities, see Chapter 5 'Starting where young people are' and Chapter 6 on 'Assessing learning in PSHE education'.

Facilitated discussion

Many PSHE education lessons require you to facilitate discussions. This is a skill that is learnt over time and needs to be practised. It is a combination of questions or tasks to focus discussion, drawing out existing thinking, using responses to extend and build young people's thinking and where necessary adding in new knowledge or perspectives that are not forthcoming, using language such as 'Imagine you knew…, how does this change your thinking?'.

Always give the class 'thinking time'. Silence may not mean a young person doesn't know the answer, just that they are thinking one up. Try counting to ten in your own head before reframing a question.

Where possible avoid telling any young person that their ideas or opinions in PSHE education are simply 'wrong'. We need a high level of trust and respect in someone else to let go of a belief on simply being told that we are wrong. The danger is that far from letting go of an idea or belief, we may 'entrench' it deeper. Wherever possible, challenge misunderstandings or inappropriate strategies by asking 'What would things be like if that were true?' or 'If we did that, what are all the things that might happen next, soon, in the future?' For example, imagine a young person said 'I think you can catch HIV through kissing.' We could say 'No you can't.' This requires them to believe that we are right. However, if we ask them 'If HIV could be passed by kissing, what would the world be like?', the answer would be that almost everyone would have HIV. We can then ask 'Is the world really like this? So do you think HIV can be passed by kissing?' We are more likely to influence new thinking if we help young people explore the consequences of their strategies or misunderstandings through challenge rather than confrontation. We also want young people to develop the thinking skill of exploring the consequences of beliefs or actions.

Home and away groups

If young people always work with their friends there is a danger that values of that group can be mutually supportive. Whilst this can be positive it can also be destructive. 'Home groups' are the young person's friends within the class; away groups are new groups where they have an opportunity to interact with others. Consider how to construct 'away groups' for different activities and without it seeming like friendships are being divided for disciplinary reasons. Simple methods include giving each young person a number or colour; they find everyone with the same number or colour and that becomes the away group for that lesson.

Market place

When different groups have done their tasks you could ask each group to report back their findings to the whole class. This takes up a considerable time for what can be little new learning. Market place is an alternative that generates far more discussion. Two young people from each group stay with their work and the rest of the group circulate and look at others' work. Ask those 'shopping' to look for ideas they agree with, want clarified, want to challenge, or to 'borrow' and take back to their group. After a few minutes, invite the groups to swap roles. Bring the groups back together to discuss ideas they have borrowed from other groups. Then take a quick 'whole class' feedback by asking a more focused question such as 'Did any group have an idea that you felt so important you wanted to 'borrow it'?

Role play

Role play is a powerful opportunity for young people to 'try on' new attributes, language or strategies in order to test what this feels like or how useful strategies are when put into practice. There is, however, a danger in role play and it should never be used without extremely careful planning and management. Role play is a powerful technique for practising positive strategies; however, others in role may be practising negative behaviours, language and strategies, some of which may be enjoyable (e.g. practising how to bully others). We recommend that you restrict role play to pair and small group activity and ask pupils where possible to adopt 'positive roles' and the teacher or teaching assistant can take the negative role.

Asking groups to demonstrate their 'role play' to a wider group also needs sensitive management. Many young people dread 'performing', and its use is seldom necessary. An alternative is to group students in threes; two who undertake the role play and one observer who will feed back observations.

It is vital to de-role everybody, to reduce the possibility of the person subsequently being confused with that character's feelings, limitations, views or negative behaviour. One way to achieve this is to ask the young person to state his or her name, and say one thing about themselves which *is* true and draw distinctions between him or her and the character they just played. For example: 'I'm Aamna, I can't stand violence, and I don't easily lose my temper like [character's name] did.'

Class debates

Debates can encourage flexible thinking and empathy, and develop research skills and structured arguments, but must be sensitively handled. With young people who might be at risk of or already have a risky lifestyle, researching and arguing the benefits of the positive choice might positively influence future choices or be the first stage in change. Inviting young people who already hold positive opinions or have made healthy choices to prepare and argue in favour of a risky behaviour may be cognitively demanding, open up unconsidered points of view and increase empathy. However, it might also install doubts in a previously strongly held 'positive' position, lower a previously strong resistance to that behaviour and result in a loss of confidence in applying previously useful strategies. It may be better to debate the strengths of two potentially healthy options or positions rather than two extreme positions. For example, debating 'This house believes minimum unit pricing of alcohol would reduce deaths from alcohol related diseases' starts from the assumption that alcohol is harmful and is better than 'This house believes alcohol is harmful, since those opposing the latter motion would have to find and put arguments to support the view that alcohol is not harmful.'

Micro debates

Rather than whole class debates where a small number of pupils may do the bulk of the work while the majority of the class are passive, micro debates are carried out in groups of four. Two present their prepared opposing cases to the other two who decide which has the more convincing argument. The pairs then swap roles. This smaller audience retains the intellectual exercise and involves everyone whilst minimising the potential nerves associated with presenting in front of a large and often passive audience. As with any debate it is also important to 'de-role' contributors afterwards. There is some evidence that unless you do this, positive feelings created towards a previously negatively held position can remain.

Carousel

The carousel technique helps young people to share ideas and explore issues, with everyone taking an active part. With the class, generate a list of questions or statements about an issue or idea. Arrange the class in two concentric circles, those in the inner circle facing a partner in the outer circle. You will need enough slips of paper for each chair in the outer circle. Write one question/statement on each slip, (repeating some if necessary) and place one on each outer chair (where it stays when students move). Each pair has a brief conversation. After a short time, ask those in the *inner* circle to stand up and move one place to their left. Repeat – and after another brief conversation ask the students in the *outer* circle to move one place to their left, onto a new question or statement. Repeat until the issue has been reasonably aired. Invite class feedback.

Forum theatre

In the forum theatre version of role play the characters in role are 'directed' by the class. They must follow the script and strategies offered by the group. A simple way to manage this is to allow different groups to control different characters, with the characters indicating a 'time out' when they need to consult their group for advice. The groups can also call for 'time out' when they want to suggest a new strategy to their character to test.

A useful technique is to 'freeze frame' the action at an important point. Anyone in the 'audience' may stop the action using an agreed signal. This still image of characters where position, expression and body language may be important is then discussed. Individuals in the freeze frame can be asked to say, in character, what they are thinking and suggest how the scene could be replayed differently. You can also allow the person who stopped the action, or another volunteer, to take the place of one of the characters to try out a different strategy within the scene, developing it along more desirable lines, or to explore other options.

Conscience alley

'Conscience alley' is a way of exploring a choice that a character must make. Divide the class into two equal groups. Ask the young people to discuss issues in a scenario with their group. One group generates statements to encourage the person to take one option (e.g. 'Talk it through with someone you trust first'), with one statement for each member of the group. The other group generates statements in favour of the other option (e.g. 'Make your own mind up – it's your life'). The groups line up opposite each other and you, or a volunteer, walk down the middle in role as the character in question and listen to alternate statements. On reaching the end of the alley the character decides what to do and explains why.

Goldfish bowl

In the goldfish bowl technique, one group completes a task whilst others observe, often with a checklist of things to watch and listen for. It helps uncover other people's thinking when faced with a problem. After a while, stop the discussion and ask the observers to feed back their comments to those 'in the bowl'. This can be useful, for example, when focusing on developing team-working skills.

Ranking

Provide young people with a series of options and ask them to rank them according to a defined criterion, such as urgency, high/low risk, usefulness, acceptability etc. The final ranking is less important than the discussion, and groups can compare and justify their rankings. The exercise can feel more relevant if the young people generate the options or topics to be ranked. If you choose to pre-prepare statements, leave one blank for the young people to add one of their own and invite them to explain why they have added this statement.

Concept mapping

Concept mapping is one of many ways of helping young people express their thinking visually. Other methods include flow diagrams, timelines and Venn diagrams. These can help capture and structure thinking and lend themselves well to baseline and end point assessment (see Chapter 6).

Chapter overview

In this chapter we have looked at the principles that underpin effective practice in PSHE education. Some apply directly to the subject whilst others provide a supportive context. We then explored the 'building blocks' of PSHE education lessons before considering how using case studies and scenarios could offer a useful route into any sensitive issues. We ended with an overview of some active learning methods employed by PSHE education teachers. It is important to now read Chapters 5 and 6, which contain an in-depth exploration of how to plan PSHE education lessons and build in assessment for and of learning.

References

Azjen, I. (1991) 'The theory of planned behaviour', *Organisational and Human Decision Processes*, 50: 179–211.

Becker, M.H. (1984) *The Health Belief Model and Personal Health Behaviour*. Thorofare, NJ: Charles B. Slack.

Berkowitz, M.W. and Bier, M.C. (2005) *What Works in Character Education: A Research Driven Guide for Educators*. Washington, DC: Character Education Partnership.

Boddington, N., King, A. and McWhirter, J. (2014) *Understanding PSHE in the Primary School*. London: Sage.

Department of Education (2015) *PSHE Education: A Review of Impact and Effective Practice*. London: Department of Education.

Durlak, J.A., Weissberg, R.P., Dymnicki, A.B., Taylor, R.D. and Schellinger, K.B. (2011) 'The impact of enhancing students' social and emotional learning: a meta-analysis of school-based universal interventions', *Child Development*, 82(1),: 405–432.

Green, J. and Tones, B.K. (2010) *Health Promotion: Planning and Strategies*. London: Sage.

Herbert, P.C. and Lohrmann, D.K. (2011) 'It's all in the delivery! An analysis of instructional strategies from effective health education curricula', *Journal of School Health*, 81: 258–64.

Jones, L.M. (2010) *The Future of Internet Safety Education: Critical Lessons from Four Decades of Youth Drug Abuse Prevention*. Boston, MA: The Publius Project, Harvard University.

Jones, L.M., Mitchell, K.J. and Walsh, W.A. (2014) *A Systematic Review of Effective Youth Prevention Education: Implications for Internet Safety Education*. Durham, NH: Crimes Against Children Research Center (CCRC), University of New Hampshire.

Kirby, D., Rolleri, L.A. and Wilson, M.M. (2007) *Tool to Assess the Characteristics of Effective Sex and STD/HIV Education Programs*. Washington, DC: Healthy Teen Network.

McWhirter, J. (2008) *A Review of Safety Education: Principles for Effective Practice*. London: Department for Children, Schools and Families/PSHE Association/ Royal Society for the Prevention of Accidents.

McWhirter, J. (2009) *The Theory and Practice of PSHE Education*. London: PSHE Association.

Mentor-ADEPIS (2014) *Quality Standards for Effective Drug and Alcohol Education*. London: Mentor-ADEPIS.

Murray, N.G., Low, B.J., Hollis, C., Cross, A.W. and Davis, S.M. (2007) 'Coordinated school health programs and academic achievement: a systematic review of the literature', *Journal of School Health*, 77(9): 589–600.

Nation, M., Crusto, C., Wandersman, A., Kumpfer, K.L., Seybolt, D., Morrisey-Kane, E. and Davino, K. (2003) 'What works in prevention: principles of effective prevention programmes', *American Psychologist*, 58(6/7): 449–56.

PSHE Association (2014) 'Ten principles of good practice in PSHE education'. Available at www.pshe-association.org.uk/content.aspx?CategoryID=1156 (accessed 14.1.16).

Public Health England (2014) *Local Action on Health Inequalities: Building Children and Young People's Resilience in School*. London: Institute of Health Equity/Public Health England.

Remembering Srebrenica (2015) 'PSHE programme of study for Srebrenica'. Available at www.srebrenica.org.uk/education-packs/ (accessed 29.10.15).

Ruiter, R.A.C., Abraham, C. and Kok, G. (2001) 'Scary warnings and rational precautions: the psychology of fear appeals', *Psychology and Health*, 16(6): 613–30.

Stewart, D., Sun, J., Patterson, C., Lemerle, K. and Hardie, M. (2004) 'Promoting and building resilience in primary school communities: evidence from a comprehensive 'health promoting school' approach', *International Journal of Mental Health Promotion*, 6(3): 26–33.

Stewart-Brown, S. (2006) 'What is the evidence on school health promotion in improving health or preventing disease and, specifically, what is the effectiveness of the health promoting schools approach?', Copenhagen, WHO Regional Office for Europe Health Evidence Network Report. Available at www.euro.who.int/document/e88185.pdf(accessed 25.1.16)

Symons, C.W., Cinelli, B., James, T.C. and Groff, P. (1997) 'Bridging student health risks and academic achievement through comprehensive school health programs', *Journal of School Health*, 67: 220–27.

Thomas, R.E., McLellan, J. and Perera, R. (2015) 'Effectiveness of school-based smoking prevention curricula: systematic review and meta-analysis', *BMJ Open*, 5(3).

Tones, K. (1987) 'Health promotion, affective education and personal-social development of young people', in David, K. and Williams, T. (eds), *Health Education in Schools*. London: Harper Row.

United Nations Office on Drugs and Crime (UNODC) (2004) *School-based Education for Drug Abuse Prevention*. New York: United Nations.

4

The Organisation of PSHE Education in the Curriculum

Aim

By the end of this chapter you will understand the different ways PSHE education is organised in the curriculum.

Learning objectives

Through reading and reflecting on the content of this chapter you will begin to:

- understand the different delivery models for PSHE education
- appreciate the advantages and disadvantages of each approach
- understand the concept of a 'whole school approach' and that of the 'healthy school'.

Before we start

Think back to your own experience of PSHE education or consider a school with which you are familiar. How was PSHE education organised? How did the organisation of the programme contribute to or limit its effectiveness?

Introduction

Secondary schools use a variety of structures to provide PSHE education for students. In this chapter the pros and cons of different approaches will be reviewed. You will be guided in how to achieve the best outcome for young people from the structure prevailing in the schools in which you teach. PSHE education is at its most effective when part of a whole school approach. The idea of a healthy school is examined and evidence reviewed. Sources of support for a whole school approach will also be examined.

Leadership and management

The vast majority of secondary schools provide a programme of PSHE education; however, the first difficulty is the plethora of names used to 'label it' from 'PSHE education' through 'life skills', 'personal development', 'learning for life', 'living and learning' plus many more. There is no subject in secondary schools that is organised in as many different ways as PSHE education.

Most schools will have one person with responsibility for leading and managing PSHE education. Again, a number of different titles are used for this role, most commonly 'PSHE education lead' or 'PSHE education co-ordinator'. While one might argue that the job title is not important, schools are increasingly adopting 'PSHE education lead' to emphasise the fact that the role is about subject leadership, having a vision for PSHE education and leading developments and improvements in its provision, rather than merely co-ordinating those teaching it, ensuring that resources are available and other more 'managerial' responsibilities. The PSHE education lead's 'status' within the school can also be highly variable. In some schools they might be a member of the school leadership team whilst in others their role can be much 'lower' in the school's leadership and management hierarchy and this in turn can present difficulties. Where the lead has status then issues pertinent to PSHE education will be a part of senior leadership discussion. Where the subject lead does not, it can often be difficult for PSHE education to be part of such dialogue. This means that PSHE education can be at the heart of one school's overall mission and strategic thinking whilst in another it is barely on the agenda or is a tokenistic add-on.

The level of seniority of the PSHE education lead can be affected by his or her own level of teaching experience and by the overall vision of the head teacher concerning the aims and objectives of their school. Unlike other subjects, the status of PSHE education in any school can be vulnerable to staff turnover, especially if the school loses a keen advocate for PSHE education who acts as champion for the subject.

This can be compounded if the outgoing lead was a member of the school's leadership team and the school uses this as an opportunity to restructure roles and responsibilities of their team. There is no guarantee that an incoming PSHE education lead will enjoy the same seniority, and the status of the subject may fall.

Who teaches PSHE education?

Because the organisation of PSHE education can be so varied, this chapter can only cover the most common models. As you will see, each has strengths and weakness. Sadly, from our collective experience, there is a 'rippling effect'. Unsurprisingly the degree to which young people value their experience of PSHE education reflects the degree to which their teachers value the subject. This in turn is reflected by the commitment of the school's senior leadership to PSHE education. Young people who have received a high-quality PSHE education frequently report that it is one of the most important subjects in their curriculum. First we need to consider who teaches PSHE education in secondary schools.

The specialist team: This approach has a team of PSHE education specialists. They will have chosen to teach PSHE education as part of their role within the school, although they may continue to teach other subjects. There is currently no initial teacher training courses in PSHE education, so in secondary schools these 'specialists' will be teachers of other subjects who have received specific training in PSHE education as part of their continuing professional development (CPD). It is likely that they will be confident in the use of interactive teaching strategies and will be knowledgeable on a variety of issues relevant to PSHE education. Some teachers may specialise in specific aspects, for example teaching relationships and sex education, careers education or economic well-being. In many respects this is no different from any other department. In some schools there will be dedicated classrooms for PSHE education, giving it a greater sense of a 'physical' department.

Form tutors: In this model form tutors are expected to teach PSHE education as part of a tutorial programme, or in timetabled lessons. This means that teachers with a huge range of subject specialisms will be required to teach a complex subject, often with little specific subject knowledge or expertise. Where *all* tutors are committed to this approach and are well trained and supported, this model can work effectively as tutors tend to know their students well. However, it is no surprise that tutors often lack confidence in teaching PSHE education or don't value it, especially if they have received little or no specific training in teaching PSHE education, which is often the case. In this model the PSHE education lead's principle task is to ensure that all tutors are adequately prepared for undertaking this work. In some schools 'heads of year', 'heads of house' and members of the school leadership team may also play a role in teaching this area of the curriculum.

A combination of PSHE education specialists and form tutors: In this model form tutors teach PSHE education in Years 7–9 and specialists teach this subject in Years 10–11. The argument is sometimes given that it is in Years 10–11 that young people need access to more specialist knowledge.

Visitors to the classroom: In this model the subject lead arranges for a series of 'visitors' or external experts or agencies to provide young people with lectures and workshops. This model is most commonly used in 'suspended timetable' or 'drop down day' events examined below.

Teachers of other curriculum subjects, teaching through their own subject specialism: In this approach, PSHE education is not taught discretely but is theoretically embedded in all subjects' schemes of work and all teachers share responsibility for meeting the learning objectives and outcomes for PSHE education as well as those of their main subject.

Consider

In 2013 Ofsted published 'grade descriptors' for the teaching of PSHE education. Whilst no longer in the public domain following the suspension of subject survey visits for PSHE education, this framework provides an insight into Ofsted's view of 'outstanding teaching in PSHE education' with this descriptor:

> Teachers demonstrate very high levels of confidence and expertise in their specialist knowledge and in their understanding of effective learning in PSHE. Clear learning objectives are complemented by explicit and appropriate learning outcomes. Teachers use a very wide range of imaginative resources and strategies to

(Continued)

(Continued)

stimulate pupils' interest and active participation and, as a result, secure rapid and sustained progress. Highly effective and responsive teaching ensures the needs of all pupils, including the most able are met. Teachers are confident and skilled in discussing sensitive and/or controversial issues. Effective discussion is a very strong feature; pupils are encouraged to investigate, express opinions and listen to others. Consequently they develop excellent critical skills, can evaluate information well and make informed judgments. Teachers communicate very high expectations, enthusiasm and passion for PSHE. They know how well their pupils are achieving, build on their previous knowledge and provide effective feedback to help them to improve further. They ensure that pupils have their attainment and progress recognised across all aspects of knowledge and skills development in PSHE.

Consider the four teaching models above in the light of Ofsted's description of 'outstanding teaching' in PSHE education. What might be the advantages and disadvantages of each model?

Consider

There is a commonly held view that the model in which form tutors teach PSHE education in tutorials helps to strengthen the relationship between the tutor and their form. The argument is made that this is because this subject teaches issues directly related to young peoples' lives.

Why might this view be simplistic? We share our own views on this below.

Some advantages and disadvantages of the different models of PSHE education teaching

There are very few disadvantages to the specialist team and numerous advantages. There are many aspects of teaching PSHE education that can be challenging and it can take time to gain both the knowledge and confidence in the subject matter to feel comfortable in teaching this subject. It can also take confidence to allow a class of young people to take a degree of control over their learning: something that is essential in this subject. If there is a disadvantage, it can be that other teachers see PSHE education as something that only happens in these specialist lessons, whereas there are many opportunities to extend and reinforce learning in PSHE education in other subjects. Good examples would be science teaching aspects of reproduction, English exploring the media, and drama helping to develop assertiveness.

Tutors are unlikely to have the subject knowledge they need to provide a comprehensive PSHE education programme and it can be challenging to equip them with all the training they need. Also subject specialists are naturally going to focus the majority of their time on their main subject. With a form tutor delivery model it is difficult to ensure that all young people receive the same quality of provision. One creative solution found by an increasing number of schools involves each tutor becoming a specialist in one aspect of PSHE education and then teaching all the forms in a year group in carousel. These schools turn all their tutors into PSHE education topic specialists. There are advantages and disadvantages to the carousel model. There is likely to be increased teacher 'buy-in' to PSHE education, as they have a degree of choice over the strand of PSHE education they teach and they only have to plan and teach a limited number of lessons which they repeat with each cohort of young people through the year. On the other hand, there will still be variation in the expertise of the tutors; some will still not feel confident or motivated to take this on – it is more difficult to build rapport between teachers and young people and to assess learning over time, as each group only stays with one teacher for perhaps six lessons. Young people may also complain that their PSHE education is dominated by the subject specialism of their tutor, for example an over-emphasis on online safety by a computing specialist.

In a worrying trend, schools are sometimes attempting to deliver PSHE education within 'vertical tutor groups' (which contain a small number of young people from each year group). Those who advocate vertical tutoring as a model for pastoral care believe it leads to tutor groups having much more of a 'family feel', providing opportunities for pupils to learn from and support each other. Tutors are more able to spend time with pupils at key points in their school life, such as transition to Year 7 and when choosing post-16 options. Vertical tutoring gives young people a chance to work and socialise with people of different ages, preparing them for the adult world and many schools feel that it improves behaviour, reduces bullying and provides relief from peer pressure.

While these are compelling arguments in favour of this model for pastoral tutoring, we would never advocate it as a model for PSHE education lessons. Effective PSHE education is taught through a spiral programme, revisiting concepts and topic areas, each time extending knowledge, deepening understanding and developing skills. To plan such a programme to be taught in groups of young people of different ages and stages would be practically impossible. Even if a teacher managed to plan a lesson or module that was appropriate for everyone in the group, what would happen next year when the current Year 11s have gone and there is a new cohort of Year 7s? Effective PSHE education is also age and stage appropriate, taking the starting point and individual learning needs of young people into account. Again this would be impossible to achieve in a 'vertical group' and in the case of some elements of PSHE education, such as relationships and sex education or drug education, could potentially do more harm than good.

We turn now to the cross-curricular approach in which teachers of other curriculum subjects teach PSHE education integrated within their own subjects. The pedagogical arguments for and against this approach are explored later in this chapter when we consider the cross-curricular organisational model.

In terms of this approach to teaching PSHE education, to be done well, all teachers of subjects through which PSHE education is being taught would need to ensure that PSHE education learning objectives and outcomes are included in their lesson plans, be familiar with the pedagogy of PSHE education and be able to assess, record and report learning in PSHE education as part of their work. Subject teachers already have high demands placed on them and it is likely that the PSHE education elements of such an approach would be lost as the pressure to cover the knowledge and understanding and possibly the examination syllabus of the subject increases.

So what about PSHE education being delivered by 'visitors' or external providers? There is a powerful place for 'visitors' in the teaching of PSHE education (see Chapter 13 for a deeper consideration). Consider for a moment the teaching of mathematics. It would be interesting to invite a bank manager in to discuss the role of interest in their work, or a member of the insurance industry to explain the place of odds in the assessment of risk. However, you would not remove our maths teachers and replace them entirely with such experts in every lesson and you would be very unlikely to leave the bank manager in charge of the group while you catch up on your marking.

The knowledge, skills, language, strategies and attributes developed through PSHE education and the opportunities young people need to explore and clarify their values and beliefs need the same continuity and progression as any other subject. What can easily become a 'parade' of experts can provide knowledge but rarely the true breadth of experience offered by a comprehensive programme.

Curriculum organisation

We now need to consider how PSHE education is organised within the timetable before exploring the benefits and challenges of each model.

Discrete PSHE education lessons: This model treats PSHE education in the same way as any other subject, with a lesson timetabled into the curriculum. There is, however, a further complexity. Some schools will attempt to 'merge' PSHE education, usually with citizenship, which is a statutory subject for maintained schools as part of the National Curriculum and occasionally also with RE to make one combined course.

Teaching PSHE education through 'tutor time': As we have seen above, this model involves form tutors teaching PSHE education within the time allocated as 'form time' or 'tutor time'.

'Rolling' PSHE education lessons: In this model a different lesson each week is replaced by PSHE education for the whole school, usually delivered by form tutors. For example, in week one, the whole school has PSHE education on Monday period 1, week two it's Monday period 2 and so on.

'Drop down' or 'collapsed timetable' events: These are different names for the same thing: instead of regular weekly lessons, a block of time is given over to PSHE education, for example a day per half term. These events usually focus on a particular 'topic area' of PSHE education, such as sex and relationships or 'enterprise', and may involve the whole school coming off their regular timetable for this period to explore issues relevant to their age range. If it is in a single year group then specialists may be able to teach all the young people; if the whole school is involved this will inevitably involve tutors.

Cross-curricular provision of PSHE education: As outlined above, this model attempts to embed PSHE education throughout the entire curriculum. In this model there are no identifiable PSHE education lessons, although there is usually a lead or co-ordinator. Through a curriculum mapping exercise the school will incorporate the learning objectives for PSHE education within other subjects' schemes of work.

Some schools employ a combination of the models above.

Consider

Again we can look at Ofsted's (2013) descriptors for PSHE education. This time we focus on what in Ofsted's view constitutes an outstanding PSHE education curriculum.

The imaginative and stimulating PSHE curriculum is skilfully designed to match the full range of pupils' needs, interests and aspirations and to ensure highly effective continuity and progression in their learning across all key stages. The programme is explicit, comprehensive and coherent. The statutory elements of sex and relationships education (SRE) are fully met. The programme for personal wellbeing is very highly regarded by pupils and enables them to lead safe and healthy lives. The curriculum provides a very strong platform for pupils' future economic wellbeing. Local data is fully taken into account when planning. The school and wider community provide high-quality and wide-ranging enrichment activities for pupils to apply and extend their social and personal skills. Where suspended timetable days are used they complement the PSHE programme extremely well because they are based on accurate understanding of pupils' needs and informed by clear and appropriate learning objectives. Pupils and teachers are fully engaged in influencing the content and evaluating the quality of the curriculum. The subject makes an outstanding and sustained contribution to pupils' spiritual, moral, social and cultural development and reinforces well a range of personal and thinking skills.

Consider the five curriculum models above in the light of Ofsted's description of an 'outstanding PSHE education curriculum'. What might be the advantages and disadvantages of each model?

Some advantages and disadvantages of models of curriculum organisation

Discrete timetabled PSHE education lessons

There is little disadvantage and many advantages to a programme taught through discrete lessons. With this model PSHE education has status and profile, is more likely to be valued by teachers and young people, and it becomes possible to deliver the subject to the same standard and with the same rigour as other subjects. There is time available to ensure comprehensive coverage and to build in continuity, progression and differentiation to meet the needs of all young people. It is also easier to organise and collect data to assess progress and measure the impact of the programme.

Sadly many schools feel the pressure of time in the curriculum, and with the current non-statutory nature of PSHE education this lesson time can be vulnerable to being reallocated to other subjects.

Teaching PSHE education through 'tutor time'

Arranging PSHE education through tutor time has a number of disadvantages. We have already discussed the challenges for tutors and we know that tutorial time can be taken up with administration and pastoral care, leaving little quality time for PSHE education. It is difficult to create the sense that this is a lesson, with the structures and seriousness that are necessary to deliver a curriculum subject to the same standard as any other. In many cases such sessions seldom progress beyond an 'interesting discussion'. It is also important that learning in PSHE education is distanced from the individual young person (see Chapter 3), whereas pastoral care is explicitly focused on the individual. It takes an extremely skilled practitioner to effectively switch from the role of pastoral tutor to subject teacher in this way, in limited time (see Chapters 12 and 13).

Tutor time is rarely longer than 20–30 minutes and is often as short as 15 minutes, which is insufficient to effectively teach a structured lesson. PSHE education taught in this way is less likely to be taken seriously by teachers or young people. Where the form tutor lacks confidence or motivation in teaching PSHE education it is too easy to avoid doing it at all, consciously or unconsciously filling the time with form administration and general discussion. Finally, if all form tutors are teaching a short PSHE education lesson at the same time throughout the school, which is often the case with this model, it is very hard for the PSHE education lead and school leadership team to monitor delivery.

Reflection and assessment are often omitted from this model, with reporting limited to a comment on the student's personality and ability to relate to others.

'Rolling' PSHE education lessons

A number of secondary schools are adopting the 'rolling lesson' model as they feel it can provide adequate time to deliver a comprehensive programme in the same way that regular timetabled lesson slots do, whilst maximising the time for other subjects. Most time slots on the timetable will only be replaced by a PSHE education lesson once a year. For example with a five-period day, there are 25 different time slots before the same period is 'hit' again, so where a school wishes to introduce or re-introduce discrete PSHE education lessons, this model may be more acceptable to teachers of other subjects as they do not feel they are giving up a regular amount of their subject time to allow PSHE education to be timetabled. In addition, this model tends to involve all teachers, so there is the potential for greater 'ownership' by staff as part of whole school approach. However, the 'rolling lesson' has disadvantages as well. Perhaps the greatest of these is that adopting this model gives a strong message that PSHE education does not warrant its own timetabled lesson but is something to be squeezed in as painlessly as possible. It is cumbersome to manage for the PSHE education lead, can feel disjointed and confusing for staff and young people and may be unpopular with teachers who still see this as 'losing a lesson', however infrequently it occurs.

'Drop down' or 'collapsed timetable' events

Collapsed timetable events at first sight can seem a good idea. There is no necessity to timetable PSHE lessons in an already crowded curriculum, some or all of the day could be delivered by external providers and they can provide a memorable experience for pupils. A whole day focused on one topic area of PSHE education can offer an opportunity to really 'dig into' an issue, but there are problems. The most obvious is that some young people will be absent. These days tend to have higher rates of absenteeism and those absent might miss their entire provision for RSE, careers education or economic wellbeing by missing that one day. Imagine being the young person who 'missed the RSE day'.

For young people who attend, one-off events can be memorable but the learning is very short-lived unless it is embedded through subsequent lessons. It is almost impossible to assess progress over time and ensure continuity and progression with this model, so it is equally difficult to identify lack of progress and future learning needs. For many of us it takes time to process our thinking and we may come up with the really significant questions a few days or weeks after the event. Will there be anyone we can ask? Some of these disadvantages can be mitigated to a certain extent by using time, either in tutor time or in other lessons, in the run-up to the event to carry out baseline or needs assessment activities (see Chapter 6). After the event, if time can again be made available to embed the learning from the event and carry out an assessment activity then it is far more likely that young people will learn and make progress as a result of the event and it will be possible to demonstrate their progress and assess future learning needs.

There are also issues of quality assurance. How can you know that what a visitor teaches is accurate and will be taught in a way that is based on the principles of effective practice in PSHE education? Will a recovered drug user really convince young people that most young people do not use drugs? Will a video on knife crime by a campaign group employ scare tactics that are known not to work? How will the road safety session, perhaps in an assembly, take account of the needs of the young people who have experienced bereavement as a result of a road accident?

In times of budget constraints some agencies, such as the NHS, may not be able to afford to do preventative work in schools and this model could become expensive. At the same time schools are less and less likely to release staff for training so that they can feel skilled and competent.

Cross-curricular provision of PSHE education

The idea that PSHE education can be integrated into the whole curriculum is seductive, not least as a means of increasing 'ownership' of PSHE education and sense of responsibility for it as part of whole school approach by all teachers. Where cross-curricular provision is more successful, this is due to an absolute commitment to make it work and 'buy-in' on the part of the school leadership team and every single teacher. However, in practice this model is very rarely effective. First, it is difficult to ensure that PSHE education learning objectives are achieved as they tend to take second place to those of the other subject. As discussed in relation to the delivery model earlier in this chapter, teachers of other subjects have so little time to really explore the PSHE education aspects of their subject, for example whilst a science teacher may teach about the nature of sexually transmitted infections, it is unlikely that they will explore how to negotiate the use of contraception with a reluctant partner or how to access local sexual health services when they are under pressure to cover the statutory curriculum or exam syllabus for their subject. As a result, this model becomes tokenistic, without any real sense that there is an equal focus on the PSHE education objectives and intended outcomes. Second, ensuring continuity and progression is little short of a nightmare for the PSHE education lead, whilst this model would mean each subject lesson having discrete PSHE education objectives and outcomes to ensure that assessment of PSHE education is not lost and progression can be measured despite the pressures of teaching the 'main subject'. Third, young people find it very hard to draw the PSHE education learning together in a way that allows them to make sense of it in relation to their own lives. Theoretically, we could teach English purely through other curriculum subjects (after all, with the exception of modern foreign languages, they are all taught through the medium of English), but without a developmental programme of English lessons the learning would be disjointed, each young person's progress would be very hard to assess over time and across subjects, and there would be no context through which to teach the theory, grammatical principles, rules of punctuation and so on in a way that allowed pupils to really process and master them.

Consider

A young person is at a party with their friends when some pills are handed round. They are now in front of them and their friends are looking at them to see what they do.

Real life frequently doesn't give us a warning that a critical moment is about to arrive. Real life has a habit of catching us by surprise. At this moment the young person may have to draw together understanding and skills learnt in separate subjects, perhaps learnt across many years, connect them up and apply them all in a matter of seconds.

Consider

Is this familiar? You are out somewhere and unexpectedly meet someone you know. They warmly greet you but there is one problem. Although you know them, at that moment you have no idea exactly who they are or exactly from where you know them. Perhaps you ask open questions such as 'How's everything?' in the hope that you will get a clue and not be embarrassed and have to admit you can't recall who they are. Perhaps you find that as they walk away you get an 'ah-ha' moment when you suddenly remember who they are.

It isn't that you didn't have the knowledge; it was encountering them suddenly in a different context. At the moment when you needed their name you couldn't access that knowledge. It was only after the encounter that the knowledge became accessible again.

We know the brain struggles to make these connections quickly and especially under stress or if the context is different. Have you ever found yourself thinking 'I knew I shouldn't have done that!' or 'I can't believe I did that!'? So why did you do it? Would you have made the same choice if you had had a just little more time to think or prepare?

Whilst academic subjects can provide academic knowledge and understanding, they seldom contextualise this learning in young people's lives. Science can teach about the process of conception and contraception, English or drama may explore negotiation, however, PSHE education draws this learning together and explores how to negotiate the use of contraception perhaps with a reluctant partner. PSHE education is where the learning provided by the academic curriculum is connected up and made relevant to young people's real lives. We can make it even more relevant by asking questions such as: 'Where can you imagine yourself using this learning?', 'Where might you be?', 'Who might you be with?', 'What might they be saying?', 'How might you reply?'

The 'whole school approach' and the 'healthy school'

The most comprehensive model for PSHE education takes the best elements of some of the models discussed in this chapter. PSHE education timetabled as a discrete lesson taught by a specialist team is supported by a comprehensive tutorial programme through which the learning from less sensitive areas of PSHE education, such as study skills or GCSE options, is further embedded and explored. This programme is enriched by 'collapsed timetable events', where it may be easier to arrange for external providers to share their expertise through talks with larger groups or through longer workshops that would not be possible to arrange in normal lesson times for all young people in a year group, for example. The learning from these enrichment activities is embedded and assessed in subsequent PSHE education lessons that build on the visitors' input.

This is made even more powerful by being set within a 'whole school approach'. So what does this mean? Take for instance the issue of bullying. In the planned PSHE education programme we can explore what is meant by healthy relationships and explore issues of physical and emotional bullying. We could explore how technology can extend bullying into the online world, together with issues such as 'sexting'. This would lead naturally into exploring areas such as abuse in teenage relationships and domestic violence.

At the same time it would be important for pupils to be fully familiar with the school's anti-bullying and behaviour policies; to know whom they can approach when they or someone they know needs support and to fully understand the subsequent actions the school will take following a request for help. In the case of serious abuse, the school will have set up lines of referral to local safeguarding teams and will have built a working relationship between professionals in the school and in social services.

The school may have publicised its approach to healthy relationships on its website, including clarifying any relevant protocols that will be followed in the event of incidents.

Most importantly, the school will have considered the way it 'models' relationships as part of their students' day-to-day lives in the school. Much of our personal and social learning is 'unconscious learning', sometimes referred to as learning that is 'caught, not taught'. A whole school approach therefore considers what is taught through the curriculum, what is 'caught' through modelling or the 'culture and ethos' of the school and what protocols and procedures are in place to support young people at risk. The 'healthy school' is one that actively plans, implements, monitors and evaluates all of these.

The healthy school provides opportunities for young people to put their healthy choices into action; for example, if the school encourages healthy eating in the curriculum, it must make it both possible and easy to choose healthy food in the school. If the school encourages physical activity in the curriculum, it must provide opportunities for young people to engage in a variety of physical activities in the school. If the school promotes the values of democracy in the curriculum, it must make a commitment to 'student voice', for example through an active, elected and representative student council.

The National Healthy Schools Programme and beyond

The National Healthy Schools Programme (NHSP) began in 1998 and set quality standards for schools to achieve in four areas:

- PSHE (it had not yet evolved into PSHE education)
- emotional wellbeing
- physical activity
- healthy eating

All to be developed through a 'whole school approach to school improvement'.

By 2008, 99 per cent of schools in England were involved in the NHSP, which was probably the most significant programme in driving forward standards in PSHE education. (It was also one of the largest 'whole school improvement activities'.)

In 2010 the national programme was withdrawn as part of the Government's cuts to spending; however, many local authorities continue to maintain local healthy schools programmes, often through their Public Health Directorates, seeing these as a vital link between health and education. The argument has been that health and education form a virtuous circle with each supporting the other. Public Health England (2014) reported:

1. Pupils with better health and wellbeing are likely to achieve better academically.
2. Effective social and emotional competencies are associated with greater health and wellbeing, and better achievement.
3. The culture, ethos and environment of a school influence the health and wellbeing of pupils and their readiness to learn.
4. A positive association exists between academic attainment and physical activity levels of pupils.

You might find that some schools are part of a different level of 'healthy schools', sometimes referred to as 'advanced healthy schools', or in some areas they may hold silver or gold healthy schools status. These schools will have already achieved healthy schools status and wish to use the model as part of continuous school improvement.

The model makes extensive use of action research and engages teachers, young people, parents and members of the community focusing on a particular aspect of school life that the school has either identified as in need of improvement or is capable of further improvement, rather than meeting a set of external or national quality standards.

Its connection with PSHE education is that this area of the curriculum can significantly support 'student voice' and PSHE education can provide a context for identifying needs, building strategy and evaluating outcomes.

At the time of writing, the future of local 'healthy schools' programmes remains uncertain and to an extent, a 'postcode lottery'.

Case studies

The following case studies describe schools judged as 'good' or 'outstanding' by Ofsted and have also been judged as having outstanding PSHE education provision. Because they are real schools, their models of both teaching and curriculum organisation illustrate their own unique way of using and combining the models explored above.

St Martin's School, Essex: An example of a tutor driven approach

This school has integrated the planned PSHE education programme into the wider 'whole school' approach to their students' personal and social development, but in doing so has lost none of the rigour that would be expected of any subject within the curriculum. Form tutors teach the programme; however, rather than expecting each tutor to teach all of PSHE education to a year group, each tutor specialises in one topic or theme that is taught in carousel. The Head of Year is also part of this team, meaning that the majority of tutors and the Head of Year teach PSHE education to virtually all young people in that year group. In the school's view this significantly contributes to developing strong relationships across the year groups.

The programme makes use of a combination of published teaching resources and resources created 'in house' focused to reflect their students' unique local priorities and needs. The entire programme is subject to robust monitoring by the PSHE education lead, who provides one-to-one and tailored team professional development.

Observations of teaching and learning and scrutiny of young people's work and progress ensure that the quality of teaching and the PSHE education lead is available to co-teach sensitive issues should colleagues lack confidence or need support. The PSHE education lead also provides comprehensive induction training for new members of staff.

The PSHE education lead is an active member of the school's pastoral team. This, along with data gathered from a variety of sources (including external surveys such as 'SHEU'– School and Students Health Education Unit, http://sheu.org.uk) and internal surveys (such as the school's behaviour and bullying logs) inform the content of the PSHE education programme which is constantly evolving to reflect young people's changing needs.

There is active involvement of young people in the teaching of PSHE education, known internally as Prefects in Peer Support (PiPS). Senior students (prefects) are attached to forms and have a role in providing elements of PSHE education. They receive comprehensive training including Bullying Intervention Training and other specific theme-based training by the PSHE education lead.

All prefects teaching these twice-weekly sessions have email contact with both the head of year and the PSHE education lead to ensure that any young people who indicate they are vulnerable or at risk are swiftly supported.

Learning in the PSHE education programme is robustly assessed against clear learning outcomes using a 'working towards, working at, and working beyond' framework of progression statements. Teacher assessment is combined with peer and young people's self-assessment.

This means that school and local health data, the individual experiences of young people, the school's development plan, the professional development of staff, the formal PSHE education programme and the assessment data it generates are one single 'system' mutually informing each other and providing a comprehensive bank of evaluation data to evidence impact.

Newent Community School and Sixth Form Centre, Gloucester: The specialist team

PSHE education programme is led by a very experienced PSHE education specialist who has been seconded part-time in an advisory role with the local authority working closely with their Healthy Schools team.

The PSHE education lead has regular contact with her school's pastoral team where the monitoring of both student behaviour and pastoral concerns can be quickly reflected in the taught PSHE education programme. The school has produced a comprehensive, developmental and highly flexible programme combining elements of published resources and those produced by the lead. All lessons have clear learning objectives and outcomes and provide illustrations of how learning can be differentiated to meet different young people's needs.

A key part of the lead's role within her local authority is the production of new PSHE education teaching material for Gloucester schools. This joint role means that resources are being developed in a school setting, allowing for rapid field trialling and a strong student engagement in evaluation.

The entire programme including enrichment material and models of assessment is available on the school's database, meaning that PSHE education teachers have immediate access to resources, a rich range of pedagogy and assessment material.

Newent's PSHE education programme is strongly 'data driven'. All schools in Gloucester undertake annual research both into their students' health behaviour and also their expressed values, beliefs and opinions.

This research has been in place for 12 years as part of the authority's healthy schools programme. Schools receive their own current data so they can see how this compares with their own historical data and make a comparison with other schools in the authority.

This wealth of data allows schools to constantly refocus their attention to reflect the changing needs, beliefs and behaviour of their young people. Access to longitudinal data enables them to monitor the impact of any intervention. This combined with the regular in-school liaison with the pastoral team means the programme is highly responsive to changing evidence. Their constant cycle of:

- baseline assessment of both need and prior learning
- planning intervention
- teaching
- assessment of the impact of both learning and behaviour
- evaluation

…brings focus to the programme.

PSHE education in this school is a 'subject' in the curriculum. The school has a two-week timetable and each week has a 50-minute dedicated lesson specifically for PSHE education spanning all school years.

The programme is enriched by 'drop down days' where the school makes use of a variety of 'visitors' bringing additional expertise of viewpoints to topics covered in the planned programme. All enrichment days are supported by both pre and post work in the PSHE education programme.

PSHE education is taught by a specialist team of seven experienced teachers, the majority of whom are full-time PSHE education specialists, and there are two dedicated PSHE education classrooms. As a department they have the same schedule of departmental meetings and CPD opportunities as all other departments.

Significantly, one member of this team is one of the school's deputy heads. His commitment to the subject and membership of the team adds credibility to the programme and ensures that the subject is fully represented at senior leadership meetings.

Although there are PSHE education specialists and a dedicated PSHE education programme, this team is part of a wider department called Personal Development and Future Choices (PDFC) that ensures continuity between PSHE education, citizenship, careers and work related learning. This larger department collaborates in the planning and teaching of the drop down days, providing learning that helps young people connect up and deepen their learning in each subject area.

The school has vertical tutor groups. Whilst this has brought the benefits of building strong relationships across year groups, the school wisely considered this setting inappropriate for teaching PSHE education that reflects the needs and readiness of young people.

The teaching of PSHE education has the same expectations concerning assessment as all other subjects. There is robust assessment undertaken through a comprehensive marking schedule, including young people's self-reflection and assessment, peer and teacher assessment. Young people have specific targets set for PSHE education, recording their learning and progress in a personal workbook.

PSHE education is subject to the same scrutiny as all other subjects, with book monitoring and lesson observations being undertaken by the PSHE education lead. New teachers joining the PSHE team are given comprehensive teaching material and one-to-one CPD, monitoring and guidance from their subject lead.

Reporting to parents takes the form of reporting on young people's attitude to learning and engagement in PSHE education. The school has no plans to introduce PSHE education examinations, arguing that this would limit the scope and responsiveness of their current provision.

The database provides the PSHE education team with a variety of assessment tools to assist young people in self-reflection and self-assessment, including material to support both pre (baseline) and prior learning and the assessment of knowledge, understanding and skills.

There are frameworks with clear learning outcomes to support peer assessment and clear, structured and comprehensive guidance to ensure that peer assessment provides the opportunity for young people to develop the skills of both good listening and giving effective feedback. In this way peer assessment is linked with both the student's and the peer-assessor's development.

Material is available to support not only the assessment of the outcome of learning but also the evaluation of the process. For example, young people are encouraged to reflect on and assess both the outcome of team working and the effectiveness of their team working and how pupils should behave if it is to improve.

PSHE education is evaluated at a number of levels. Young people evaluate the overall programme at the end of each term for its relevance and usefulness and the programme is adapted in light of this evaluation. The use of both immediate and longitudinal data collected in the school and processed in the local authority enables the PSHE education lead to understand the changing needs of the young people and adapt and refocus the programme in the light of this data. The provision of longitudinal data then enables the school to evaluate the impact of the programme on pupils' understanding, beliefs and behaviour. Monitoring of school-based data such as the school's behaviour log enriches this external process.

Hurworth School, Darlington: Tutor driven

Twenty-five tutors led by an experienced and committed PSHE education lead provide a comprehensive, developmental PSHE education programme. The PSHE education programme is subject to robust evaluation by both senior leadership and young people.

The expectation of outstanding teaching and learning in PSHE education is the same as that expected for all other subjects. In their 2014 scrutiny the school leadership team who undertake regular lesson observations judged the quality of teaching in PSHE education as 'good with outstanding features', using the Ofsted framework to guide their own judgements. As part of the monitoring of young people's progress against outcomes, workbooks are also subject to regular scrutiny by the PSHE education lead and members of the school's senior leadership team.

The programme is highly 'data driven', making use of data gathered externally from the local authority and internally to ensure that learning is planned and undertaken in contexts that are relevant to the young people.

PSHE education is fully integrated into the planned opportunities for personal and social development offered by the wider curriculum and through the school's 'healthy schools' ethos.

The scheme of work for PSHE education is subject to review by the school's senior leadership team, and there are calendared pastoral meetings to provide form tutor feedback and dedicated management time for the PSHE education lead. This systematic approach further helps to focus the PSHE education programme. This includes a large variety of additional planned learning opportunities that enrich young people's learning in the school's planned PSHE education programme.

Although the programme is taught by tutors, the scheme of work, subsequent lesson plans and resources are provided by the subject lead and are constantly monitored and reviewed by the school's SMSC co-ordinator and the member of the school leadership team with specific responsibility for PSHE education. The programme has been designed 'in house' to best meet the needs of the students and to address issues brought up through the robust data gathering.

The taught PSHE education programme is also enriched by specific interventions that target pupils with additional needs. For example, the PSHE education lead and the assistant special educational needs co-ordinator (SENCo) work together to provide relevant material to pupils with additional educational needs.

The school has a strong commitment to staff development in PSHE education. The member of the school leadership team with oversight of PSHE education also co-ordinating the school's CPD programme supports this. PSHE education updates are offered in twilight Inset sessions, and all staff have the opportunity to complete external accreditation in PSHE education.

Learning in PSHE education is assessed in line with the school's assessment policy and tutors assess young people's learning in each module of the programme. Marks are collated on the school's information management system and are included in reports to parents.

Consider

- Although the models illustrated above are all different, do they have anything in common?
- Can you see any vulnerability in their approach to PSHE education?
- Has the school taken any steps to address this vulnerability?

Did you notice how the case study schools have sought to capitalise on the advantages of some models and minimise the disadvantages of others? For example, two make use of tutors for the teaching of PSHE education, a model that has some serious disadvantages discussed above. However the commitment of the school's leadership teams to have high expectations for the quality of the provision and robust monitoring both of teaching and learning are minimising these potential disadvantages.

They illustrate that the commitment of the school's senior leadership team and teachers to high-quality PSHE education is critical and may matter more than the teaching and curriculum models that are used.

What is clear is that in all these schools there is an experienced and committed PSHE education lead supported by a school leadership team and committed teachers who all recognise the contribution a comprehensive PSHE education plays in their vision for their school. Those that use a tutor driven programme have spent time and resources ensuring their tutors are equally committed to providing high-quality learning in PSHE education.

All of these approaches may be vulnerable to a change either of the leadership of PSHE education or in the school's leadership team. No matter the model, it takes time to embed and is always vulnerable to change.

Chapter overview

In this chapter we have considered two overlapping themes: who teaches PSHE education and how PSHE education is organised in the curriculum. We have seen that there are a number of different ways both staffing and curriculum time are organised and that there are advantages and disadvantages to all, although some have far greater benefits or challenges than others. We have also seen that in the 'real world' of schools sometimes models are blended to create a unique method of delivery for that school. Whatever model is finally chosen, it is important to continue to offer young people a programme of PSHE education that reflects the principles of effective practice explored in Chapter 3.

Further reading

Ofsted no longer undertakes individual subject survey visits, however, the Ofsted Supplementary Inspection Guidance remains one of the most comprehensive descriptions of good practice in PSHE education. It is available from the PSHE Association at www.pshe-association.org.uk/curriculum-and-resources/resources/ofsted-grade-descriptors-pshe-education.

References

Public Health England (2014) 'The link between pupil health and wellbeing and attainment: A briefing for head teachers, governors and staff in educational settings', PHE publications gateway number 2014491. Available at www.gov.uk/government/uploads/system/uploads/attachment_data/file/370686/HT_briefing_layoutvFINALvii.pdf (accessed 26.10.15).

Ofsted (2013) Personal, Social, Health and Economic (PSHE) education survey visits: Generic grade descriptors and supplementary subject-specific guidance for inspectors on making judgements during visits to schools. London: Ofsted.

5

Starting 'Where Young People Are': Planning Learning in PSHE Education

Aims

This chapter will explore the importance of starting teaching with an understanding of young people's prior learning, in order to plan schemes of work and lessons that build on this starting point and are tailored to young people's needs.

Learning objectives

Through reading and reflecting on the content of this chapter you will begin to:

- understand why gauging young people's prior learning is so important
- be able to use some quick action research strategies that can be used in PSHE education
- understand how these can provide both baseline assessment and a powerful teaching resource
- understand the principles of designing PSHE education schemes of work
- be able to plan an engaging PSHE lesson that meets young people's needs.

Before we start

This chapter covers one of the most important aspects of PSHE education: establishing young people's starting point before planning or teaching anything new cannot be underestimated.

Activity

For this activity you will need three friends.

Each working alone, write down the first ten words you and your friends associate with the word 'relationships'. Now compare your lists. What words do you have in common? What words are only on some peoples lists? Does any list have something unique?

In the light of this, why do you think an understanding of young people's prior learning is essential to providing high-quality PSHE education?

Introduction

We each construct our own reality and without understanding how our young people are constructing theirs it is highly likely that lessons we believe are being clearly taught are actually being received by young people in many different ways. The nature of PSHE education also means that we can never predict or assume, on the basis of their age and year group, the prior knowledge, understanding, skills, beliefs and attitudes that our young people bring with them in relation to any particular aspect of the PSHE curriculum, in the way we can in most other subjects.

For any learning to be easily acquired it is essential that young people see it as relevant to them in either their immediate lives or that they can see it having a value in their futures. One of the hardest challenges for teachers is trying to engage young people with any learning that they see as irrelevant.

Because PSHE education draws on young people's real life experiences it is difficult, if not impossible, to control the development of their learning. Their personal, social, health and economic development is happening all the time and is not restricted to the classroom.

With most academic subjects our young people are seldom extending their learning in their day-to-day lives. They seldom encounter the need to balance a new equation or spontaneously encounter an event that extends their understanding of the Tudors, for example. PSHE education isn't like that as life experiences, challenges, encounters and events constantly feed into the development of a young person's sense of identity, their understanding, beliefs, language, strategies and skills. Some experiences will be affirming, some neutral and some destructive. All we can say with any certainty is that every young person in a class of 30 will be totally unique in terms of the prior experiences they bring to PSHE education.

The second issue is of 'readiness', which is different from 'age'. Even if we are going to teach a lesson on a topic that we know is relevant to our students, we need to pitch the specifics of the learning at the right level. A teacher of modern foreign languages who is about to teach a new Year 8 'top set' for the first time in September will have a clear and fairly accurate understanding of what the young people already know, understand, can do and can say. The same teacher, about to teach their new Year 8 group for PSHE education, will not be able to make the same assumptions of the young people's existing knowledge, understanding, language, skills, beliefs and attitudes in relation to their physical and mental health, sex and relationships, drugs, alcohol and tobacco, economic wellbeing or risk management, for example. A quick online search will provide the teacher with a range of lesson plans 'suitable for Year 8', but what are the chances that any one of them will in fact start from where those young people actually are and meet their learning needs?

Many young people have told us that PSHE education covers the right topics but the level of learning within that topic can be so mis-timed as to be at best irrelevant and at worst almost insulting. Sadly, once young people believe that you don't understand their real lives, their capabilities and their anxieties, you risk losing credibility. Young people may accept that you are doing your best and generally appreciate your efforts but no longer see you as a credible source of new learning.

Starting where young people are

It is possible to gain insights into young people's current understanding about a topic or issue really easily, but this does not mean it lacks rigour or validity. We have included two references for further reading, but be warned: from our experience classroom based action research can become addictive as each enquiry usually generates a lot more questions!

Getting real

In the real world, teachers do not have time to undertake comprehensive action research projects with young people every time they start a new module or unit of work, but it is possible to generate a huge amount of useful data by applying deceptively simple and quick research methods that do not sacrifice validity. We have included a number of examples in Appendix III.

To help with planning, many PSHE education teachers use these research methods at two different times: at the start of a module of work as baseline assessment, or some time before a module is due to start. Baseline assessment and its importance in PSHE education are explored in Chapter 6.

Exploring existing behaviour

It is tempting to carry out internal surveys to explore the health behaviour of young people; for example, their experience of using a drug such as cannabis, their alcohol consumption or their eating habits. However, this needs to be approached with great care as it can seem intrusive.

There is a wealth of data already available through organisations such as local public health directorates, and many schools either individually or within a cluster already undertake surveys as part of the general life of the school, a common example being the School and Students Health Education Unit's 'Health Behaviour Survey'.[1]

Behavioural data tells us 'What young people are doing, at what age and perhaps where and when', which can help local authority public health directorates allocate resources and help you as a teacher identify priorities (see Appendix IV).

However, teachers need to understand 'Why are young people at this age choosing to do this? What are they thinking and feeling?' and then 'What prior learning do we need to put in place to either prevent it (if it is something that is potentially harmful) or further encourage it (if it is potentially beneficial)?'.

So how can we gain these insights?

Exploring existing knowledge, attitudes, understanding and language

Let us imagine that you will shortly be teaching about bullying.

---

[1] School and Students' Health Education Unit: http://sheu.org.uk (accessed 18.3.16).

Activity

- Draw a quick picture of someone who bullies others. How would you describe them to others? What words would you use? Write down the words you would use to describe what it is they do when they bully others. How are they feeling?
- Draw a quick picture of someone who is being bullied. What are all the things that could have been happening to them? Write the words you would use to describe how they might be feeling.

(And in case you were wondering...!) You may feel that asking young people in secondary schools to 'draw a picture' is a little patronising and when we started using these techniques ourselves we shared this concern. What we found was that secondary students were very comfortable being asked to do this and would often include drawings even if this was not specified.

'Bullying' is a complex word because it can mean so many different things to different people. Imagine a young person has a restricted understanding of 'bullying', perhaps limited to physical assault or name-calling. They may not recognise that being deliberately excluded from activities they are entitled to join by their peers may constitute bullying; is unacceptable and worthy of support from their teachers.

Clearly the illustration above could be extended. But there are also some ethical rules if you are going to use this yourself:

- Ensure that young people can do the activity anonymously, perhaps just indicating their class name.
- Allow young people to 'opt out' if they wish.
- Ensure that they know who will see their work and explain why you need their help (e.g. you and a colleague will use it to help plan lessons that will be relevant or helpful to them).
- Do not agree total confidentiality. It is possible you will be able to identify a pupil and may feel concerned about their wellbeing, in which case this must always take priority and safeguarding protocols followed.

So what are we looking for? For example, how rich was your description of the bully's behaviour? Did it include verbal, physical and emotional bullying? Did it include 'bullying by omission', constantly being ignored or 'left out' that some young people experience? Did it include the use of technology or 'cyber bullying' – the hurtful behaviours that can now be used 24-hours a day seven days a week and ensure that even a young person's own bedroom is no longer emotionally safe? Did it include homophobic, sexist, disablist or racist bullying? Bullying in relation to body shape, academic ability, family background or gender identity?

Imagine you asked a class to do this activity. You would gain an understanding of what:

- they already know and understand that can be shared
- they 'almost' know and understand that can be developed or clarified
- appears to be understated (perhaps not by all young people but with the majority)
- is missing that perhaps you feel could be explored
- they feel and believe in relation to bullying and being the target of bullying?

Have a look at their drawings. Are the pictures 'stereotypes'? For example, are the people who bully 'recognisable people' or could they be anyone? Do the words tell a more nuanced story? Is there a risk that some of these young people are seeing people who bully as 'someone else' and do not recognise that we are all capable of some degree of 'bullying behaviour'?

With the young people's permission, feeding back their data can become a powerful teaching activity. For example:

I noticed that most of you included....in your answers about what behaviours are bullying, however, only one or two of you included...

- Why do you think that is?
- Do you think they are right to include it?
- Why do you think that?

Consider

Perhaps the simplest research tool is the 'brainstorm' or 'first thoughts' activity. Imagine you were going to teach a module on drug use. Before you teach this module you have put up two large sheets of flipchart paper on the classroom wall and invited the young people from your class to complete two sentences:

- 'Drugs are...'
- 'Drug users are...'

Imagine most responses focus on substances such as cocaine, heroin and ecstasy. There is no mention of tobacco, caffeine, alcohol or even cannabis. There is also no mention of over the counter or prescribed medicines.

Imagine their responses to 'drug users' are highly stereotyped, focusing predominantly on 'addicts' who they see as 'bad people'. The chances are they have all drawn young, rather scruffy-looking males.

How would you plan your teaching in the light of these data?

Exploring existing skills and strategies

Let us take this a little further.

Activity

Looking back at your drawings from the activity above:

- Now imagine the young person who is experiencing bullying asks you for your advice – what would you say?
- What will happen if they follow your advice?
- Do you think it would be easy for them to follow your advice?
- Why – what would help them? Why not – what might prevent them?
- What if they said they will not follow your advice and ask you to promise not to tell anyone what is happening to them? What will you do? Why?

Imagine we have asked this of our class. We can now start to gain insights into our students' existing strategies. Do they appear to be generally positive and likely to help resolve the problem ('I think you should talk to a teacher and I will come with you'); are they well intentioned but misguided ('I think you should ignore it, they are not worth worrying about') or are their suggested courses of action totally terrifying ('Don't worry, I'll get my mates to sort them out!')?

Do they appear to know the school's anti-bullying policy? Perhaps more importantly, do they appear to have confidence in that policy? Could they suggest ways to rewrite it? This might make a useful assessment activity.

Do they appreciate the complexities involved in getting help? Can they empathise with the anxieties of the person being bullied or does the solution seem simple or obvious?

How do they address the request not to tell anyone? Do they respect this or do they recognise that they have a responsibility to get help?

Again this can become a teaching activity:

> In your responses some of you said that you would respect the person's request not to tell anyone about what is happening to them whilst others said they would tell someone in order to get them help. In groups of four discuss what might happen next, the good and not so good things:
>
> • If you do respect their wishes not to tell?
> • What might happen next if you get them help?
> • On balance, which is the better outcome? Why?

A useful technique is to provide groups of young people with a blank 'story board' – simply a set of empty boxes drawn like a comic strip. Ask them to put the dilemma, in this case the request for confidentiality, in the first box and then draw and caption how the story will develop depending on how they propose to resolve the dilemma.

Exploring existing understanding of complex concepts

Some of the concepts that we explore in PSHE education can be very complex and abstract, such as 'bigotry', 'risk', 'prejudice', 'consent', 'equality and inclusion', 'justice' or 'health'. Without understanding how young people are already interpreting these terms any discussion can be filled with misunderstanding. It is quite possible that a young person will hear something either subtly or even entirely different from what you think you are saying.

Consider

Imagine an 'alien' has come down from another world. Theirs is a world of clones; they are all identical. They have heard about something on Earth called 'prejudice' but they don't know what it is.

How would you explain it to them?

It would be tempting to simply place a dictionary definition of 'prejudice' on the board and tell young people this is what it means. The only snag is you would probably end up using words that would also need to be defined. It is better to let young people process this for themselves through discussion. We could ask different groups to share their thinking and come up collectively with a class definition and perhaps then compare it with dictionary definitions to see the extent to which we agree.

The 'alien' can be really useful as it is a totally 'naïve' character. It has permission to ask the 'naïve questions' such as 'So why do people behave in this way towards others?'.

In Boddington et al. (2014) (see Chapter 3) there is a consideration of other classroom action research techniques to help you start from where your students are. These include 'circle time', focus groups and photography.

Using your understanding of the young people's starting point to plan relevant, engaging PSHE education lessons.

Whether it be due to inexperience in PSHE education, lack of time to plan your PSHE education lessons, lack of confidence in your ability to teach certain aspects of PSHE education or a combination of all of these, the net result can be that beginning teachers either reach for a 'ready-made' lesson plan that just happens to be on the 'topic' you are due to be teaching, or look for a particular resource or activity which you think will be an engaging use of the time. As we have already seen in this chapter, this approach is highly unlikely to result in a relevant lesson that meets the young people's needs, builds on previous learning and prepares for what is coming next.

An effective PSHE education lesson plan has to be born of the combination of a good scheme of work and an understanding of young people's starting point and progress. The lesson plan is therefore the final stage of the planning process, not the beginning. As a beginning teacher, the chances are that you will not be involved in planning the entire PSHE education programme and schemes of work for your school; however, to plan an effective lesson requires an understanding of the planning process.

From 'programme of study' to 'scheme of work' to your 'lesson plan'

The first stage in the planning process (see Figure 5.1) is the overarching programme of study that describes the scope of everything that might be included in a school's PSHE education programme. For most subjects these

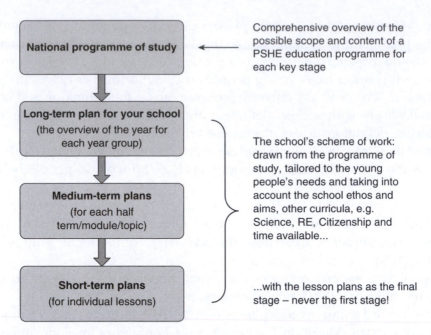

Figure 5.1   The four stages of planning a PSHE education programme

are contained within the National Curriculum (Department for Education, 2014). However, at the time of writing there is no longer a National Curriculum programme of study for PSHE education. The Department for Education now signposts instead to the PSHE Association's (2014) 'Programme of Study for PSHE education' (Key Stages 1 to 4).

However, most schools would need to do away with subjects such as maths and English if they were to have time to adequately cover everything in a national programme of study for PSHE education; such is the nature of the subject. In addition, it would not be possible to plan lessons directly from such a programme of study that together provided a developmental, coherent programme for young people. It is therefore necessary to use the programme of study as the starting point for the long- and medium-term plans that constitute the scheme of work, or scheme of learning, tailored to the school and its young people's needs.

Long-term planning

While its layout will differ from school to school, the long-term plan provides an overview of the programme for each year group by term, half-term, unit or module. Teachers at the start of their career would not be expected to produce this but it should be available from your PSHE education lead.

An effective long-term plan is matched to young people's needs: those they share with all young people and those specific to the school and local community. It is also enriched by activities, such as focus days or events, visiting speakers and other outside providers. These should not be 'one-offs': such events and inputs must build on prior learning and be embedded through subsequent learning.

Most important of all, there should always be an emphasis on developing young people's learning across time within a spiral programme: revisiting themes, building on prior knowledge, deepening understanding and further developing skills. In this way the learning is built up in layers each time a concept or theme is revisited in an age and stage appropriate way.

Consider

Imagine teaching young people in Year 11 who have received absolutely no PSHE education before to recognise and manage unhealthy or abusive relationships now or in the future. I think you would agree this presents quite a challenge. Now consider the prior learning that you would wish these young people to have gained on their journey from Key Stage 1 to Key Stage 4, so that what you teach them in Key Stage 4 is simply another small step in their learning. Note down what you would want them to have already learned. What should they know and understand? What should they be able to do and say? What personal attributes would you want them to have been given opportunities to develop by the end of Key Stage 4?

Now look at your list and think about what that learning might look like in each previous key stage, within a spiral curriculum.

We might summarise it like this. In early years and Key Stage 1 we would want children to have learned to recognise feelings, developing a vocabulary to describe their feelings and their bodies; the importance of not keeping adults' secrets, only surprises that everyone will find out about eventually; and to judge what kind of physical contact is acceptable and unacceptable and how to respond (including who to tell and how to tell them). If they have been taught the importance of playing co-operatively together and that people should care for those close to them, it becomes easier for them as they continue their learning journey through Key Stage 2 and into Key Stage3 to recognise why

(Continued)

(Continued)

bullying is wrong. Teaching strategies for handling situations where they or someone they know is being bullied, lays the foundations for them to develop strategies for handling abusive relationships. To do this, we would want them to learn to recognise a positive, healthy relationship and when a relationship is unhealthy, how to manage this or whom to go to and what to say if they need support. We would want a good understanding of rights and responsibilities in relationships to help them to build on their early learning about consent, understanding that the legal and moral responsibility for ensuring that consent is actively given rests with the person seeking consent. In addition, we would want them to develop an understanding that relationships can be abusive in any context, including within friendships and families, that abusive behaviour may include emotional, physical, economic or sexual abuse, and that all are unacceptable. And throughout their PSHE education, from Key Stage 1 onwards, as part of this learning we would wish them to have received regular opportunities to rehearse and develop the skills of communication, negotiation, assertiveness, identifying sources of support available to them, initially within their circle of trusted adults and later locally, nationally and online, developing the ability to critically evaluate the reliability and appropriateness of such sources. We would also want them to have had opportunities to develop personal attributes such as empathy, resilience, an understanding of their own moral compass and a sense of self-worth.

   This complex learning needs to be developed gradually by revisiting the theme of relationships year by year, each time assessing the young people's starting point and building on it in an age and stage appropriate way.

Medium-term planning: The key to an effective scheme of work

Models of delivery for PSHE education vary from school to school. In some schools the PSHE education lead will plan every PSHE education lesson that's taught, while in others the lead will plan the schemes of work and the teachers will plan their own lessons based on those schemes. Either way, the medium-term plans, which lie at the heart of the schemes of work, are the key to ensuring that the lessons that take place, together form a coherent, developmental programme of learning and that the young people's progress in those lessons can be meaningfully assessed.

Some schools will take their schemes of work from a published course book or programme. While this can save the PSHE education lead a great deal of time and effort, the disadvantage of this is that, as we have seen in this chapter, to be effective PSHE education must always start from where the young people are and meet their specific needs. It is far better, therefore, to use an understanding of young people's starting points in terms of their knowledge, understanding, skills, beliefs and attitudes to inform the planning of medium-term schemes of work. Through this understanding the PSHE education lead or the PSHE education team can identify the learning objectives and intended learning outcomes for each year group and then choose resources that will enable young people to achieve those objectives and outcomes (see Chapter 13 for more on selecting resources).

A really effective medium-term plan for PSHE education will maintain a balance between increasing knowledge and developing skills and personal attributes. It will clearly set out the learning objectives and intended learning outcomes for each lesson or series of lessons. Again, terminology will vary from school to school but in this context we are using 'learning objectives' to express what we want the young people to learn. They help the teacher and young people to see the point of the lesson or series of lessons. The simplest way to think of these is in terms of 'What are young people going to learn about? What are they going to learn to do?'. 'Intended learning outcomes' express what we intend the young people to be able to do as a result of the learning. If we have met our objectives, what will the young people know, understand, feel, be able to do or say by the end of the lesson or lessons that they did not or could not before?

Activity

Imagine you have been given schemes of work for your new Year 8 PSHE education group and you see that for the next half-term the theme is mental health and emotional wellbeing. The scheme of work looks something like Table 5.1.

(Continued)

(Continued)

Table 5.1   Year 8, Spring term 2: Mental health and emotional wellbeing (Scenario 1)

Lessons	Topic	Learning objectives
1–6	• Emotional wellbeing – what it is and how to promote it • Self-harm • Eating disorders	• To have a better understanding of mental health issues and emotional wellbeing, including how to improve emotional wellbeing and cope with difficult feelings • To understand unhealthy ways of coping, such as self-harm and eating disorders

If this is all you are given to work from when planning your lessons, what are the challenges? How easy would it be to plan lessons from this scheme of work?

Now imagine you were given the scheme of work in Table 5.2 for the same series of lessons.

Table 5.2   Year 8, Spring term 2: Mental health and emotional wellbeing (Scenario 2)

Lessons	Learning objectives	Intended learning outcomes
1 and 2	To learn: • about emotional wellbeing • how to promote emotional wellbeing	Students will be able to: • explain what emotional wellbeing is and why it is important • identify ways to promote their own emotional wellbeing • explain who, how and why to ask for support when it's needed • identify sources of support in school, the community and online • explain or demonstrate how to be a supportive friend and how to promote others' wellbeing
3 and 4	To learn: • about unhealthy coping strategies, including self-harm and eating disorders • how to get help for myself or someone else	Students will be able to: • understand that self-harm and eating disorders are unhealthy coping strategies • identify some of the things that might trigger them • explain the signs to look out for in a friend • identify where and explain how to get support for themself or a friend
5 and 6	To learn: • healthy ways to manage difficult feelings	Students will be able to: • identify a range of difficult emotions young people might experience • demonstrate and use a range of strategies for managing difficult emotions • explain where and how to access further support

Source: Adapted from PSHE Association, 2015

Would this scheme be easier to plan lessons from? Why? Could anything else be included in the scheme of work that would support teachers in planning their own lessons?

The scheme of work in Table 5.2 is clearly more detailed but it is not only the quantity but also the quality that makes this scheme so much easier to plan from. The learning objectives are simple and clear but it is the intended learning outcomes that really support effective planning. The more concrete and precise the learning outcomes, the easier it is to plan a lesson from them and the easier it is to assess young people's learning. Using verbs such as *identify, describe, explain, demonstrate, analyse* and *evaluate* really help to pin down the teaching and learning required in the lesson in order to achieve the objectives and also what we will be looking for in terms of assessing young people's learning (see Chapter 6 on assessing learning).

Many schemes of work will also identify the resources available in the school that teachers might draw on in planning their lessons. It is important that the resources to be used are chosen *after* the learning objectives and outcomes are identified, not before. An understanding of the young people's needs and starting point, taking into account the school ethos and other curricula (e.g. science, RE and citizenship) and the curriculum time available, allows the learning objectives and intended learning outcomes to be identified in the medium-term schemes of work. Once these have been defined, resources can be designed or chosen. This becomes especially important as we go on to think about the lessons you will be planning from the medium-term plan.

Short-term planning: The individual lesson plans

When starting to teach PSHE education, teachers are often provided with lesson plans, either from a published scheme or that have been written by the school's PSHE education lead. For the lesson to be effective, you need to take 'ownership' of the lesson plan and adapt it to meet the needs of your students, as there is no such thing as a 'one size fits all' PSHE education lesson. But before considering how best to do this, it is important to understand how to plan an effective PSHE education lesson from scratch.

It is vital that we take as our starting point the lesson objectives and intended learning outcomes identified in the medium-term scheme of work, rather than the resources available.

The golden rule is:

Choose resources that will allow you to meet the learning objectives, rather than planning learning that will allow you to use a particular resource.

By starting with learning objectives that form part of a developmental scheme of work and intended learning outcomes that are determined by the young people's starting point, rather than starting with the activities or resources, planning a lesson that meets our young people's learning needs and allows us to assess their progress becomes much more straightforward.

Lesson plans will look different in every school and it may be that you will be using a standardised school template for PSHE education lessons; however, the features of an effective PSHE education lesson plan remain the same, whatever the format in which it is written.

Table 5.3   An effective PSHE education lesson plan

Criteria	Notes
1. Has clear and precise 'learning objectives'	We can see the point of the lesson and what young people are going to learn. Often worded: Students will learn (or 'We are learning') about …/ how to …
2. Has clear, precise and measurable 'intended learning outcomes'	It is clear what the young people will be able to do as a result of the learning. Often worded: Students will be able to (or ' I can …') identify/demonstrate/describe/explain/evaluate …
3. Shows how the teacher will gauge the young people's starting point	The lesson begins with an activity that allows young people to reconnect with previous learning and allows the teacher to gain an insight into their existing knowledge, understanding, skills, beliefs and attitudes in relation to the learning objectives.
	There is flexibility within the plan to adapt it as necessary once young people's starting point has been established.
4. Creates a safe teaching and learning environment from the outset	The lesson starts with the establishment or re-visiting of 'ground rules' for the group (to which the young people have had the opportunity to contribute).
	The learning is 'distanced' so young people can explore the issues in an objective way.
	Questions are encouraged and there is the opportunity for young people to submit questions anonymously if they prefer.
	(See Chapter 3 for more on creating a safe teaching and learning environment).
5. Uses activities and resources that are appropriate to achieve the intended learning outcomes	Activities and resources are carefully matched to the objectives and intended learning outcomes, are engaging and ensure interactive learning. There are opportunities for young people to work independently and/or collaboratively and to take responsibility for their own learning.
6. The activities and resources are differentiated for young people's differing needs	The lesson includes differentiation for the less able, which goes beyond just being able to access the lesson content via modification of materials and matches the learning outcomes to their social and emotional needs.

Criteria	Notes
	The lesson includes differentiation for the most able, providing sufficient challenge in their learning outcomes so that they remain engaged and can demonstrate that they have extended their learning.
7. Has assessment *for* and *of* learning built in as an integral part of the plan	There are explicit opportunities for young people to critically reflect on what the learning means to them in their own lives.
	There are explicit opportunities for self-, peer- and/or teacher-assessment, which provide assessment *for* learning and assessment *of* learning.
	Young people and/or teacher are able to evidence the progress made from the starting point.

Using an existing lesson plan

While it is best practice to plan each lesson from a scheme of work that has been designed with the specific needs of the young people you teach in mind, there may well be times when you are given or choose to use an existing lesson plan. The understanding you now have of how to plan a PSHE education lesson from scratch will enable you to take ownership of the lesson plan, adapting it for your group. We can adapt Table 5.4 to apply the principles of planning an effective lesson to adapting an existing lesson plan. Look at the lesson plan and ask yourself the questions presented in Table 5.5

Working through these steps to adapt an existing lesson plan to meet your group's needs will allow you to really get to grips with the lesson you are going to teach. It will result in a much more engaging and effective lesson for the young people as it will assess and meet their needs and become a much more enjoyable lesson for you to teach than if you had simply used the original plan. It will probably also lead you to think 'It would have been easier to plan this from scratch myself'!

Activity

Taking the medium-term scheme of work in Table 5.3, use the flow chart in Table 5.4 to help you plan the first lesson of this series of lessons. When you have finished, use Table 5.3 as a checklist to assess your lesson plan.

(Continued)

(Continued)

Table 5.4   Planning a PSHE education lesson

Identify the learning objectives and intended learning outcomes

Learning objectives: What do you intend the young people to learn about, or learn how to do?

Learning outcomes: What will the young people be able to do as a result of the learning? Identify …? Demonstrate …? List …? Describe …? Manage …? Analyse …? Evaluate a…?

↕

Plan an activity to establish the young people's baseline

What knowledge, understanding, experience, skills, beliefs and attitudes do the young people already have?

Do they have any special needs? What implications does this have for planning?

If possible, carry this out before planning the lesson and use it to help identify the learning outcomes. If this is not possible, start the lesson with this and adjust the teaching accordingly.

↓

Plan activities that will allow young people to achieve the intended learning outcomes

Always start by revisiting ground rules to ensure a safe learning environment.

Ensure that all activities are in line with best practice (see Chapter 3).

Consider how the activities might need to be differentiated for individual young people.

Identify the resources required.

↓

Incorporate assessment for learning and opportunities for young people to reflect on what the learning means for their own lives

This might include planning key questions, mini-plenaries between activities, questions for private reflection, opportunities for feedback and identifying next steps.

↓

Plan an activity that allows young people to demonstrate progress

How will you know that the objectives have been achieved?

How can young people demonstrate progress? Consider revisiting the baseline activity.

Do you need or want to measure attainment? If so, what will 'good' look like? Define the success criteria.

Is self-, peer- or teacher assessment the most appropriate and useful in this case?

(See Chapter 6)

Table 5.5   Adapting and existing PSHE education lesson plan

Questions to ask yourself	Possible actions
1. What are the objectives and intended learning outcomes for this lesson? 2. Are the learning outcomes clear, precise and concrete? 3. Are they appropriate for this group?	Adjust the learning objectives and outcomes if necessary, to ensure they are worded in a way that is clear, precise and measurable and that they are appropriate for your young people.
4. How will I find out the starting point of the young people in my group?	If the lesson plan does not include a baseline assessment activity and flexibility to adapt the lesson according to the young people's starting point, you will need to insert one. Go back to the learning objectives and think about how young people could show you their existing knowledge, understanding, skills, beliefs and attitudes in relation to these. Possible activities might include brainstorming, mind-maps, draw and write activities, role play, storyboards or sorting activities (see Chapter 6).
5. Can I think of better activities to achieve the intended outcomes for my group?	If the lesson plan does not make reference to establishing or revisiting ground rules, insert this yourself so it is not missed. Bring your own expertise to the lesson; for example, perhaps you would rather change the discussion to a role play, or perhaps you are familiar with an innovative online tool that would make the presentation task more engaging. Think about how you need to differentiate the activities for the young people in your group to provide appropriate learning and sufficient support and challenge for them all.
6. Does the plan allow young people to reflect on their learning?	If not, make sure you build in time for reflection. This could be through plenary questions for paired discussion or private reflection, or writing in personal learning journals.
7. Is assessment for learning built into the lesson plan?	If not, incorporate opportunities for assessment for learning, such as mini-plenaries between activities, targeted, structured questions, feedback and feedforwards. Decide whether you will use teacher, self- and/or peer-assessment.
8. Does the plan include an activity that allows young people to demonstrate their progress?	If not, think how the young people could show what has been learned: what will the evidence of the learning be? Young people could revisit the baseline activity, for example adding to their mind-map, or draw and write activity in a different colour. Or they might prepare a presentation, or gauge their starting and finishing point along a continuum linked to the intended learning outcomes. (See Chapter 6)

Activity

Look at the PSHE education programme in a school with which you are familiar. If possible, talk with the school's PSHE education lead. Remembering that the terminology may differ from that used in this chapter, explore the following questions:

- Does the programme revisit themes progressively through a spiral curriculum, gradually extending thinking, expanding knowledge and developing skills?
- How has the school attempted to match it to young people's needs: those they share with all young people and those specific to this school and community?
- Has the school used an understanding of young people's starting points to inform the schemes of work and lesson plans?
- Do the medium-term schemes of work and individual lesson plans always identify the learning objectives and clear, precise, measurable intended learning outcomes?
- Do the schemes of work and lesson plans allow teachers to assess and demonstrate young people's learning and progress in PSHE education?
- Would a teacher new to the school be able to plan effective, engaging PSHE education lessons, in line with best practice, using only the schemes of work and other planning materials provided with this school's programme?

Chapter overview

In this chapter we have considered the importance of starting where our young people are when planning any PSHE education. With that key tenet of effective PSHE education practice as our own starting point, we have followed the planning stages from the overarching programme of study, to the school's long-term and medium-term schemes of work and ultimately the individual lesson plans.

Further reading

McWhirter, J. (2014) 'The draw and write technique as a versatile tool for researching children's understanding of health and wellbeing', *International Journal of Health Promotion and Education*, 52(5): 250–59.
The draw and write technique is invaluable in both planning and assessing PSHE education. This paper describes some of the early work carried out using draw and write, and some more recent studies.

Boddington, N., King, A. and McWhirter, J. (2014) *Understanding Personal Social, Health and Economic Education in Primary Schools*, Ch. 4. London: Sage.
Written primarily for student teachers and their mentors in primary schools, this is the companion text to this book, with material that will be useful for those teaching PSHE education at any phase.

PSHE Association (2014) 'PSHE Education Programme of Study (Key Stages 1–4)'. Available at: https://pshe-association.org.uk/resources_search_details.aspx?ResourceId=495&Keyword=&SubjectID=0&LevelID=0&ResourceTypeID=3&SuggestedUseID=0 (accessed 24.1.16).
The National Curriculum no longer includes a programme of study for PSHE education, however the Department for Education signposts this. It provides a suggested programme of study expressed through three 'core themes', with notes and guidance on possible content at each key stage.

References

Boddington, N., King, A. and McWhirter, J. (2014) *Understanding Personal Social, Health and Economic Education in Primary Schools*. London: Sage.

Department for Education (2014) 'The National Curriculum for England to be taught in all local authority maintained schools'. Available at www.gov.uk/government/collections/national-curriculum (accessed 24.1.16).

PSHE Association (2014) 'PSHE education Programme of Study (Key Stages 1–4)'. Available at https://pshe-association.org.uk/resources_search_details.aspx?ResourceId=495&Keyword=&SubjectID=0&LevelID=0&ResourceTypeID=3&SuggestedUseID=0 (accessed 24.1.16).

PSHE Association (2015) 'Preparing to teach about mental health and emotional wellbeing'. Available at https://pshe-association.org.uk/resources_search_details.aspx?ResourceId=570&Keyword=&SubjectID=0&LevelID=0&ResourceTypeID=3&SuggestedUseID=0 (accessed 24.1.16).

6

Assessing Learning in PSHE Education

Aim

To understand assessment *for* and *of* learning in the context of effective PSHE education.

Learning objectives

Through reading and reflecting on the content of this chapter you will begin to:

- understand the importance of assessing learning in PSHE education
- understand different methods of assessment and when each is appropriate
- be familiar with some practical examples of assessing learning in PSHE education.

Before we start

There are two pieces of information we'd like you to remember whilst you are reading this chapter. The first is that we are supposed to eat at least five portions of fruit and vegetables a day to stay healthy; and the second is that in one of the counting systems in Korean, the number 3 is 'sam' (as in 'Samsung', which means 'three stars'). Got that? Five portions of fruit and vegetables a day and 'sam' is 3 in Korean.

Don't worry: this will make sense later!

Introduction

First of all, let's be clear about what we mean by 'assessment' in this chapter. The terms 'assessment' and 'evaluation' are frequently spoken in the same breath and sometimes used interchangeably but they are two different activities and this chapter will focus on assessment. Evaluation is about the process: it is answering questions such as 'How effective were those activities?', 'How engaging did the students find that lesson?', 'Was that film clip suitable and did it work well as a discussion stimulus?', 'What will I change next time I teach this?'. Evaluation is vital and is the basis for development or improvement planning but, crucially, what it does not tell us is what has been learned. That is where assessment comes in. Assessment is everything we and the students do to gauge what has been learned and what still needs to be learned. The information assessment gives us will feed into the evaluation process so the two work together and we do need both, but teachers have tended to find evaluating PSHE education easier than assessing it and therefore we frequently see students asked to evaluate the lesson at the end using handy acronyms such as WWW/EBI (what went well/even better if), with the focus on the amount of effort they made, what they enjoyed and what they feel could be improved or built upon next time. Very useful information. but this evaluation rarely constitutes assessment for or of the learning, unless the teacher expressly instructs young people to focus on what they learned and still need to learn.

Why do we say that teachers tend to find evaluation easier than assessment in PSHE education? We think there are several reasons, not least the range of opinions on how 'do-able' or desirable assessing learning in PSHE education is to begin with. Some argue that PSHE education will never have the same status or be valued in the same way as other subjects unless it is a GCSE subject, examined like any other, whilst others feel that PSHE education is far too personal a subject to assess and to do so would be inappropriate. Somewhere in the middle are those who feel that we can and should assess the factual knowledge and understanding but that assessing the skills, strategies and personal attributes we aim to develop through PSHE education is far more problematic. There is an element of truth in each of these arguments. We constantly aim to achieve the same status and recognition for PSHE education as for any other subject, and qualifications do seem to convey a message about the seriousness with which a subject is viewed. But do we really want to put young people in a position where they could 'fail' a subject that so closely reflects their personal development? We have no problem at all admitting that we were never any good at chemistry but would we be as happy to admit we only just scraped a pass in a subject that includes relationships and sex? Furthermore, would we want an examination syllabus to lead the learning in PSHE education, rather than the needs of our young people in our school?

Addressing the second view that assessing PSHE education is inappropriate in some way: yes, it is a personal subject, operating within the young person's reality in a way that no other subject does, so assessment that comprised nothing but doing tests and marked written work might not always be appropriate. But giving opportunities for students to reflect privately on their learning and what it means to them in their own lives is also assessment, and there will be times when this will be the most appropriate way to assess a lesson. The final view is hard to argue with: assessing knowledge is straightforward but in PSHE education the skills, strategies and personal attributes students are developing are as, or arguably more, important than factual knowledge. These are harder to assess, but once we understand the principles of assessment as they relate to PSHE education, we will see that this is possible and can be achieved in a meaningful and manageable way.

Add to these more philosophical arguments the lack of time given to PSHE education lessons, and the fact that it is often squeezed into tutor time, or off-timetable events. Furthermore, for most teachers it is a subject they have neither chosen nor been trained to teach and it is little wonder that in its 2013 report into PSHE education in England Ofsted stated that: 'by far the weakest aspect of teaching was the assessment of pupils' learning which was often less robust for PSHE education than for other subjects.'

Even where teachers agree that we *should* assess PSHE education, ask them 'how?' and most will agree that they lack confidence when it comes to assessing PSHE education, that they are not sure how to do it or what exactly 'it' should look like.

To understand how to assess PSHE education, we need to start by answering the question '*Why* assess PSHE education?'. Identifying our aims and priorities in assessing PSHE education will help us to identify the types of assessment that are appropriate and also *who* should be involved in the process. Together, this understanding makes it much easier to answer the question '*How* do we assess PSHE education?'.

Why assess PSHE education?

Take a minute to think of all the reasons that could be given for *why* learning in PSHE education should be assessed. Here is a selection, although you may be able to think of others:

- To classify young people or give them a grade.
- To provide statistics for the subject or for the school.
- To lead to qualifications.
- To allow the leadership team, parents, governors and Ofsted inspectors to see the impact PSHE education is having for young people and for whole-school outcomes.
- To give teachers something meaningful to write about in PSHE education reports.
- To raise the status of PSHE education and to set clear expectations for standards and achievement.
- To increase motivation and improve learning in PSHE education.
- To help young people to reflect on and identify what they have learned and what they need to do to continue their learning.
- To give teachers feedback about the progress and achievements of the young people they teach, and how their learning might be improved.

Now look closely at the list. If you were asked to put them in order, bearing in mind everything you know and believe about PSHE education, with the one that *for you* is the most compelling reason at the top and the one that is least compelling for you at the bottom, how would you order them? The chances are that if we were to reverse the list above, your list would then look quite similar. When thinking about assessing learning in PSHE education, most teachers find the reasons towards the bottom of this list far more compelling than those at the top. When asked why, they will typically say it is because these are more student-centred, they're about the young people's learning and about promoting that learning, whereas those at the top of this list are more quantitative, about the school, about record keeping, and they do not feel as appropriate for such a personal subject.

So what? How does this help us understand how to assess learning in PSHE education? The main reason is that this activity gives us a sense of the types of assessment that we need to use to ensure that we are assessing for the purposes we have identified as the most compelling and important for us and our students, without losing sight of those that might be less compelling but are still part and parcel of the education system in which we teach.

Types of assessment

Before we go any further, let's clarify some terminology. 'Assessment *for* learning' (AfL) can be defined as: 'any assessment for which the first priority in its design and practice is to serve the purpose of promoting pupils' learning' (Black et al., 1990). The term 'formative assessment' is often used interchangeably with AfL but they're not exactly the same. Formative assessment is central to AfL and, as the name suggests, it is assessment that is used for shaping the learning by informing changes to teaching in the longer term. If it does not have an immediate impact in adjusting the teaching and learning, then it is not AfL, as that is 'dynamic and concerned with the immediate future through the daily adjustment of teaching based upon feedback' (Spendlove, 2009).

Summative assessment, or 'assessment *of* learning' (AoL), measures learning, telling us where the young person has got to at a given point in time; for example, at the end of a unit of work, a period of time, or a course of study. This is useful, especially when it comes to writing reports, showing evidence of impact and celebrating achievement, but that's all it tells us. Summative assessment could be likened to the full-time football score – it tells us who is the winner and loser and where they might be in the league or cup, but not how the game went, if the play was dirty or clean, if the referee was ineffective or how the crowd urged on their team or abused individual players. Whilst we can sometimes use evidence from a summative assessment in a formative way (if the summative results indicate that few in the class have understood a particular concept, then perhaps we need to teach it differently in future), summative assessment alone does not tell us the cause of any learning difficulty, or how to improve and make further progress.

Returning to our list of possible reasons for assessing PSHE education, we can say that, broadly speaking, the reasons most of us find more compelling (those towards the bottom of the list above) tend to relate to AfL, whilst those we seem to find least compelling in relation to PSHE education relate more to AoL. But does this then mean that AoL is not needed or important in PSHE education? Absolutely not. Summative assessment will help us provide evidence of progress, give us evidence for reports, help us to recognise and celebrate success and, in some schools, provide external accreditation. Furthermore, we work in an education system that relies heavily on summative assessment and arguably values it more. Schools, teachers and young people are judged on results, grades, attainment (with or without levels). If we wish to show the impact of PSHE education as a curriculum subject like any other, then we need PSHE education to fit into this system too, whilst not losing sight of the valuable, meaningful and vital contribution that AfL makes.

Who should be involved?

Given the personal nature of PSHE education and the importance of AfL within the assessment process, it is clear that assessing learning in PSHE education is not just something for the teacher to do: self- and peer-assessment should play an integral part. In AfL the involvement of the young person in the assessment process is central: assessment is done with them, not to them. The personal nature of the subject means that sometimes it is just not appropriate for the teacher to assess their students. For example, if a young person has started to feel differently about their sexual orientation, or has recognised for the first time that views their parent holds and that they have grown up with, are prejudiced and hurtful to others, then it would not be appropriate for the teacher to ask them to write that down and hand it in for marking, but it is very important that the young person is given the time and space to reflect privately on this learning. In addition, PSHE education aims to develop transferable skills such as critical thinking, communication and negotiation skills, whilst the processes of assessing one's own achievement and learning needs, and of giving and receiving constructive criticism to a peer, provides opportunities to practise these skills in a real context.

Consider

At the end of a module focusing on developing skills for employability, young people in a Year 10 PSHE education group have written the first draft of personal statements to accompany their work experience applications. They have brought their drafts to the lesson and their teacher asks them to find a partner and peer-assess each other's personal statement. Assuming these are the only instructions given:

1. How are the young people likely to approach the task?
2. What elements of their partner's work are young people likely to feedback on?

(Continued)

(Continued)

3. Will they all give the same sort of feedback and focus on the same aspects of their partner's work?
4. What is the outcome likely to be: do you think this will be an effective peerassessment activity?

For the next lesson the young people write the final version of their personal statements and hand them in to the teacher. Looking at their work, the teacher feels that peerassessing their first drafts has not been effective: the final statements are little better than the drafts. Imagine the teacher were to ask your advice on what to do next time to ensure that peerassessment is more effective. What would you advise?

Peerassessment in PSHE education needs to be approached and prepared for with care, otherwise we risk an ineffective, or worse, hurtful or negative experience for young people. There needs to be a relationship of trust between the young people; ground rules need to be negotiated and consistently applied, such as no personal comments and commenting on the peer's work rather than the individual person. Assessment criteria are key: what is it exactly that they are assessing? All peer assessors need to fully understand the criteria against which they are giving feedback or making judgements and young people need to be taught and practise peerassessing, including having the language to recognise and build on the positives and be able to offer strategies for improving.

Of course teacher assessment remains important too: not to 'check' or moderate self- or peerassessment but in order for us to have a clear understanding of our young people's progress, to gather evidence of that progress, to evaluate the effectiveness of our teaching and to inform our planning by identifying what still needs to be learned.

What does assessment in PSHE education look like in practice?

We now know why we should assess PSHE education, what types of assessment we should use and who should be involved in the process. Now we are ready to think about what assessment looks like in practice in PSHE education.

In education, assessment is most often either norm-referenced or criterion-referenced (see Figure 6.1). A norm-referenced assessment compares the young person's performance against his or her peers. This is useful, for example, when deciding which young people are to be put into sets according to ability in a particular subject. A criterion-referenced assessment measures the young person against external criteria, for example those of a particular GCSE syllabus. Thinking back to our young person-centred priorities for assessing learning in PSHE education and taking into account the personal nature of the subject, does either of these types of assessment 'feel right' for PSHE education? Taking everything we have already considered in relation to assessment in PSHE education, the model of assessment that we would advocate is a third type, sometimes called 'ipsative assessment'. An ipsative assessment in an educational context compares the young person's results against his or her previous results in a similar way to an athlete measuring today's performance against their own previous performance.

To demonstrate or measure learning and progress in PSHE education we measure each young person's progress against their starting point. It is not and should not be about passing an exam, or being given a level, percentage or grade.

As we approach each new 'piece of learning' (topic, module, series of lessons or maybe just a single lesson), let's imagine each young person standing on a giant ruler. Their position on the ruler is determined by their existing knowledge, understanding, skills, strategies, beliefs and attitudes in relation to the learning you're about to provide. Our aim will be to use AfL to establish their starting point and promote their learning and finally at the

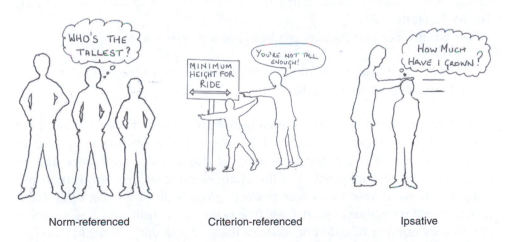

Norm-referenced   Criterion-referenced   Ipsative

Figure 6.1 Norm-referenced, criterion-referenced and ipsative assessment

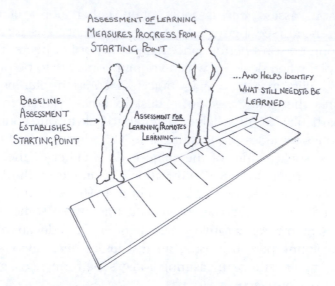

Figure 6.2   A model for assessing learning in PSHE education

end of the lesson or series of lessons to measure the distance travelled from their starting point through our AoL (see Figure 6.2).

Why baseline assessment is crucial

To assess PSHE effectively, it is vital that we establish the knowledge, understanding, skills, strategies, beliefs and attitudes our young people already have before we teach anything new. We would argue that baseline assessment is more important in PSHE education than in any other subject. Let us illustrate why.

We would like you to answer the following questions:

1.   How many portions of fruit and vegetables should we eat a day?
2.   What is the number 3 in Korean?

If you answered 'at least five portions' and 'sam' then well done – absolutely correct. But how did you know the answers? The obvious response is 'Because you told me at the beginning of the chapter and asked me to remember them.' For question 1, the chances are that this is not the only reason you were able to answer correctly. You will almost certainly have learned that we should eat at least five portions of fruit and vegetables a day from a number of different sources: the government, the health service, the media, food advertisers, packaging, to mention a few. In the case of question 2, it is quite likely that you were only able to answer the question because we told you the answer at the beginning of the chapter (i.e. unless you happen to already speak Korean, you know it because we taught you it). If we were teachers of Korean in a school in the UK, we could confidently give our students an assessment task at the end of each module, term or year and the results would be a clear indication of their progress and of the impact of our teaching, because in most cases they will not have received any learning in Korean from anywhere else during that time. Whereas if we were to give our PSHE education classes an assessment task at the end of a module on healthy eating, the results would not give a true reflection of the progress young people were making, or of the impact of our teaching, unless we had established their starting point before teaching them anything at all on the subject. The nature of PSHE education means that their learning will have come from any number of sources and will vary hugely from young person to young person. If we want to demonstrate or measure progress in PSHE education we *have to* start with baseline assessment. It will ensure that our lessons are suitable and relevant to each group's needs and abilities. It will help us to identify what young people already know, understand, believe, can do, can say; it helps us clarify learning needs, identify any special educational needs, determine where to start and decide how the work should be developed, including selecting appropriate language and resources.

Imagine

You are going to start a series of lessons with your Year 8 group on developing a healthy lifestyle. Time yourself for two minutes and see how many different activities you can think of that you could do with the group to give you an insight into their starting point in terms of their existing concept of health.

Your list will probably include activities such as questioning, brainstorming, drawing a mind map or spider diagram, a graffiti wall/working wall (where we invite young people to write everything they know, think, feel, want to know, want to ask about the topic on sheets of paper along the wall), quizzes and questionnaires. Another activity that works really well for establishing young people's baseline is 'draw and write'. If you have not come across this before try it.

Activity

Draw and write

Imagine you are a young person in Year 8. You don't yet know it but you are about to start a module on developing a healthy lifestyle. Your teacher asks you to work on your own, without any discussion with your neighbours for this activity: no sharing of ideas until afterwards. They add that there are no right or wrong answers, and not to worry about spelling. You are asked to draw a healthy person. Do a quick drawing now of what you would have drawn – don't worry if you're no Rembrandt, a rough sketch will do. Draw or write around your picture all the things that make or keep this person healthy. Now write around your picture why or how these things make them healthy.

Now imagine you are the teacher and you have collected in everyone's draw and write activity. What sort of information might you get about the young people's starting point in their concept of health from looking at these? (See Figure 6.3.) You might see some stereotypes emerging that you will need to challenge, for example if their 'healthy people' all have 'six packs' and rippling muscles, or if they identified 'being very thin' as a factor of being healthy. You will gain an insight into whether their concept of health confuses health with fitness, is focussed more on physical health than mental health, and includes the importance of relationships and other contributing factors to emotional wellbeing. You will see whether they have misconceptions and gaps in their understanding. Often 'draw and write' activities can give us insights and answers to questions we had not thought to ask and can be applied to any number of PSHE themes such as drug education, relationships, health, risk, bullying and keeping safe. The key is not to prompt or teach about the topic prior to doing the baseline 'draw and write' activity, to keep the instruction neutral and open-ended so as not to lead them in any way (e.g. 'draw someone who uses drugs' rather than 'draw a drug addict/drug user'), to ensure that everyone works on their own without sharing thoughts and ideas and finally to resist the teacher's instinct to support and scaffold or guide young people's responses. If asked for help, repeat that you want their ideas. For more on the use of 'draw and write' see Boddington et 'al. (2014).

'Draw and write' example

Katie   10ᵗʰ October

Figure 6.3   'Draw and write' example

What does this young person's response (Figure 6.3) to the draw and write activity above tell us about their current concept of health? What is missing? What is right but needs extending further? Are there any misconceptions? If this young person's classmates' draw and write responses were broadly similar to this, what learning objectives and intended learning outcomes would you identify for the series of lessons to follow? (See Chapter 5 for more on learning objectives and outcomes.)

Building in assessment for learning

Baseline assessment is an important element of AfL. It should inform our planning and enable us to adapt our teaching to promote young people's progress. It allows us to provide learning that starts from where they are, building on their existing knowledge, understanding, skills, beliefs and attitudes. But this is just one way in which we should incorporate AfL into our PSHE education teaching. First we must share the learning objectives and intended learning outcomes with the young people (see Chapter 5): they need to know where we intend them to go and how we expect them to get there. It may be that we need to share these after we have carried out a baseline assessment activity rather than before, to give us a truer insight into their starting point before any teaching takes place. Equally central to AfL are effective questioning and feedback and feed-forwards between teachers and young people.

Effective questioning for assessment for learning

Questioning is a skill that is often overlooked, but spending time thinking about and planning the key questions you will use to structure your discussions in a PSHE education lesson will greatly enhance your AfL. Through questions we find out what young people know, understand, believe, can do and can say. It allows us to identify misconceptions and gaps in understanding and skills, allowing us to adjust our teaching accordingly.

Questionning

In a Year 7 lesson on peer influence, the teacher has written a short scenario to open the discussion, which she reads to the class:

> When Mala started senior school she didn't know anyone else as she had recently moved to the area. A group of really popular kids in her class has started to let her hang out with them sometimes but she still feels a bit of an 'outsider' and really wants to fit in. On the way home from school one day she sees them hanging around. 'Hey Mala! Over here,' calls Stacey. Mala's really pleased they've acknowledged her and hurries over to join them. As she reaches them Stacey says, 'We're going back to mine but we're going to the corner shop on the way to pinch some sweets – it's dead easy there – we've done it loads of times. You coming?' Mala's never stolen anything and doesn't want to, but she does want to be one of Stacey's crowd.

Try to think of some questions you might use to structure the discussion from this point that will allow the teacher to build on the young people's current point in their learning.

What did you come up with? Often the best way to engage with a scenario, story or film clip in PSHE education is using a 'timeline' technique to explore the present, the future and the past. This was covered in greater depth in Chapter 3 but here we consider its application for AfL. We can explore the present through questions such as:

- How do you think Mala is feeling right now? Could she be having lots of different feelings at the same time?
- Do you think what she's feeling and thinking is different from what she's saying and doing? Why?
- If someone who really cared for her was watching her now, what would they be feeling? Is it different? Why?
- Imagine that suddenly Mala can see you, but the rest of the world is 'on pause'. Mala asks your advice. What would you tell her to do? She thinks for a minute and then asks you 'why?' Could you convince her? What more would you like to know/need to know to really convince her?

We can explore the future through questions such as:

- What do you think will happen next? Is that good or not so good?
- Will anyone be 'at risk', who could get hurt? Their body? Their feelings?
- What do you think might happen tomorrow, next week, in the future depending on the decision Mala makes now?
- What would be the best way this situation could develop?
- For that to happen, what has to be said or done now? Who has to do it? What might push them forward? What might hold them back?

Depending on the scenario, especially when using film clips or pictures where nothing is known about the lead-up to this moment, we might want to explore the past with questions such as:

- If we could turn the clock back, what do you think might have happened before this situation?
- Could there have been a critical moment when someone could have said or done something different that could have stopped this situation from happening?
- Would it have been easier to have said or done something then rather than now?

Only if we feel it is appropriate, depending on the scenario we are using, we can carefully take the group into the situation on a more personal level with questions such as:

- Could we ever imagine this happening to us?
- Where might we be? Who might we be with?
- What would we be feeling? Saying? Doing?
- Can we have more than one feeling in a situation like this?
- What would be the risks for us, now, tomorrow, soon? How do we feel about this?
- Do we think we know enough to make a good/healthy/safe choice? One we would be happy to live with tomorrow, next week, the future? If not, what would we like to know?

We can also think about questioning in AfL through the lens of Bloom et al.'s (1956) taxonomy. Try using a selection of the following in 'mini-plenaries' as you move from one activity to another (see Table 6.1).

Table 6.1   Mini-plenaries (based on Bloom's taxonomy)

Looking for knowledge:

- Tell me five… [illegal drugs, types of contraception etc.].
- What is a…[CV; uterus etc.]?

Looking for understanding:

- How would you explain/describe…?
- What's the difference between…?
- What does this tell us about…?

Looking for application:

- Can you think of another example of…?
- In what other situations might this [information/skill etc.] be useful? How?
- Based on what you know, what would you change if…?

Looking for analysis:

- What might happen if…?
- Why might someone …?
- Can you explain why you think…?
- How can we be sure of that?

Looking for synthesis:

- What are the best ways to…?
- How many ways can you think of to…?
- What happens if…?

Looking for evaluation:

- How would you judge which is the best solution/decision?
- Do you think… is a good or not so good thing/decision/idea?
- Why might some people believe…?
- How do you feel about…?
- Is it always/ever true that…?
- How can we be sure of that?

Assessment *of* learning: Demonstrating and measuring progress

We have gauged our young people's baseline in terms of their knowledge, understanding, skills, strategies, beliefs and attitudes; we have built assessment *for* learning (A*f*L) into our teaching and now we come to the end of the lesson, series of lessons, module or unit and it is time to demonstrate and measure the progress young people have made in their learning.

Measuring progress

Earlier in this chapter, when thinking about baseline assessment, we asked you to imagine you were going to start a series of lessons with your Year 8 group on developing a healthy lifestyle. We asked you to time yourself for two minutes and see how many different activities you could think of that you could do with the group to give you an insight into their starting point in terms of their existing concept of health.

Now imagine you are at the end of the series of lessons. Give yourself another two minutes to think of as many activities as you can that would allow the young people to demonstrate the progress they have made in their learning since you carried out the baseline assessment.

I'm sure you have a long list that might include activities such as quizzes, role plays and scenarios, presentations, discussions, annotated photos, written work including leaflets, projects, displays, mock TV or radio interviews, blogs, podcasts, videos and so on.

Possibly the simplest and most effective way of demonstrating progress is to either repeat, or better still, revisit the original baseline activity. We looked earlier at the example of a 'draw and write' baseline activity where the young people were asked to draw a healthy person. If at the end of the series of lessons we give each young person their work back, ask them to take a different colour pencil or pen and add to it and make any changes they now want to make, we and they will be able to clearly see how far they have come in their learning.

Draw and write progress

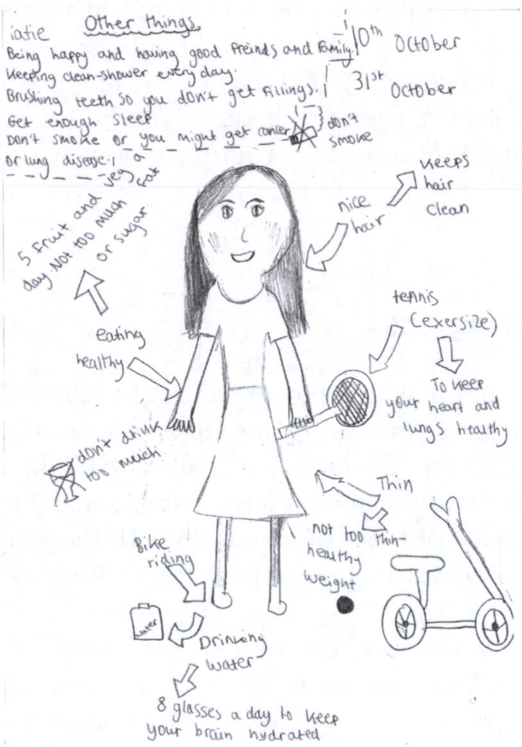

Figure 6.4 Example of a 'draw and write' baseline assessment activity revisited to demonstrate progress

Here (Figure 6.4) the same young person has added to their original drawing of a healthy person in a different colour pen. What progress has been made?

The same technique can be used with many baseline activities including mind maps and brainstorms, storyboards and quizzes.

Alternative draw and write techniques

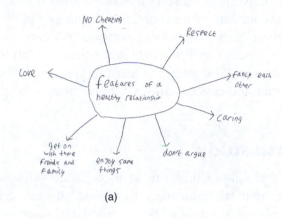

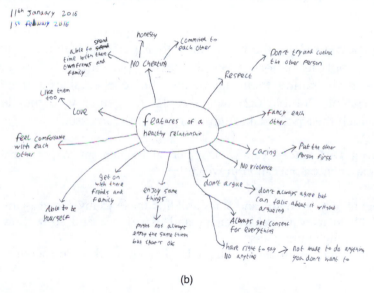

Figure 6.5 Example of a mind map on healthy relationships

In this example (Figure 6.5) a young person in Year 9 was asked to draw a mind map to show their understanding of 'healthy relationships' at the beginning of a series of RSE lessons and to return to it at the end, again making changes, adding to it or expanding on their original ideas in a different colour.

Baseline activities repeated or revisited in this way provide evidence of progress that can be used as a record of where young people are at the end of a piece of learning, to celebrate achievement, or formatively to help us plan the next steps in our teaching. However, we might also want to measure and record their attainment more formally. If this is the case, then we need to move to a more criterion-referenced model, which means we will need something to measure the young people's work against: some success criteria. These might take the form of 'I can ...' statements, or better still, a set of descriptors for 'working towards ...', 'attaining ...' or 'working beyond/exceeding' the intended learning outcome. The terminology is less important than the process and will differ from school to school.

Mini case study

Here is an example of how one school carried out quite a formal piece of assessment in PSHE education that used success criteria that allow for young people's attainment to be recorded and their work to be 'marked' in a meaningful way.

Earlier in the chapter we looked at peer assessment in the context of a Year 10 group peer-assessing the first draft of their personal statements to accompany their applications for a work experience placement. Before the young people started drafting their statements, the teacher shared the intended learning outcome (Table 6.2) with the class, together with the descriptors against which their personal statements would be assessed:

> **Learning Outcome**: I can write a personal statement to accompany my work experience application in which I:
>
> - identify my strengths and skills and link these to my career plans
> - highlight relevant achievements and experience and show how these link to my future plans
> - demonstrate an understanding of last lesson's work on 'presenting myself positively'.

Once the young people had completed their personal statements the teacher decided which descriptor in each row most closely reflected each young person's work and finally made an overall judgement on whether, on balance, the young person was working towards, attaining or working beyond the intended outcome for this piece of work.

Assessing a piece of written work can be problematic in PSHE education. Without clear, precise intended learning outcomes and success criteria, the

Table 6.2   Intended learning outcome

Working towards the learning outcome	Attaining the learning outcome	Working beyond the learning outcome
The student can ...	*The student can ...*	*The student can ...*
identify some of their personal skills;	recognise and analyse their personal skills in order to explain which they enjoy using and which are likely to be advantageous at work;	show well-developed career ideas, based on realistic thinking about the links between their personal skills and interests and the demands of particular occupations;
identify simple targets and plans to help them make progress;		
with comprehensive support and guidance, recognise the significance of their main experiences and achievements in relation to their future plans;	with minimal guidance, assess the significance of their experiences and achievements in relation to their future plans;	use an independent and thorough assessment of the significance of their experiences and achievements to inform future choices in education, training and employment;
with comprehensive support and guidance, use this to inform their personal statement.	with minimal guidance, use this assessment to inform their personal statement.	independently produce a personal statement, in which a critical evaluation of their experiences and achievements is clearly related to their future plans.

tendency is to focus and feedback on aspects such as spelling, grammar, presentation, neatness and effort. These are of course important, but it is the intended outcomes and success criteria that clarify for the teacher and young person the PSHE-specific learning that is being assessed.

The success criteria in this example were adapted from the PSHE Association's 'Progression Frameworks for Planning and Assessment in PSHE Education' (2010), but there is no reason why teachers cannot identify their own. Always start with the intended learning outcome: What will young people be able to do by the end of the lesson(s) that they could not do before? What will they be able to demonstrate, explain, identify, say, understand, evaluate, if we have achieved our learning objective (see Chapter 5)? And if the intended learning outcomes have been based on the findings of the baseline assessment, rather than plucked from the air or from a textbook, then they are far more likely to be relevant and meaningful. Some teachers find it helpful to identify success criteria in terms of what they expect all young people to be able to do, what they expect most to be able to do and what they expect only some to be able to do. Thinking of the personal statement activity above, this might result in something like this:

All students will produce a personal statement in which they identify their strengths, skills, interests, achievements and experiences.

Most students will also be able to identify some career ideas and relate these to their strengths, skills, interests, achievements and experiences.

Some students will also be able to demonstrate how an analysis and evaluation of their strengths, skills, interests, achievements and experiences has informed their career plans.

The terminology and format used for success criteria is a matter of personal preference or of what is most meaningful and manageable for the individual school; however, it is important that there is consistency within the school, rather than each teacher adopting a different approach. The key questions are: Does this enable me and/or the young people to demonstrate the progress they have made? Does it allow me and/or the young people to measure their attainment in relation to our intended learning outcomes?

Choosing assessment activities

If we define an assessment activity as any activity that gives us information about what has been or still needs to be learned, then it is difficult to think of any activity we might use in a PSHE education lesson that is not potentially an assessment activity (with the exception, perhaps, of copying from a book, watching a DVD or listening to a speaker for the entire lesson). This is an important point, as one reason that is often given for not assessing learning in PSHE education is lack of time. But assessment should not be an add-on: it is not about squeezing in an extra activity but rather being smarter in the activities we choose, planning activities that allow us to gather our evidence.

The type of activity we choose will depend on the aspect of young people's learning we wish to assess. The easiest aspect to assess is knowledge. How many class A, B or C drugs do our students know? Can they list the side-effects of each? Do they know the legal age of consent and the law relating to the sharing of sexual images of someone who is under 18? Can they list the different methods of contraception available? To find out would be a simple matter of using questioning, setting a quiz or a test, and there might be times in PSHE education when we want to do just that. But if we think for a moment about the possible situations in which young people might need to call on and apply that knowledge, we begin to see that whilst assessing knowledge might be the most straightforward to do, knowledge is not always the most important aspect of learning in PSHE education on which to focus our assessment.

If a young person finds themself in a situation where they are being offered a pill of some sort at a party, their knowledge of drugs will be very useful. However, to successfully and safely manage the moment at which that pill is offered, they will need to call on a combination of skills (including risk assessment and management, decisionmaking, communication and negotiation skills, critical thinking, strategies for managing peer influence, exit or avoidance strategies) and personal attributes (including self-confidence, self-esteem, assertiveness and a sense of their own 'moral compass', values and identity). Likewise, for a young person in the early stages of a relationship whose partner seems keen for the relationship to become sexual but less keen to discuss contraception, a comprehensive knowledge of different forms of contraception and sexually transmitted infections will be vital, but again, what will most support the young person to manage the situation in a way that is best and safest for them will be those same skills and attributes: risk assessment and management, decisionmaking, communication and negotiation, critical thinking, strategies for managing peer influence, exit or avoidance strategies, self-confidence, self-esteem, assertiveness and a sense of their own 'moral compass', values and identity (see Chapter 3).

It is clear, therefore, that if we are to assess what is of value in PSHE education and not simply value what is easy to assess, then we must find a way to assess skills and attributes as well as knowledge.

Role play activities are an excellent way of giving young people the opportunity to rehearse real life decisions and choices and explore attitudes and feelings. But they can also be used as a baseline assessment to demonstrate existing skills and strategies before starting a new piece of learning, or to demonstrate progress: the skills and strategies young people have developed as a result of their learning. Assessing skills does not have to depend solely on role play, however. Some young people will respond better to writing a script for a role play, or a cartoon strip or storyboard showing the strategies their characters might use in different scenarios. Whichever activity we choose, we need to take care that we and the young people are very clear about the intended learning outcomes and success criteria in relation to the skills and strategies we wish to assess, so that our assessment is not just focussed on dramatic ability, creativity or artistic ability. It is also important to draw out what young people have learned or discovered afterwards and provide time and space for reflection on how they might use these skills themselves, to avoid the activity being viewed as a bit of light relief and the real life connections not being made.

Activities such as preparing and making a presentation to the class can be useful as a means of assessing a combination of knowledge, skills and personal attributes. Presenting their knowledge and understanding through this medium allows young people to rehearse and demonstrate their communication skills whilst building their confidence and self-esteem. Video diaries, mock TV or radio interviews, podcasts and debates all offer similar opportunities.

Table 6.3 Planning a PSHE education lesson

Identify the learning objectives and intended learning outcomes
Learning objectives: What do you intend the young people to learn about, or learn how to do?
Learning outcomes: What will the young people be able to do as a result of the learning? Identify …? Demonstrate …? List …? Describe …? Manage …? Analyse …? Evaluate a…?

Plan an activity to establish the young people's baseline
What knowledge, understanding, experience, skills, beliefs and attitudes do the young people already have?
Do they have any special needs? What implications does this have for planning?
If possible, carry this out before planning the lesson and use it to help identify the learning outcomes. If this is not possible, start the lesson with this and adjust the teaching accordingly.

Plan activities that will allow young people to achieve the intended learning outcomes
Always start by revisiting ground rules to ensure a safe learning environment.
Ensure that all activities are in line with best practice (see Chapter 3).
Consider how the activities might need to be differentiated for individual young people.
Identify the resources required.

Incorporate assessment for learning and opportunities for young people to reflect on what the learning means for their own lives
This might include planning key questions, mini-plenaries between activities, questions for private reflection, opportunities for feedback and identifying next steps.

Plan an activity that allows young people to demonstrate progress
How will you know that the objectives have been achieved?
How can young people demonstrate progress? Consider revisiting the baseline activity.
Do you need or want to measure attainment? If so, what will 'good' look like? Define the success criteria.
Is self-, peer- or teacher assessment the most appropriate and useful in this case?
(See Chapter 6)

Personal attributes are arguably the hardest aspect of learning to assess. How can a teacher accurately assess a young person's self-esteem, confidence or sense of their own identity and values? The answer may well be that they cannot, at least not with any real meaningfulness. However, young people themselves *will* be able to judge, for instance, whether they feel more confident or have a firmer sense of their own beliefs and opinions as a result of their learning in PSHE education than they did before. This might not and probably should not ever be something that is written down and handed in for marking, but giving young people the time and space within PSHE education lessons to reflect on this, either privately or through discussion, is a vital ingredient of the assessment process.

Building in, not bolting on: Integrating assessment into lesson plans

Assessment should never be a bolt-on and will not be effective if it is. If each lesson is planned from the outset with assessment *for* and *of* learning in mind, not only will it be straightforward to assess and provide evidence of progress but the lesson will also provide learning that is relevant, meaningful and which meets young people's learning needs.

Look again at the step-by-step guide to planning a PSHE education lesson in Table 6.3 that we also considered in Chapter 5 (Table 5.4). This time, note particularly the process of integrating assessment *for* and *of* learning into the lesson plan.

Chapter overview

In this chapter we have considered why assessment is important in PSHE education, the importance of incorporating both assessment for and of learning, through self-, peer- and teacher-assessment and how this works in practice. We end with some key messages:

- Do not teach anything new until you have assessed the young people's baseline in terms of their existing knowledge, understanding, skills and attitudes.
- Remember that assessment in PSHE education is not a question of whether a young person has passed or failed, achieved a grade A or E but is about the progress they have made in their learning from their own starting point.

(Continued)

(Continued)

- Remember to assess progress in skills and attributes as well as knowledge.
- Ensure that assessment activities do not judge the worth, personality or value of an individual young person.
- Ensure that assessment is planned as an integral part of teaching and learning and is not a bolt-on.
- Ensure that assessment activities reflect the range of learning styles and the learning and achievements of *all* young people.
- Remember to involve young people as partners in the process.
- Assess the learning that has value in PSHE education; do not value only that which is easy to assess.
- Finally, there is no single correct way to organise assessment in PSHE education. If you are not sure whether you are 'getting it right' then ask yourself: 'Do I and the young people I teach know what they have learned, the progress they have made and what they still need to learn?' If the answer is 'Yes' and you have borne in mind all the points above, then you are!

Further reading

Blake, S. and Muttock, S. (2004) *Assessment, Evaluation and Sex & Relationships Education*. London: National Children's Bureau.
This is a collection of generic activity ideas for assessment and evaluation that can easily be adapted to any aspects of PSHE education.

Boddington, N., King, A. and McWhirter, J. (2014) *Understanding Personal, Social, Health and Economic Education in Primary Schools*. London: Sage.
Written primarily for student teachers and their mentors in primary schools, this is the companion text to this book, with material that will be useful for those teaching PSHE education at any phase.

Race, P., Brown, S. and Smith, B. (2005) *500 Tips on Assessment*. London: Routledge.
Although written with teachers and lecturers in further and higher education in mind, anyone entering secondary school teaching, or

even those who have been teaching for some time, will find this offers practical, down to earth guidance on assessment.

Smith, I. (2007) *Assessment and Learning Pocketbook*. Alresford: Teachers' Pocketbooks.
Highly accessible and easy to read with many practical ideas for assessment for and of learning.

Spendlove, D. (2009) *Putting Assessment for Learning into Practice*. London: Continuum International.
A practical guide to effective strategies for improving learning through assessment for learning (AfL) that engages learners and teachers as partners in the process of teaching and learning.

References

Black, P., Harrison, C., Lee, C., Marshall, B. and William, D. (1990) *Working Inside the Black Box: Assessment for Learning in the Classroom*. London: Letts.

Bloom, B.S., Engelhart, M.D., Furst, E.J., Hill, W.H. and Krathwohl, D.R. (1956) *Taxonomy of Educational Objectives: The Classification of Educational Goals – Handbook I: Cognitive domain*. New York: David McKay.

Boddington, N., King, A. and McWhirter, J. (2014) *Understanding Personal, Social, Health and Economic Education in Primary Schools*. London: Sage.

Ofsted (2013) 'Not yet good enough: personal, social health and economic education in schools'. Available at www.ofsted.gov.uk/resources/not-yet-good-enough-personal-social-health-and-economic-education-schools (accessed 15.3.16).

PSHE Association (2010) Progression Frameworks for Planning and Assessment in PSHE Education. Available at https://pshe-association.org.uk/resources_search_details.aspx?ResourceId=336&Keyword=&SubjectID=0&LevelID=0&ResourceTypeID=3&SuggestedUseID=0 (accessed 24.1.16).

Spendlove, D. (2009) *Putting Assessment for Learning into Practice*. London. Continuum International.

Part Two

In this part we focus on some of the ways in which young people take risks and distinguish between risk taking and being at risk. We know, however, that students and newly qualified teachers ask for support in these aspects of PSHE education in particular. We are not able to include chapters on every element within PSHE education, but the advice we provide here is transferable to almost any topic. This does not mean that PSHE education should always be broken down into separate topics – far from it. Many opportunities, challenges and choices facing young people and that are explored through PSHE education do not fit neatly into 'topics' but are influenced by a complex variety of different factors; for example, alcohol use may influence personal safety, economic wellbeing or relationships, and teaching should reflect this.

7

Understanding Risk During Adolescence

Aim

To review what is understood about adolescent risk taking behaviour in the context of their overall development.

Learning objectives

Through reading and reflecting on the content of this chapter you will begin to:

- explore how being 'at risk' and risk taking are related
- understand risk and risk taking behaviour among young people
- reflect on risk taking and brain development in adolescents
- be able to plan and implement effective approaches to risk education within a whole school approach to PSHE education.

Before we start

Draw a picture of someone, who is about your own age, doing something risky. (A stick person will do!)

Now write briefly:

- what is happening in the picture
- what makes it risky
- what you would be doing or saying if you were there while this was happening.

Keep this picture and notes with you while you read this chapter as we will come back to it several times.

Introduction

Adolescence is a period in our lives which many will associate with increased physical, social and emotional risk taking. Adults have good reasons to be concerned about risk taking as they begin to share responsibility for a young person's safety, with a young person whose behaviour may appear reckless at worst and careless at best! Parents, carers and teachers want to reduce the short-, medium- and long-term harm that can result from young people's risky behaviour. Legal, social and cultural restraints support these efforts. However, we need to keep in mind that risk taking is a normal and necessary part of adolescence that should be encouraged. Risk taking can promote health, creativity and a better quality of life.

Consider

The author and journalist Luke Jennings has written about how he overcame his fears to climb a tree in the grounds of his school in the 1960s. Climbing this particular tree was a rite of passage for his peer group. This is how he describes what that achievement meant to him:

> It was more than just the thrill of altitude, it was the sense that we had climbed beyond the reach of authority, that what lay before us was a map, bearing any number of alternative routes, all of them vanishing into the future. To my 12 year old self, swaying amongst the pine needles, it looked like freedom. (Jennings, 2012)

How might this rite of passage be dealt with by a school today? What might be the consequences, good and bad, for banning risk taking by young people, not only for them but for our whole society?

This chapter will help to put adolescent risk taking in context of our overall development. Why do adolescents take risks? Do all young people take risks? How can secondary schools maximise the benefits of risk taking while minimising possible harms for individuals, their families and communities?

What is risk?

Vocabulary of risk

To fully understand risk, young people (and their teachers!) need a vocabulary of risk that bridges the gap between everyday language and the technical language used by health and safety experts. Here are some definitions of words which are used differently by lay people and experts. In this chapter we will use mainly the technical language used by safety professionals – although we take a different view when it comes to the definition of risk.

Hazard – an object or behaviour with the potential to cause harm.

Risk assessment – a calculation of the likelihood that a hazard is associated with harmful outcomes. This includes an assessment of the probability that harm will occur and the severity of the outcome, and for whom.

Risk management – steps taken to minimise the possibility of harmful outcomes.

Some definitions of risk, particularly those cited by the safety industry, focus only on negative outcomes, for example:

- Risk is the probability of harm (Health and Safety Executive).
- Risk is a situation involving exposure to danger (Oxford English Dictionary).

However, as Holton (2004) points out, risk actually has both of these components: uncertainty and exposure. A dangerous situation (such as jumping from a great height without any means of breaking the fall) involves no uncertainty as the only possible outcome is death. According to Holton, to be risky a situation must involve some uncertainty about the outcome.

Researchers interested in adolescent risk taking acknowledge the potential for benefit in accomplishing something risky. Gullone and Moore state that risk behaviour

> is the participation in behaviour which involves potential negative consequences (or loss) balanced in some way by perceived positive consequences (or gain). (2000)

Here, perhaps, is a clue to young people's risk behaviour: it is the possibility of reward that encourages young people to take risks, even when some of the potential outcomes could involve physical injury, failure or personal embarrassment.

What it means is that in PSHE education we must recognise the possibility of both positive and negative outcomes when we are thinking about what risk means:

> Risk is the uncertainty that a particular behaviour will have a harmful and/or beneficial outcome.

It also means we must focus on behaviour and not just on physical hazards: cliffs are not inherently dangerous; standing on a cliff edge on a windy day after heavy rainfall is to risk life and limb.

What is the problem?

In other chapters we look at the epidemiology of health issues for young people including substance misuse (Chapter 9), sexual health (Chapter 10), social and mental health (Chapter 8 and 12 and Appendix III). Those data suggest there is an increase in risk-taking behaviour which coincides with the onset of puberty (Steinberg, 2008). All these health issues involve risk for young people – and some, such as the use of social media, are a present-day cause for concern. However, we will look first at one of the leading causes of death and serious injury among young people: accidents.

The Health and Safety Executive (HSE) defines an accident as 'any unplanned event that resulted in injury or ill health of people, or damage or loss to property, plant, materials or the environment or a loss of business opportunity' (HSE, 2014).

The Royal Society for the Prevention of Accidents (RoSPA) takes the view that accidents are preventable. RoSPA has examined Office for National Statistics (ONS) and NHS data on preventable causes of death, the causes of injury reported to accident and emergency departments (see Figure 7.1) and estimated the number of years of life lost (YLL) as a result. While their analysis shows that accidents were the leading cause of preventable premature death for people of all ages from 0 to 60 years in England and Wales in 2010, the pattern of A&E attendances for adolescents and young adults is strikingly different from that for under 5s and those aged 30+.

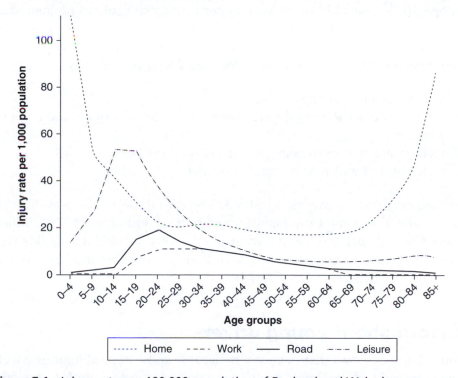

Figure 7.1   Injury rate per 100,000 population of England and Wales by age group, 2010

Consider

Take a look at your drawing of someone your own age doing something risky. Does it fall into one of the four broad categories of home, work, road or leisure? Does your picture reflect the most likely causes of injury for your age group? Are the outcomes in your picture certain or uncertain? What, if any, are the potential benefits from the risky situation in your picture? Is your view of risk synonymous with danger or with the possibility of loss or benefit?

Among adolescents most injuries happen during leisure activities, the majority of which are minor, although sports such as horse riding and rugby can result in life changing injury.

Although the workplace is a far safer place than it was 50 years ago, across Europe 18–24 year olds are at least 50 per cent more likely to be injured at work than older people. Young people are also more likely to suffer from an occupational illness. The European Agency for Safety and Health at Work (2009) has identified several reasons for this. Young people may:

- lack skills and training
- be unaware of their employer's duties, and their own rights and responsibilities
- lack confidence in speaking out if there's a problem
- lack physical and psychological maturity

Preparation for work experience should consider these issues as well as all the benefits that come from familiarity with the world of work. The British Safety Council (2016) offers an award for 14–19 year olds that builds students' awareness of important health and safety issues before they embark on work experience or their first job.

A word about young drivers

Figure 7.1 also shows that there is a noticeable spike in road injuries which begins in early adolescence, reaching a peak among late adolescents and young adults. This peak coincides with young people becoming drivers. However, all younger road users (including cyclists and pedestrians) are vulnerable: in 2013 a quarter of all deaths among 15–19 year olds in Great Britain occurred on the roads (Department for Transport, 2014). However, recently qualified drivers (and their passengers) are particularly vulnerable. In 2013, almost 1,300 young drivers aged 17–24 were killed or seriously injured on Britain's roads.

Classroom research task

Draw and write about risk (based on McWhirter, 2007)

This draw and write is a more formal version of the task described in the introduction to this chapter and has been used in several large-scale research studies as well as school-based enquiry used in planning PSHE education (McWhirter and South, 2004). If possible, try this out with a range of year groups.

As with all draw and write techniques intended to establish the starting point for your teaching (assessment for learning), ask the young people to work independently but quickly on the following activity.

Don't give any prior explanation about what you mean by 'risk'. If a student asks what risk means, tell them that it is OK to write 'I don't know'.

- Invite students to draw someone their own age, doing something risky.
- Next, ask them to write what is happening in the picture.
- Then, ask them to write what makes it risky.
- Finally, ask them to draw themselves in the picture.
- What are they saying or doing to help?

You can carry out a simple analysis of the findings with the students by categorising the hazards they have depicted. Among the highest scoring categories, you can expect extreme height (cliff tops, bungee jumping and parachuting) and misbehaviour (everything from naughtiness and disobedience to lawbreaking and physical violence). You will also find more everyday hazards such as crossing the road, drinking and driving, as well as smoking, drinking alcohol and amongst older groups, risks associated with sexual behaviour, social media and violence by others.

How do these findings compare with your response to the similar task at the beginning of this chapter?

In large studies using this 'draw and write' tool, many of the scenarios young people describe have the most severe (but often least likely) consequence, which suggests that young people tend to confound 'risky' with 'dangerous'. However, we have seen that in dangerous situations there is little uncertainty about the outcome, and very little possibility of benefit (Holton, 2004).

Young people also often depict scenarios where they are flouting adult authority and social convention, where the risk is being caught, found out or punished (and where the benefit is the thrill – or relief – of getting away with it).

Once you have completed the simple analysis, you can reflect with the young people on the hazards most associated with harm for young people of their age. They may be surprised to find that being a road user (whether as a pedestrian, cyclist, passenger or recently qualified driver) is one of the riskiest activities for their age group.

However, there is more to learning about risk than knowing the language to use or being informed about the causes of death and serious injury for your age group, as we will see later in this chapter.

Who are the risk takers?

Although accidents (especially road accidents) are the leading cause of serious injury and death amongst young people of secondary school age, that is only part of the pattern of risk taking among young people. There is an overlap between the young people who take the most risk on the road (e.g. by speeding or drink-driving) and those who get into difficulties with drugs, those who have risky or unprotected sex, and those who are involved in acts of aggression and self-harm.

In fact, young people involved in multiple risks account for most of the adolescent risk taking recorded. For example, in a study of young people in the USA, among the 12 percent of students reporting regular tobacco use, 85 percent were multiple risk-takers (Duberstein Lindberg et al., 2000).

This 'cluster effect' was first noted by Jessor and Jessor (1977), who showed a correlation between a range of 'problem' behaviours including criminality and 'social protest'. They suggested that these behaviours were manifestations of a syndrome, common among adolescents, which reflected a rejection of social convention (Donovan and Jessor, 1985). The association between health risk behaviours and being anti-authority is part of the reason why risk taking by adolescents attracts so much negative attention from adults.

Consider

In Jessor's early work, he described young people's risk taking as problem behaviour or a 'syndrome' (a term used by doctors to describe a collection of related symptoms or a disorder). For whom is multiple risk taking by adolescents a problem? Do you think that young people can be cured of this disorder?

What these data suggest is that some young people are more likely to become multiple risk takers than others, and that there are likely to be many 'risk' and 'protective' factors associated with risk taking among adolescents.

The Health Behaviour in School-aged Children (HBSC) is an international survey that has been implemented across Europe and other countries such as the USA, Canada and the Russian Federation by the World Health Organization (WHO) since the 1980s and has been carried out separately for England, Wales, Ireland and Scotland. The last published international findings are based on data collected from 11, 13 and 15 year olds in 2009–10 and consider young people's health behaviours in the context of 'risk factors' such as age, gender and other social factors including a family's financial status (Currie et al., 2012). National reports are published more frequently; for example, the most recent report for England was published in 2015 (Brooks et al., 2015)

The HBSC survey has shown that internationally, risk taking behaviour is generally greater amongst boys from poorer households, increasing with age from 11–15 years. Within this general picture there are variations, however. For example, in England, 15 year old girls are more likely than boys to smoke at least once a week and to report having been drunk more than twice, while the prevalence of cannabis use is similar among boys and girls aged 15. Boys aged 11–15 in England are both more likely than girls to report having been injured and to be involved in fighting, and to report having bullied someone at school (Brooks et al., 2015).

Most young people under 16 in the UK do not smoke, drink to excess or use drugs (see Fuller and Hawkins, 2014 and Chapter 8), and most young people (70 per cent) wait until they are 16 or older before they have sexual intercourse for the first time (Mercer et al., 2013), so the cluster effect highlights that it is a subset of the adolescent population who are most likely to become involved in multiple risk taking and experience negative outcomes as a result.

A word about social media and risk taking

Recent studies suggest that the factors involved when young people use social media in risky ways are similar to those correlated with other 'problem behaviours' of the pre-internet era. For example, boys are more likely than girls to report that they have viewed sexually explicit online material and play video games which are inappropriate for their age group (Peter and Valkenburg, 2006; Nikken and Jansz, 2006). Boys from single parent families are most likely to report that they have 'friended' people they don't know in any other way, shared personal information and/or photos with people they only know through social media sites (SMS) and pretended to be a different kind of person than they really are (Notten and Nikken, 2014). However, Notten and Nikken have shown that the gender effect is explained when the personality trait of 'sensation seeking', digital skills and frequency of usage are taken in to account.

Although young people whose parent(s) have a higher level of education are less likely to use the internet in risky ways, parents from any educational background who co-use and monitor their adolescents' use of social media reduce the likelihood that young people will take risks on the internet. Somewhat counter-intuitively, young people living in countries where access to the internet is more widespread (i.e. with greater exposure) are less likely to take risks on SMS. This could be because adults are themselves more familiar with social media, so more able to encourage safe usage, and there is also less novelty involved for adolescents (Notten and Nikken, 2014).

Why do some young people take more risks than others?

Over the last 40 years, Richard Jessor has explored the factors that influence the development of problem behaviours. This model specified three factors, which typically interact with one another:

- demographic
- perceived social environment
- personality.

Within each category there were both proximal (immediate) influences on behaviour and more distal influences. Each category has both risk and protective factors involved. For example, within an adolescent's social environment, parental smoking would be a risk factor, while peer disapproval of smoking would be a protective factor. These may both be 'proximal' or close influences, while a cultural environment which discourages smoking in public places not frequented by young people would be distal (more remote). Statistically these risk and protective factors account for around 30 per cent of the variation in a specific risk behaviour, but importantly, the risk factors for smoking, drinking and unsafe driving are similar and hence we refer to some young people as being more 'at risk' of problem behaviour than others.

It is important to point out, however, that the associations between risk factors and behaviour are correlational and not causal (i.e. a young person may experience more risk factors and fewer protective factors than his or her peers and not be involved in 'problem' behaviours and vice versa).

An awareness of the risk and protective factors suggest that manipulating the social environment could make a difference to young people's risk taking. Recently there has been a focus on parenting styles in preventing problem behaviour (Michael and Ben-Zur, 2007). Schools are also a convenient setting in which to identify and support young people to reduce the likelihood that they will come to harm. Indeed, the psychologist Laurence Steinberg (2008) believes that manipulating the social environment is likely to be more effective than educational interventions.

Consider

What risks did you take as an adolescent that you would no longer take? Ask yourself what were the personality, social and demographic factors involved. How strong were the influences of friends compared with family? What (if anything) has changed? It is unlikely that your demographics (apart from age!) or personality have changed much – what are the social influences that shaped your behaviour then, and now?

What role does brain development play in young people's risk behaviour?

While Jessor's work has helped us to understand social factors which affect young people's involvement in problem behaviour, there is growing evidence that what happens in our brains during adolescence means we are actually 'hard-wired' for risk taking to some extent.

In Chapter 2 we saw how the limbic system (which is responsible for sensations of pleasure and reward) develops more rapidly in adolescents than the frontal cortex. The frontal cortex is responsible for 'executive functions' such as impulse control, planning, selective attention and working memory, all of which contribute to decision making. One of the processes by which the frontal cortex matures is known as 'synaptic pruning' – the loss of connections between neurones which are not reinforced by neuronal activity. Interestingly, testosterone inhibits synaptic pruning and may slow (but not prevent) brain development for boys in comparison to girls of the same age.

However, Steinberg (2008) cautions us not to attribute changes in adolescent emotion, cognition or behaviour solely to puberty, appealing though that might be.

Steinberg has highlighted the changes in the dopaminergic system which mediates social information and reward processing in the adolescent brain. One hypothesis is that these changes result in a 'reward deficiency syndrome', leading to increased sensation seeking behaviour and the pursuit of novelty. An alternative hypothesis is that the adolescent brain becomes transiently hypersensitive to dopamine and that rewarding stimuli are experienced more intensely than before.

The changes in the dopaminergic system occur around the time of puberty but can also be seen in animals whose gonads (sex organs) have been removed. This suggests that behavioural and sexual maturation are distinct but interacting processes; that is, these processes don't necessarily mature simultaneously, although they usually do (Sisk and Foster, 2004).

Differences in the timing of these two processes could help to explain why those young people who mature physically earlier than average (when their brains are relatively immature) report higher rates of drug and alcohol misuse, delinquency and other problem behaviours (Collins and Steinberg, 2006).

Where the sex hormones do appear to play a more direct role is in the development of memory for social information and social bonding and this effect appears to be mediated by the hormone and neurotransmitter oxytocin. Oxytocin is well known for its role in bonding between mothers and newborn babies. In adolescence, changes in the density of oxytocin receptors in the brain coincides with rises and falls in self-consciousness and the emergence of the 'imaginary audience'. The imaginary audience is the name given to a phenomenon observed among adolescents when they perceive that others pay as much attention to them as they pay to themselves. Social information is an essential tool in developing and sustaining social bonds which in turn provide positive feedback to the self-critical teenager (see Chapter 2).

In other words, different parts of adolescent brains are developing at different rates. The timing of these changes can have an effect on their emotional and social wellbeing and desire for novel and exciting experiences and for the development of attachment with their peers. It is important not to be deterministic about this, however. Young people have the capacity for amazing maturity and responsibility 'beyond their years' as well as apparently reckless and thoughtless behaviour. We know that the social environment also plays an important part in shaping young people's behaviour (see Chapter 2).

Steinberg and colleagues have carried out a range of revealing tests with adolescents and young adults between the ages of 10 and 30 years (see Albert et al., 2013, for an overview). They were able to show that scores for sensation seeking and risk preference increase from the age of 10 to 13–16 years and then decline, whereas other scores such as impulse control, future orientation, punishment sensitivity and resistance to peer influence continue to increase linearly across the same age range. However, we have seen that accident and other risk behaviours peak much later in the late teens and early twenties. This disparity may be because of the strong social controls and laws which have developed to limit young people's opportunities for risk taking in their mid teens, when they may be most vulnerable.

A key feature of adolescent risk taking when compared with that of adults is not, as we might expect, that young people lack all knowledge or awareness of hazards, but that risk taking more often occurs in groups. Teachers will be well aware how important it is to young people that their friends engage in similar activities. The extent to which a young person's peer group uses drugs or alcohol is the strongest predictor of a young person's own use (Chassin et al., 2009). A young person is more likely to be sexually active if their immediate peers are also sexually active, or if they perceive that their peers are sexually active, whether they are or not (East et al., 1993).

A recent study (Knoll et al., 2015) suggests that just labelling an opinion as coming from an adolescent is enough to influence the views of other adolescents. Visitors to the Science Museum in London were asked to rate a range of situations for their riskiness and then asked to reconsider, based on the opinions of others. These opinions were in fact randomly generated so were not based on the actual opinions of any group. Younger children and adults were more likely to modify their responses based on opinions apparently coming from adults, while adolescents were more likely to modify their views based on the views identified as those of other adolescents.

How peers influence one another is interesting, but it has some important everyday consequences. For example, the mere presence of young passengers in the car of a novice driver significantly increases the risk of an accident (Simons-Morton et al., 2005).

This association could be coincidental (i.e. that young people spend more time with their own age group). Alternatively it could be that the presence of peers activates the neurological reward systems and this encourages sensation seeking behaviour.

These alternatives were tested by Gardner and Steinberg (2005) in simulated driving tasks which reflect differences in risk behaviour among different age groups. Three groups – adolescents, youth and adults (mean ages 14, 20 and 34) – took the tests, either alone or in the presence of two friends. When the participants were alone while they did the simulated driving test, the levels of risk taking were similar in all age groups. However, in the presence of friends, risk taking behaviour doubled among adolescents, increased by 50 per cent in youth and was unchanged in adults.

More recently Chein et al. (2011) repeated this experiment while the participants were scanned using fMRI. When adolescent participants knew that their peers were able to observe their responses to the simulated driving task on a monitor in another room, signals from the parts of the brain associated with reward systems were amplified for adolescents. This effect was not observed among older participants.

Simulations are never the same as the real world, but the overlap between these simulated driving scenarios and the accident statistics suggests there is a powerful mechanism at work here.

In the modern world this 'reward for risk' system has some obvious negative consequences, but in evolutionary terms, the importance of bonding with your own generation and cutting ties with the older (soon to be dead) adult generation makes a lot more sense: humans are social animals who depend on one another for survival.

For PSHE practitioners this work helps us to understand the difference between peer pressure (when a young person is actively encouraged or coerced into a form of risk taking) and peer influence, where just being part of a peer group affects how you respond. The 'herd' mentality often associated with adolescence is not an excuse for our sometimes 'bad behaviour', but it does help us to understand that this is a normal, natural consequence of our evolution as human beings.

Consider

Teaching young people to resist peer pressure is a common activity in PSHE education, but tackling peer influence requires a more subtle approach. Helping young people to understand peer influence and how their susceptibility to peer influence changes during adolescence (see Chapter 2) could form part of drug education, sex and relationships education and or lessons on internet safety.

   Plan a lesson for Year 9 students with the following learning outcome:

- Students will understand the difference between peer pressure and peer influence.

Include experiential learning opportunities and opportunities for assessment for and of learning and reflection. (See also Chapters 5 and 6.)

Teaching safety

What can safety education as part of PSHE education do to reduce risk taking behaviour among young people?

Safety education is part of PSHE education and is best described as a universal intervention (i.e. it is aimed at all young people, whether or not they are at risk of becoming involved in risky behaviours). Safety education has the benefit of increasing knowledge and reinforcing the intentions of most young people to keep themselves safe and maintain healthy behaviours. Conventional safety education focuses on specific hazards and what young people can do to stay safe in that situation. Road safety education is a good example of this, with its emphasis on specific knowledge and skills needed to cross the road safely, cycle safely and then learn to drive.

   However, because safety education is related to specific situations the learning is not easily transferable to other situations. Some forms of safety education which are aimed at reducing the harm from rare but very risky situations can be counterproductive. A high focus on rare events can make these events seem more common and therefore create a false 'norm' (see Chapter 8).

   'Stranger danger' is an unfortunate example of this. Primary school aged children are often taught to be aware of strangers who might do them harm, but children are actually more at risk of abuse from people who are well known to them, or those who are well known and respected in their communities and so not recognised as 'strangers'. As recent events have shown, the results of this approach have been profound, with children more, not less, at risk of abuse. Some celebrities later convicted of child abuse have even backed stranger danger campaigns (Evans, 2014).

What can risk education as part of PSHE education do to reduce risk taking behaviour among young people?

We have seen that most young people are not 'risk takers' (i.e. they do not become involved in multiple high risk behaviours). Of course many young people do occasionally experiment with harmful behaviours (e.g. with alcohol) and most can describe near misses or minor accidents which could have had more serious outcomes, so all young people can benefit from 'risk education'. Risk is also a generic concept, transferable across different health behaviours. In its 2013 statement on PSHE education, the Department for Education says:

> [W]e expect schools to use their PSHE education programme to equip pupils with a sound understanding of risk and with the knowledge and skills necessary to make safe and informed decisions. (Department for Education, 2013)

However, Steinberg argues that risk education aimed solely at increasing knowledge or improving decision making skills may be misguided:

> 'I don't want people to think that education should not continue,' he says. 'I just think that it alone is not going to make much of a difference in deterring risky behavior. Some things just take time to develop, and, like it or not, mature judgment is probably one of them.' (Steinberg, 2007)

One reason why risk education may not be very effective is that too few definitions of risk acknowledge the potential for benefit in accomplishing something risky. So the aims of risk education in PSHE education must recognise that young people's risk behaviour is influenced by the possibility of reward. In our view the aim of risk education is to improve young people's risk decision making so that they can act on their intentions to behave in safe and healthy ways through:

* awareness of hazards
* assessing the probability of both beneficial and harmful outcomes associated with a particular activity or behaviour
* knowing and developing competence in measures to maximise benefits and minimise harm.

Taking a whole school approach to risk education as part of PSHE education encourages young people to develop their competence while providing the social support and control needed for their developing brains.

Teaching decision making skills

Consider

If the adolescent brain finds risk taking is rewarding, is it possible to teach young people to make healthier, safer decisions?

Just as in many examples of social science, there are at least two schools of thought on the answer to the above question. All agree that decision making is a dual process – it involves reasoning (the head) and intuition (the heart, or gut). Where theorists differ is in their interpretation of how these two systems operate – and the implications for how we educate young people.

One dual process model, known as 'prototype willingness', describes how adolescent risk taking behaviour differs from adults in that it is most accurately predicted not by young people's *attitude* to risk, or their *intention* to take a particular risk (driving while drunk, smoking a joint) but by their *willingness*, in a given situation, to act on their intentions. In studies, students were asked if they would be willing to smoke a joint at a party where there are no adults. Those who agreed were more likely to have smoked a joint six months later than those who said they were not willing. This willingness is shaped partly by images or 'prototypes' of young people who are thought to behave in this way. So if cannabis smoking is seen in a positive light, the more willing another young person might be to adopt the same behaviour even if they do not intend to do so. The prototype forms part of the meaning of 'joint smoking', rather like the term 'migrant' forms the meaning many people attach to refugees from war zones. And risk behaviour, once initiated, has the potential to form part of the adolescent identity, leading to other risk taking.

Meg Gerrard and Frederick Gibbons, who are the leaders in this field, argue that to counter the impact of positive images of unhealthy choices, education needs to encourage reflection on real life situations where decisions and choices are made, and to try to influence the positive features of prototypes (Gerrard et al., 2008).

They also take the view that rational decision making is at least equal to intuition during adolescent development and that adults more often reason rationally than intuitively when faced with important decisions. They argue that as a young person gains experience, they are more able to make rational decisions.

However, there is an alternative view which suggests that intuitive reasoning is superior to rational reasoning. According to these theories, adults tend to rely on intuition rather than rational processes, whereas adolescents try to weigh up the pros and cons before reaching a decision. Valerie de Reyna (2004) cites experimental studies where adolescents and adults were asked if they would play Russian roulette for a $1,000,000 stake. Both adults and adolescents made the same choice (not to play), but the adults reached their decision faster than the adolescents. This, de Reyna argues, is because the adolescents stopped to weigh up the odds before deciding the risk was not worth taking, while adults understood more quickly the meaning, or gist, of the gamble.

De Reyna (2004) derived her dual process theory from studies of memory, which suggest that memories are stored in two ways. Memories are stored like video tape or 'verbatim' form (which are recalled during analytical or rational decision making) and also as the meaning or 'gist' which is stored and recalled differently. This dual process is known as 'fuzzy trace' theory. According to fuzzy trace theory, familiarity with a situation informs the meaning of an experience and enables gist-based reasoning, but cognitive development (the ability to think in abstract ways) also plays an important part.

So does any of this matter? Whether we accept the arguments of fuzzy trace theory or prototype-willingness models is of more than academic interest, since each suggests different approaches to helping young people avoid the worst outcomes from risk taking. Fuzzy trace theory suggests that there are developmental boundaries to gist-based reasoning and that as a consequence we should do all we can to prevent young people gaining experience of risk taking until they are capable of rapid intuitive choices. For example, de Reyna would support abstinence approaches alcohol education, rather than a gradual introduction to alcohol with adult supervision. De Reyna would also recommend that we steer young people away from detailed and complex rational decision models of risk assessment and towards more categorical good choice–bad choice reasoning. In contrast, Gerrard et al. (2008) would encourage young people to use rational risk analysis models when making choices and encourage the development of positive images of adolescents who don't take risks with their health.

In practice, in PSHE education we tend to work with both processes (see e.g. the ten principles of effective practice in PSHE education in Chapter 3,

Section 1). We inform and explore with young people the many social controls on their behaviour – the legal age at which alcohol can be drunk in public, for example, or the age at which a young person can begin to learn to drive, while at the same time using a social norms approach to show that most of their peers conform with these norms, creating a positive environment in which young people take crucial decisions. We also offer them opportunities to weigh up the pros and cons of possible future decisions in safe and supportive environment. At the same time we encourage the development of 'gist-based reasoning' or 'intuition' with reflection, modelling safe and healthy behaviour and promote forms of risk taking which are fun, exciting and beneficial so that young people can develop their personal meaning of risk.

Into practice

As a follow-up to a lesson on peer influence, invite students to suggest examples of risky behaviour for their age group (or use examples from the classroom research activity in Appendix III). Write one on each of eight sheets of A4 (landscape) in large lettering. Include driving a car as well as other examples they might not have included, such as sexting or being inactive (lack of exercise).

Ask students to choose one of the risk behaviours and to take a position on an imaginary line in the classroom between high risk and no risk.

They will need to compare their risks with others in the line to decide their final position. Now invite the students to say why they have chosen this position. Do the other students agree with the relative riskiness of the activities? Suggest that someone who disagrees with the position of a particular activity can take the same card. Do they choose to stand in the same

Figure 7.2 Continuum of risk

or a different position? This activity illustrates the subjectivity of risk – what seems risky to one person may not seem so risky to another.

Give the student holding 'driving' a new sheet of paper 'driving with passengers'. Ask the class to say whether they think this makes driving more or less risky. Explain that driving with passengers is more risky for young drivers than for older drivers, and that changes in the development of the brain may explain this.

Now ask the students in the line to reflect on what influenced their decision to stand in this position. Was their decision mainly influenced by what they know (head) or by how they feel (heart)? Ask each student to take one step forward for 'head' and one step backward for 'heart'. Again, different people may have different responses to this for the same risky activity.

Now introduce the idea to the class that their brains develop rationally and emotionally at different rates and the effects this can have on everyday choices and decisions as they grow and mature.

How well do young people understand risk taking in adolescence? How would you assess the students' learning at the end of this session (see Chapter 6)?

Targeted interventions

Some schools offer targeted approaches to risk education for young people most likely to become involved in multiple risk taking.

A targeted approach

The PreVenture Programme was developed in Canada and targets vulnerable young people at risk of substance misuse which occurs alongside other emotional or behavioural disorders. It is a prevention programme which aims to reduce risk taking behaviour by reducing anxiety, sensitivity, sensation seeking, negative thinking and impulsivity, which are known risk factors for early onset substance misuse. The programme is delivered by teachers who have been trained to deliver interactive group sessions with students aged 13–16 years. The group sessions focus on what motivates students to participate in risky behaviours and provide them with coping skills to improve their risk decision making. A study by Kings College London found improved scores for a range of outcomes including reduced impulsivity, anxiety, depression and thrill seeking behaviour as well as reduced binge drinking when compared with a control group (Castellanos et al, 2006; King's College London, 2016).

Risk-Avert is an intervention for secondary school students developed in the UK intended to help young people to improve their 'risk decision making'. Like the PreVenture Programme, young people are screened to determine their risk profile. Those who are at high risk of involvement in multiple risk behaviours (but are not yet involved) are offered a chance to take part in a six-week programme which is delivered by trained teachers in their own school. The programme is based on small interactive workshops and encourages young people to reflect on their own behaviour and experience and to develop their decision making skills. It also encourages them to feel supported by their school through the involvement of staff who are known to them. While the effectiveness of the programme in reducing risk taking behaviour is yet to be demonstrated in a controlled trial, young people who have taken part in pilot studies report greater confidence in managing risky situations and that their relationship with teachers has improved. Teachers report they have a greater understanding of young people's risk taking behaviour as a result of delivering the programme in their schools.

Teaching safely

Schools are also workplaces with a duty of care for staff and visitors as well as students, so this 'diversion' into health and safety or 'teaching safely' is a vital part of a whole school approach to risk – and can give us some surprisingly interesting opportunities for teaching and learning. Of course, teachers have a moral and legal responsibility to teach in such a way that keeps young people safe, but responsibility also rests with governors, local authorities, academy chains or other proprietors. On a day-to-day basis this responsibility will be delegated to a member of the senior leadership team who must take all reasonable, practicable steps to ensure students' safety while on the school premises and when learning outside the classroom.

Your school will have a wide range of policies and routine practices which provide you, and the children you teach, with a safe environment in which to work and learn. These policies should be reviewed regularly by senior staff and governors. Because safety is so well regulated in our society, the provision for 'health and safety' has gained a reputation for being bureaucratic and overly burdensome. As a result we are in danger of having a 'tick box' approach, where health and safety issues are addressed because they have to be, rather than seen as a shared responsibility of one human being for another – a responsibility which must be shared with young people as they develop.

Perhaps because the responsibility for teaching about safety and 'health and safety' policies are split, it could appear that 'teaching safely' and 'teaching safety' have very little to do with one another on a day-to-day basis. However, Ofsted looks at both through inspections of behaviour and safety across all aspects of school. We hope to show you how teaching safely and teaching safety are integral parts of a whole school approach to safety.

Case study – Jamila's story

Read the following case study and use your understanding of PSHE education to reflect on what happens.

Jamila was looking forward to her first day at secondary school. Her parents took lots of photos of her in her new school uniform before she set off. Although she was nervous about meeting new people, Jamila had never felt so grown up before.

Jamila's first lesson was science and she was excited by all the sights – and smells – of this new environment. The teacher introduced himself and handed out a photocopied worksheet showing a cartoon of a science classroom, with lots of crazy accidents happening or about to happen. The teacher then asked the class to colour in all the hazards they could see. Jamila quickly coloured in all the hazards correctly. Once she had finished she noticed that some of the boys were messing about and not doing what they had been asked. The teacher collected in the sheets and then told the class the safety rules for working in the 'lab', which they copied into their new science exercise books.

Jamila's next lesson was PE and she changed proudly into her new PE kit before joining the others in the gym. The lesson began by the teacher talking about how to lift heavy objects without hurting themselves. Then the students practised what they had been learning by getting out all the equipment they would be using. By this time the lesson was almost over so they spent the rest of the time putting all the equipment away again.

After lunch, which was in a huge, noisy room, Jamila went to design and technology. In this room there were lots of strange looking machines and tools she had never seen before. The teacher began by explaining that it was important to learn how to keep safe in this new environment. The teacher divided the class into groups, each with a clip board, paper and a pencil. Next she explained that a hazard is something which could cause harm to someone. She asked the groups to begin in different parts of the room and to write down any hazards they could identify, and any safety messages they could see.

Each group read out their findings and talked about what could happen in this classroom and how likely it was that someone could injure themselves if they did not follow safety instructions. The teacher then explained that what they had done was a 'risk assessment'. Each group was asked to write one sentence about keeping safe in their design and technology lessons. At the end of the lesson the whole class and the teacher voted for the sentence they thought best summed up how to be safe in their next lesson, when they would be using some of the equipment to make their first project – a nutcracker.

Think about the three lessons. Each teacher has a responsibility for 'teaching safely' as well as 'teaching safety'. Each lesson has been planned to make sure the students understand how to keep themselves safe in a variety of new and unfamiliar environments before any subject teaching begins. Were the intended learning outcomes similar even though the subjects were different? Was any of the learning transferable from one subject to another?

Although fictionalised, these lessons reflect real experiences of Year 7 students being introduced to science, PE and design and technology for the first time. One student we spoke to did three colouring-in 'spot the hazard' sheets in his first week at secondary school.

Now ask yourself, how did Jamila feel at the end of each lesson? Did being asked to 'colour in' match her expectations of being a student at secondary school? What did she actually learn in each situation, about safety and risk – and about each teacher's perception of her and her classmates as they entered Year 7? Although none of these lessons

(Continued)

(Continued)

were PSHE education, is there anything the teachers could have learned from the ten principles of PSHE education (see Chapter 3, Section 1)?

Now think about how you would plan a PSHE education lesson about keeping safe for Year 7 entrants in this new and exciting environment of secondary school. Where might you begin, and how could this lesson help your colleagues teaching other subjects to 'teach safety' more effectively?

Chapter overview

Adolescence is associated with a greater incidence of accidental injury and the onset of health risk behaviours such as smoking, drinking and using social media in risky ways. However, most young people do not become involved in deliberate, extreme or multiple risk taking. Brain development and social context play important roles in shaping a young person's risk profile. Adolescent risk taking differs significantly from adult risk taking in that it is more likely to occur in groups. Being with peers is inherently rewarding for young people, and they may perceive benefits to risky behaviour which are not apparent to adults. Universal risk education within PSHE education should differentiate between danger and risk and recognise both the possibility of benefit and harm. Targeted approaches to risk education could help young people who are more likely to become involved in risk taking. Being able to identify, assess and construct strategies to manage risk is only part of the overall picture. Since we may be making these decisions in a social context, we may need to draw on our vocabulary and interpersonal skills to ensure that we can turn *our* decision into action. This is why risk education needs to be set in a wider PSHE education programme.

Further reading

Leather, N. (2009) 'Risk taking behaviour in adolescence: a literature review', *Journal of Child Health Care*, 13(3): 295–304.
This is an accessible review of the literature linking risk-taking behaviour with developmental tasks outlined in Chapter 2.

Gardner, D. (2009) *Risk: The Science of Politics and Fear*. London: Virgin. This book explores how our understanding (and misunderstanding) of risk can be exploited to create a climate of fear and mistrust and argues for a more rational approach to understanding risk.

European Agency for Safety and Health at Work (2006) *Preventing Risks to Young Workers: Policy, Programmes and Workplace Practices*. Luxembourg: Office for Official Publications of the European Communities, Available at https://osha.europa.eu/en/publications/reports/TE3008760ENC (accessed 21.3.16).
These publications will be of interest to teachers with responsibility for coordinating work experience.

References

Albert, D., Chein, J. and Steinberg, L. (2013) 'The teenage brain: peer influences on adolescent neurocognition', *Current Directions in Psychological Science*, 22: 114–20.

British Safety Council (2016) 'Entry level award in workplace hazard awareness'. Available at www.britsafe.org/qualifications/entry-level-award-workplace-hazard-awareness (accessed 21.3.16).

Brooks, F., Magnusson, J., Klemera, E., Chester, K., Spencer, N. and Smeeton, N. (2015) *HBSC England National Report 2014*. Hatfield: University of Hertfordshire.

Castellanos, N. and Conrod, P. (2006) 'Brief interventions targeting personality risk factors for adolescent substance misuse reduce depression, panic and risk-taking behaviours', *Journal of Mental Health*, 15: 1–14.

Chassin, L., Hussong, A. and Beltran, I. (2009) 'Adolescent substance use', in Lerner, R. and Steinberg, L. (eds), *Handbook of Adolescent Psychology, Vol. 1* (3rd edn) (pp. 723–63). Hoboken, NJ: Wiley.

Chein, J., Albert, D., O'Brien, L., Uckert, K. and Steinberg, L. (2011) 'Peers increase adolescent risk taking by enhancing activity in the brain's reward circuitry', *Developmental Science*, 14(2): F1–F10.

Collins, W.A. and Steinberg, L. (2006). 'Adolescent development in interpersonal context', in Damon, W. and Eisenberg, N. (eds), *Handbook of Child Psychology: Vol. 4, Socioemotional Processes* (pp. 1003–1067). New York: Wiley.

Currie, C., Zanotti, C., Morgan, A., Currie, D., de Looze, M., Roberts, C., Samdal, O., Smith, O.R.F. and Barnekow, V. (eds) (2012) *Social Determinants of Health and Well-being Among Young People: Health Behaviour in School-Aged Children (HBSC) Study – International Report From the 2009/2010 Survey* (Health Policy for Children and Adolescents, No. 6). Copenhagen: WHO Regional Office for Europe, 2012. Available at www.euro.who.int/__data/assets/pdf_file/0003/1638 57/Social-determinants-of-health-and-well-being-among-young-people.pdf?u a=1 (accessed 20.11.15).

de Reyna, V., (2004) 'How people make decisions that involve risk: a dual processes approach', *Current Directions in Psychological Science*, 13(2): 60–66.

Department for Education (2013) 'Guidance: personal, social, health and economic education'. Available at www.gov.uk/government/publications/personal-social-health-and-economic-education-pshe/personal-social-health-and-economic-pshe-education (accessed 24.11.15).

Department for Transport (2014) 'Reported Road Casualties Great Britain'. Available at www.gov.uk/government/uploads/system/uploads/attachment_data/file/359311/rrcgb-2013.pdf (accessed 20.11.2015).

Donovan, J.E. and Jessor, R. (1985) 'Structure of problem behavior in adolescence and young adulthood', *Journal of Consulting and Clinical Psychology*, 53(6): 890–904.

Duberstein Lindberg, L., Boggess, S., Porter, L. and Williams, S. (2000) *Teen-risk Taking: A Statistical Portrait*. Washington, DC: Urban Institute. Available at www.urban.org/research/publication/teen-risk-taking-statistical-portrait/view/full_report (accessed 26.11.15).

East, P.L., Felice, M.E. and Morgan, M.C. (1993) 'Sisters' and girlfriends' sexual and childbearing behavior: effects on early adolescent girls' sexual outcomes', *Journal of Marriage and Family*, 55(40): 953–63.

European Agency for Safety and Health at Work (2009) *Preventing Risks to Young Workers: Policy, Programmes and Workplace Practices*. Luxembourg: Office for Official Publications of the European Communities.

Evans, M. (2014) 'Rolf Harris starred in video warning children about paedophiles', *Telegraph*, 30 June. Available at www.telegraph.co.uk/news/uknews/crime/10935963/Rolf-Harris-starred-in-video-warning-children-about-paedophiles.html (accessed 21.3.16).

Fuller, E. and Hawkins, V. (ed.) (2014) *Smoking, Alcohol and Other Drug Use by Young People in England in 2013*. London: Health and Social Care Information Centre. Available at www.hscic.gov.uk/catalogue/PUB14579/smok-drin-drug-youn-peop-eng-2013-rep.pdf (accessed 21.3.16).

Gardner, M and Steinberg, L. (2005) 'Peer influence on risk taking, risk preference, and risky decision making in adolescence and adulthood: an experimental study', *Developmental Psychology*, 41: 625–35.

Gerrard, M., Gibbons, F.X., Houlihan, A.E., Stock, M.L. and Pomery, A. (2008) 'A dual process approach to health risk decision making: the prototype willingness model', *Developmental Review*, 28(1): 29–61.

Gullone, E. and Moore, S. (2000) 'Adolescent risk-taking and the five-factor model of personality', *Adolescence*, 23(4): 393–407.

Health and Safety Executive (2014) Health and Safety Toolbox: Accidents and investigations. Available at www.hse.gov.uk/toolbox/managing/accidents.htm (accessed 11.04.16).

Holton, G. (2004) 'Defining risk', *Financial Analysts Journal*, 60(6): 19–25.

Jennings, L. (2012) *Blood Knots*. London: Atlantic Books.

Jessor, R. and Jessor, S.L. (1977) *Problem Behaviour and Psychosocial Development: A Longitudinal Study of Youth*. New York: Academic Press.

King's College London (2016) 'PreVenture'. Available at www.kcl.ac.uk/ioppn/depts/addictions/research/legacyprojects/PreVenture.aspx (accessed 21.3.16).

Knoll, L.J., Magis-Weinberg, L., Speekenbrink, M. and Blakemore, S-J. (2015) 'Social influence on risk perception during adolescence', *Psychological Science*, March. Available at http://pss.sagepub.com/content/early/2015/03/24/0956797615569578.full (accessed 24.11.15).

McWhirter, J. (2007) 'It's a bit risky is this!', *Safety Education Journal*, Spring. Available at www.rospa.com/school-college-safety/teaching-safety/risk/ (accessed 20.11.15).

McWhirter, J. and South, N. (2004) *Young People and Risk*. London: Report for Government Office East.

Mercer, C.H., Tanton, C., Prah, P., Erens, B., Sonnenber, P., Clifton, S., Macdowall, W., Lewis, R., Field, N., Datta, J., Copas, A.J., Phelps, A., Wellings, K. and Johnson, A.M. (2013) 'Changes in sexual attitudes and lifestyles through the lifecourse and trends over time: findings from the British National Surveys of Sexual Attitudes and Lifestyles (Natsal)', *Lancet*, 382: 1781–94.

Michael, K. and Ben-Zur, H. (2007) 'Risk-taking among adolescents: associations with social and affective factors', *Journal of Adolescence*, 30(1): 17–31.

Nikken, P. and Jansz, J. (2006) 'Parental mediation of children's videogame playing: a comparison of the reports by parents and children', *Learning, Media and Technology*, 31(2): 181–202.

Notten, N. and Nikken, P. (2014) 'Boys and girls taking risks online: a gendered perspective on social context and adolescents' risky online behaviour', *New Media and Society*, October: 1–23.

Peter, J. and Valkenburg, P.M. (2006) 'Adolescents' exposure to sexually explicit online material and recreational attitudes toward sex', *Journal of Communication*, 56(4): 639–60.

Royal Society for the Prevention of Accidents (RoSPA) (2012) *The Big Book of Accident Prevention*. Birmingham: RoSPA. Available atwww.rospa.com/RoSPAWeb/docs/public-health/big-book/index.html (accessed 24.11.15).

Simons-Morton, B., Lerner, N. and Singer, J. (2005) 'The observed effects of teenage passengers on the risky driving behavior of teenage drivers', *Accident Analysis and Prevention*, 37(6): 973–82.

Sisk, C.L. and Foster, D.L. (2004) 'The neural basis of puberty and adolescence', *Nature Neuroscience*, 7, September: 1040–47.

Steinberg, L. (2007) 'Teenage risk-taking: biological and inevitable?', *Science Daily*, 12 April. Available at www.sciencedaily.com/releases/2007/04/070412115231.htm (accessed 21.3.16).

Steinberg, L. (2008) 'A social neuroscience perspective on adolescent risk-taking', *Developmental Review*, 28(1): 78–106.

8

Understanding the Role of PSHE in Promoting Mental Health and Emotional Wellbeing

Aim

This chapter will attempt to unpick the complex relationship between PSHE education as a subject within the curriculum and the wider role schools play in promoting the mental health and emotional wellbeing of young people. In a chapter of this length it is impossible to cover all aspects of mental health education, so here we focus on the key principles.

Learning objectives

Through reading and reflecting on the content of this chapter you will begin to:

- understand the role PSHE education can play in promoting the mental health and emotional wellbeing of young people
- understand the role of PSHE education in helping raise young people's awareness of mental illness and reduce stigma associated with mental illness
- understand how PSHE education can signpost support for young people who are experiencing mental ill health.

Before we start

- 1 in 10 children and young people aged 5–16 suffer from a diagnosable mental health disorder in Great Britain (Green et al., 2005) – that is, around three children in every class.
- Between 1 in every 12 and 1 in 15 children and young people deliberately self-harm (Mental Health Foundation, 2006).
- Nearly 80,000 children and young people suffer from severe depression (Green et al., 2005).
- The number of young people aged 15–16 in the UK with depression nearly doubled between the 1980s and the 2000s (Nuffield Foundation, 2013).
- 4.4 per cent or about 195,000 young people have an anxiety disorder (ONS, 2004).
- 1 in 150 15 year old girls and 1 in 1,000 15 year old boys will experience anorexia (RCPsych, undated).

Introduction

In a 2014 survey the PSHE Association asked its members what issues most concerned them as teachers of PSHE education. It was not the sensitive issues traditionally associated with PSHE education, for example drug misuse, sex education or safeguarding, but the mental health of young people that emerged as their major concern. The statistics above go some way to explaining why this should be and why it is so important that we should address young people's mental health. Mental health education should be considered part of a school's responsibility to safeguard young people.

Poor mental health is also likely to significantly impact on young people's ability to concentrate, learn and achieve as well as they might. It may inhibit their ability to make and keep friends, cause problems in their families and inhibit their ability to live a constructive, independent life.

Difficulties with mental health can range from 'Something is playing on my mind', through to overwhelming, immobilising thoughts or emotions that prevent us from almost any meaningful interaction with others. It can also manifest in unhealthy coping strategies such as self-harm and eating disorders.

Consider

Why do you think that at a time when figures for smoking, alcohol consumption, drug use and teenage conception are falling, there is increasing concern over the rise in mental health issues amongst young people?

Possible triggers for mental illness

The reasons are not clear but there is no doubt that young people are growing up in a rapidly changing world with many new challenges. These include fear of failure, bullying and abuse, the online or virtual environment, messages about body image, sexual pressures and challenging employment prospects.

Family relationships; difficulties with relationships with peers; witnessing unhealthy coping mechanisms used by peers or people in the media; trouble in school; work and exam pressures; family illness; transitions between schools; moving home; anniversaries of difficult events or being part of a vulnerable group are just some of the potential triggers for unhealthy responses which may lead to self-harm, eating disorders, suicidal feelings, panic attacks, phobias, obsessions and compulsions, anxiety or depression.

Deconstructing the role of PSHE education in relation to mental health and emotional wellbeing

PSHE education can support the mental health of young people in a variety of ways:

- Prevention, including developing individual protective factors.
- Awareness raising and challenging stereotyping and stigma.
- Signposting to sources of credible support and empowering young people to seek help for themselves or others.

Let's consider these in more detail. First, PSHE education can provide opportunities for learning that develop 'protective factors'; in other words, a range of skills and attributes that can increase young people's resilience to mental and emotional health problems and increase their ability to promote their own emotional wellbeing. These include skills such as communication and problem-solving skills, and being able to build and maintain healthy relationships. Teaching healthy coping strategies such as 'mindfulness' to help young people better manage stress and helping young people to develop more effective study skills and positive strategies to cope with and 'reframe' setbacks or failure can all help to protect young people's mental health and emotional wellbeing. They also include attributes such as positive self-esteem, the knowledge, skills and confidence to seek help, the ability to recognise, describe, understand and manage both their own and others' emotions in healthy constructive ways.

We can also promote a 'growth mind-set': the belief that we are not innately good or bad at problem solving but that we are in control of our skills and abilities and with perseverance can change. This challenges any feelings of helplessness or inevitability that young people may have and can enhance their resilience (Dweck, 2007).

This is all part of a comprehensive PSHE education programme and will be gradually developed across all the key stages supported by the wider curriculum. It is important that we don't think of mental health and emotional wellbeing simply as a discrete 'topic' to be taught in our PSHE education programme. Mental health and emotional wellbeing should be a recurring theme building on prior learning. For example, helping young children to have the skills and confidence to ask for help in the classroom lays foundations for them to be able access local community based support services.

In this way, developing the skills and attributes above should run through all elements of a spiral programme (see Chapter 5), and then at certain points in the programme you may choose to focus on more explicit learning around an aspect of mental health. In the secondary phase this discrete learning might focus on the nature of mental health disorders that most commonly affect young people, for example on anxiety and depression, and unhealthy coping strategies such as eating disorders and self-harm.

Second, in addition to developing protective characteristics, PSHE education can, through an explicit focus on mental health, raise awareness of common mental health difficulties by providing a forum for discussion and a place in the curriculum where stigma and stereotyping can be challenged. It can be a place where young people can understand the true extent of mental illness and draw what remains a 'hidden issue' into the open. The casual use of derogatory language related to mental health (e.g. 'He's such a 'tard') can be highlighted and challenged and common myths about mental illness dispelled.

This work can be immensely reassuring for many young people who may have been suffering alone and holding a belief that they were unique in their experience. It is not an exaggeration to say that schools and especially PSHE education could be in a position to create a generation of young people with a far more open and positive attitude towards mental illness.

Third, PSHE education's role in signposting sources of support within the school, in the community and nationally cannot be underestimated. But it is not enough just to identify sources of support and make young people aware of them. We can help young people to develop criteria for evaluating such sources of support and more importantly, it can help young people to develop the confidence, strategies and skills they need to get this help either for themselves or someone they are concerned about.

It is important that you feel sufficiently well prepared to teach mental health within PSHE education, that your colleagues within your school are aware that these lessons are taking place, especially those with responsibility for pastoral care, and that you have their support. Always work on the principle that at least one young person in your class is currently experiencing difficulties with their mental health as this will help you to ensure a safe learning environment and an inclusive approach.

Be alert to pupils whom you know to be affected that a particular topic is going to be discussed in the next lesson. Depending on the circumstances, you may choose to discuss the content with them, ask them what they feel their peers should know and understand and possibly give them the option of not attending the lesson, or having a pre-arranged way of removing themselves from the lesson if they feel they need to. Clearly these lessons need particularly careful planning, so make sure you have read Chapters 3 and 5 before teaching this complex area of the PSHE education curriculum.

The wider school context

Promoting or responding to young people's mental health cannot be restricted to a series of lessons in PSHE education. It has to be part of a whole school approach set in a wider 'health promoting school' that reflects on how its day-to-day management and 'the way we do things here' is conducive to young people's mental health.

For example, PSHE education can offer young people strategies to reduce stress but this is unlikely to be effective if the school's overall assessment policy is not in line with best practice or where there is a disproportionate emphasis on the importance of academic success at all costs. There is little benefit from discussing ways of addressing bullying or abuse in PSHE education if the school does not have clear protocols for managing incidents of bullying.

How to teach mental health safely and effectively in PSHE education

See our recommendation for further reading at the end of this chapter which goes into far greater depth, but here we summarise the key points from the PSHE Association's guidance (2015) to bear in mind when teaching any aspects of mental health and emotional wellbeing:

- It is essential to have established a safe classroom climate before commencing any teaching in this area. Established 'ground rules' (see Chapter 3) are absolutely essential to have in place and being respected. It is important to create a climate of openness and honesty; however, it is important to agree that these lessons are not an appropriate place to directly discuss personal experiences or those of others. This is why it is essential to have support available after the lesson.
- Be aware of any pupils who may be at risk and ensure that there is someone available to help any vulnerable young person or a young person who may become distressed. If necessary, withdraw these young people from the lesson.
- Assume there are some of whom you are not aware, who will be affected by the topic under discussion.
- Be able to signpost young people to sources of support, initially in school but also in the community and online following your lessons. (See below and Chapter 3 for more on the safe use of online support.) Your school may have a lead contact for mental health issues in line with official recommendations (Department of Health/NHS England, 2014).
- Start from where young people are, providing opportunities for them to share their prior learning with you to help you assess their current level of knowledge, understanding, skills, beliefs and attitudes. Without understanding how they are already making sense of the issue it is difficult to plan relevant learning that reflects the group's needs.
- Use distancing techniques (see Chapter 3) to prevent learning from feeling too personal for young people; for example, the use of fictional case studies, scenarios or images that can act as stimulus for young people to explore.
- Always offer time for young people to reflect on their learning and for you to assess their progress (see Chapter 6).
- Ensure that teaching is non-judgemental, focusing on what young people can do to keep themselves and others healthy and safe. It is perfectly acceptable to challenge a young person's opinion, preconceived ideas or point of view but without appearing to judge the young person. There may, however, be instances when a young person says something that alarms or worries you, in which case you should share it with your school's designated safeguarding lead.
- Look after your own mental health and emotional wellbeing. You may find some of this work has personal connections, so make sure you

have any support that you need. It is important that you talk through your planning with your colleagues and identify any aspects where you feel you lack confidence or need further professional development.

- These lessons can explore emotionally challenging issues, which can be emotionally draining. Try to build in a light-hearted – but not trivial – closing activity and if possible be around after the lesson for any pupil who may wish to discuss their own concerns or those of someone they care about.

Visitors to the classroom have much to offer mental health education; however, their input needs careful management. The use of visitors is covered in depth in Chapter 13.

When teaching about issues such as eating disorders, self-harm or suicide ensure that you:

- Do not inadvertently provide detailed methods or instruction (see Chapter 3). It can be easy to do this accidentally; providing information to help the majority of young people increase their awareness or understanding may be providing instructions in an unhealthy behaviour for vulnerable young people.

For example, we might state that self-harm may include cutting, burning or self-poisoning but we would not be more explicit. We would not talk explicitly and in detail about different methods of weight loss or methods of hiding self-harm or weight loss from family or peers. We would not discuss specific methods of suicide.

- Do use non-emotive language, images or video material. Be factual rather than dramatic, especially in your choice of teaching material. Using extreme images in an attempt to shock can seriously backfire if young people see these as inspirational or mistakenly believe that they must reach a similar condition before they require or are entitled to receive help.
- Do explore the dangers of laxative misuse or vomiting. This is one exception and should be restricted to Key Stage 4 being taught in a straightforward way focusing on imparting the factual risks associated with these behaviours and signposting sources of support.
- Do address wound care. There is a strong possibility that at least one young person in your class is self-harming and it is appropriate to ensure that all young people know the importance of wound care, without focussing on specific ways of self-harming.
- Do explore criteria for evaluating credible sources of support and signpost to these.

Chapter overview

This chapter has considered the role of PSHE education in supporting young people's mental health and emotional wellbeing. It has considered some of the possible triggers for mental illness, some broad key points for teaching about mental health safely and effectively and has looked at some key issues in more depth.

Further reading

Hymer, B. and Gershon, M. (2014) *The Growth Mindset Pocketbook.* Alresford: Teachers Pocket Books.
A practical and succinct explanation of how a growth mindset can be developed in students.

Nuffield Foundation (2013) *Social Trends and Mental Health: Introducing the Main Findings.* London: Nuffield Foundation.
A useful source of data about young people's mental health.

References

Department of Health/NHS England (2014) 'Future in mind: promoting, protecting and improving our children and young people's mental health and wellbeing'. Available at www.gov.uk/government/publications/improving-mental-health-services-for-young-people (accessed 15.1.16.)

Dweck, C.S. (2007) *Mindset: The New Psychology of Success.* New York: Ballantine.

Green, H., McGinnity, A., Meltzer, H., Ford, T. and Goodman, R. (2005) *Mental Health of Children and Young People in Great Britain 2004.* London: Palgrave Macmillan.

Mental Health Foundation (2006) Truth hurts. Available at www.mentalhealth.org.uk/sites/default/files/truth_hurts.pdf (accessed 26.04.2016).

Nuffield Foundation (2013) *Social Trends and Mental Health: Introducing the Main Findings.* London: Nuffield Foundation.

Office for National Statistics (2004) Mental health of children and young people in Great Britain. Available at https://discover.ukdataservice.ac.uk/catalogue/?sn=5269 (accessed on 26.4.2016).

PSHE Association (2015) 'Teacher Guidance: Preparing to teach about mental health and emotional wellbeing'. Available at https://pshe-association.org.uk/resources_search_details.aspx?ResourceId=570&Keyword=&SubjectID=0&LevelID=0&ResourceTypeID=3&SuggestedUseID=0 (accessed 15.1.16).

Royal College of Psychiatrists (RCPsych) (Undated) 'Anorexia and bulimia'. Available at www.rcpsych.ac.uk/healthadvice/problemsdisorders/anorexiaandbulimia.aspx (accessed 22.1.16).

9

Understanding Drug Education within PSHE Education

Aim

To review what is understood about drug education as part of PSHE education

Learning objectives

Through reading and reflecting on the content of this chapter you will begin to:

- explore your own attitudes to drugs
- review data on drug misuse by young people of school age
- understand why some young people misuse drugs
- be able to plan and implement effective, inclusive approaches to drug education within PSHE education, supported by a whole school approach.

Before we start

Activity

Draw and/or describe in words a young person who has a problem with drugs.

How old is the young person you are thinking about?

Why does this young person have a problem with drugs?

What are the risks involved for the young person?

If possible, compare your responses to those of other student teachers or school staff.

How similar or different are your responses to the others?

At the end of this chapter we will ask you to return to your picture of a young person who has a problem with drugs to see how much or how little it changes.

Introduction

First a word or two about terminology: *in this book we will use the term 'drugs' to apply to any substance which changes how a person thinks or feels*. This catch-all definition includes medicines, including over the counter and prescription drugs, 'legal highs' (also known as novel psychoactive substances or NPS), vapours, tobacco, e-cigarettes (or shisha pens), alcohol and illegal drugs (those controlled under the Misuse of Drugs Act 1971). You will find that some drug education resources do not use such inclusive language and may use the term drugs only to apply to illegal drugs. We take the view that the knowledge, skills and attributes needed to live safely in a world which includes illegal drugs are similar to those needed to manage a range of other substances.

We also refer to drug, not drugs, education. This is because drug education is not just (or even mostly!) about the drugs people use.

While drug education is not statutory in all parts of the UK it is an established part of PSHE education, appearing in the curriculum under a number of different names including substance misuse education, drug and alcohol education and drugs, alcohol and tobacco education (DAT).

We define drug education as: *the systematic and planned provision of learning opportunities that help children and young people develop the knowledge, skills, attitudes, understanding and competence to manage situations which might involve drugs now and in the future.*

Curriculum guidance for schools

Non-statutory guidance for schools in England on drug education was published in 2004, based on the best evidence available at that time and this has been not been superceded. It states that the aim of drug education is to

> enable pupils to develop their knowledge, skills, attitudes and understanding about drugs and appreciate the benefits of a healthy lifestyle, relating this to their own and others' actions.(DfES, 2004:27)

The most recent advice from the Department for Education is published with the Association of Chief Police Officers (now known as the National Police Chiefs' Council) and focuses on drug incidents, powers to search for and confiscate drugs and liaison with parents, rather than drug education (DfE/ACPO, 2012). The PSHE Association (2014) has published a national programme of study for PSHE education for Key Stages 1–4, which integrates drug education into all three core themes of 'Health and wellbeing', 'Relationships' and 'Living in the wider world'.

In Scotland substance misuse education forms part of the 'curriculum for excellence' and sets out a spiral curriculum for schools based on a range of experiences and outcomes (Education Scotland, 2015).

The Welsh government has issued more recent statutory guidance to schools (DfES, 2013).

Drug education also forms part of the statutory curriculum in Northern Ireland: Drugs: Guidance for Schools in Northern Ireland (CCEA, 2015).

There are considerable similarities among all these sources with regard to their understanding of effective approaches to drug education. There is also significant overlap between these standards for teaching and learning in drug education and the ten principles for effective PSHE education set out in Chapter 3, Section 1 and with the ADEPIS quality standards in alcohol and drug education (2015).

Effective practice in drug education

The following summary of effective practice in drug education is adapted from the ADEPIS quality standards in alcohol and drug education (2014) which is based on a recent synthesis of evidence from effective programmes around the world and on existing guidance for schools. You will notice an overlap with the ten principles for effective PSHE education as described in Chapter 3, Section 1.

Provide a safe learning environment: Drug education, if done effectively, will raise a range of issues which could be sensitive for some young people. It is important that the classroom environment respects young people's need to feel and be safe. This includes establishing and revisiting ground rules and respecting the different experiences young people bring to their drug education, which may include risky behaviour. Young people should understand that a teacher who becomes aware of something that suggests a vulnerable person is at immediate risk of harm cannot promise confidentiality, but that the young person making the disclosure will be consulted about what happens next.

Reinforce positive social norms: Young people (and the public in general) may hold views about the prevalence of drug and alcohol misuse which are misleading. Drug and alcohol misuse is much lower among young people than many believe it to be. There are a range of strategies for establishing the norms within a school or community and there are national sources of data which can be used to reinforce the largely negative attitudes towards drug misuse held by young people. This is a key element of effective programmes and we will come back to this later in this chapter.

Clear and relevant learning objectives and learning outcomes are set and assessed: This is a given in any lesson planning and should be no surprise to teachers (see Chapter 5 for planning and assessment in PSHE education). In order for drug education to be relevant there should be an assessment of the needs of the young people you are planning to teach as well as ongoing assessment for learning and assessment of their progress at the end of each stage of their drug education. This chapter includes several examples of strategies which can be used for needs assessment and Chapter 6 explores assessment for and of learning in detail. It is also the teachers' responsibility to ensure that this quality standard is adopted by visitors to the classroom such as police officers, representatives of drug charities or faith groups.

(Continued)

(Continued)

Learning (and therefore teaching) is interactive: Teachers (and peers where appropriate) facilitate learning. In drug education, and throughout PSHE education, there is an emphasis on interactivity. Young people benefit from an opportunity to engage actively with the subject matter, to question what they are being taught and to reflect on what this means in terms of their own experience and values. Some skills such as decision making and recognising when and how to respond in a range of scenarios require practice in a safe and structured environment.

Learning is evaluated: Both the overall approach to drug education and the lessons themselves should be evaluated against the broad aims for drug education in the school.

Helpfully, the ADEPIS quality standards also point out approaches to drug education for which there is no supporting evidence, or for which there is evidence of harm (i.e. approaches that have the opposite result to those intended). These approaches include those which rely on non-interactive methods such as lectures and assemblies, on fear arousal, or which focus only on life skills, social and emotional skills or values education without any content. Programmes delivered by representatives of external agencies such as police officers have frequently been found to be ineffective, for a range of reasons. These approaches may be well intended, memorable and even emotionally compelling, but on their own they are not a substitute for a planned, school based programme, delivered by trained teachers.

Whole school approach

To enable young people to develop the competence to manage situations involving drugs, their drug education needs to be supported by a whole school approach, with an emphasis on their overall wellbeing. The ADEPIS guidance sets out how the curriculum should be supported by a whole school approach. This includes how drug incidents involving young people should be managed. Advice for schools on managing drug incidents and the care and support of young people involved in drug incidents strongly suggests that the welfare of young people should be a school's first concern:

Pupils affected by their own or other's drug misuse should have early access to support through the school and other local services.

Schools are strongly advised to have a written drugs policy to act as a central reference point for all school staff.

It is helpful for a senior member of staff to have responsibility for this policy and for liaising with the local police and support services. (DfE/ACPO, 2012: 3)

Young people and drugs

Key to all these documents is the expectation that teachers offering drug education should be non-judgemental with regard to young people and drug use. This does not mean that you should approve of or encourage drug use, but to see drugs as the problem, not the young person.

Problems with drugs can have a profound effect on a young person's life chances and finding that a young person has used illegal drugs can be a cause for concern for adults who have personal or professional responsibility for their wellbeing. Before we go any further, let's look at some case histories of young people who have had problems with drugs while still at school.

Case studies: Kate's story

Kate is 15. She lives in a small town and likes horse riding and netball and hanging out with her friends. Recently she has started to go to parties at the weekends. Her parents always take her and pick her up as they want to make sure she is safe. At one party she notices two of her friends sharing a spliff in the garden. Kate feels a bit left out by her friends as she has no one else to talk to, so she joins them in the garden. Soon they are all laughing and having fun. After a while Kate asks if she can try the spliff. It feels a bit scary and also a bit exciting. She knows her parents would not approve and she is worried about the possible smell of the smoke on her clothes, but they don't seem to notice anything when they come to give her a lift home. She notices feeling really hungry but does not experience any harmful effects. She begins to wonder why her parents and teachers are so anti-drugs; it seems like a cool and safe thing to do, as long as she is with her friends.

(Continued)

(Continued)

Leon's story:

Leon is 12. He lives with his Mum and older brother Conrad in a large city, in a high rise block of flats. Conrad has been in trouble with the police because of his involvement with a local gang. He doesn't work but he always seems to have plenty of money. Leon is well behaved at school and neither his Mum nor his teachers have any concerns. One evening Conrad asks Leon to take a package to a friend's house. Leon really wants to play on his games console but agrees when his brother offers him £5.00. Gradually Leon delivers more and more packages for his brother all over the estate, and uses the money he is given to buy new games. One evening Conrad says he has not got any money and gives Leon some pills instead, saying he can sell them to his mates. Leon decides he won't deliver any more packages for Conrad but keeps the pills, intending to throw them away. The next day the pills fall out of his bag at school and the police are called to interview him.

Martina's story:

Martina is 13 and lives with her family in a large house in north London. She and her younger sisters are doing well at school. Her Mum is a housewife and her Dad works in the city. Martina's Dad leaves home for work early every day and is often home late. Martina's parents both drink heavily: Dad drinks after work and in the evenings, while Martina's Mum often drinks with friends at lunchtime, or alone at home during the day. Martina worries that her Mum will be stopped by the police for drinking and driving when she picks the girls up from school. Sometimes Martina has to cook for herself and her sisters, when her Mum goes to bed feeling ill. Martina often hears her parents arguing and sometimes she can hear her Mum crying. One day she notices her Mum has bruises at the top of her arms. Martina begins to 'forget' things she needs for school so she can ring and check on her Mum several times a day.

None of these young people are doing poorly at school or have what might be called behaviour problems, so how might you as a PSHE teacher (or as a form tutor) become aware of the difficulties Kate, Leon and Martina are having with drugs? How would your placement or school you are teaching in respond to one of these situations if they became aware of it? Ask to see the school policies on drugs, but also those on inclusion and support for young people. Take a look at Chapter 12 where we help you to differentiate between the different responsibilities you might have as a PSHE education teacher and as a form tutor.

We tend to think about people affected by drugs as users, dealers and victims. Kate could be described as a drug user, Leon a drug dealer and Martina a victim of hidden harm (of parental drug or alcohol misuse). You could also say that Kate is a typical teenager, needing to feel part of a group and choosing to share the same experiences as her friends, Leon is a victim of hidden harm and Martina is a young carer. Whatever your perception of these case histories, these are just a few of the many ways in which young people in your school could be affected by drugs and to which your school's drug education (and policies) should be able to respond, always with the young person's welfare in mind.

Drug education, as part of PSHE education, has a necessary focus on preventing young people using drugs or minimising the harm that drug use might have, but often the harm is indirect as in the case of Leon and Martina. For these reasons drug education should have a broad scope and, strengthened by a whole school approach, ensure that young people have the knowledge, understanding, skills, resilience and support to manage a range of situations where drugs might be involved, but also to be able to tell adults how drugs used by other people affect their lives.

Drug use by young people of school age

How typical are Kate's, Leon's and Martina's stories? Let's start with Martina: alcohol hidden harm is surprisingly common; it is estimated that 1 in 5 children under the age of 1 year live in a family where a parent drinks hazardously. Leon's story may not be so common, but his experience makes him especially vulnerable (Topping, 2014).

Is it common for young people of Kate's age to use illegal drugs? The statistics make for very interesting reading, especially when put beside some newspaper headlines! Two independent research organisations, NatCen and NFER, conduct an annual survey on smoking, alcohol and other drug use[1] by young people in Years 7–11 (this is done in the autumn term so pupils are mostly under 16 years; Fuller et al, 2014).

---

[1] The list of substances covered by this term in this survey includes those covered by the Misuse of Drugs Act 1971 and subsequent amendments as well as some other psychoactive and volatile substances such as mephedrone, poppers, glue and solvents.

In 2014, 6,173 young people in 210 schools in England completed these anonymous questionnaires. This survey revealed that most young people of school age have never used illegal drugs: 15 per cent of young people aged 11–15 had taken drugs in their lifetime, 10 per cent had taken drugs in the last year, and 6 per cent had taken drugs in the last month.

One possible criticism of these figures is that the survey takes place at school. Schools have to agree to take part and so may not be representative of schools across the country. The survey may not include some young people who were absent from school because of truancy or exclusion (i.e. at higher risk of substance misuse).

The Crime Survey for England and Wales is a similarly well respected survey of 50,000 adults aged 16–59 which is carried out over the phone and so is more likely to include at risk groups. This survey suggests that illegal drug use among 16–24 year olds in 2013–14 is similar to that of 15 year olds (19 per cent of 15 year olds and 18.9 per cent of 16–24 year olds had used illegal drugs in the last year; ONS, 2015). From these data it appears that drug misuse is much less common among young people of school age than some might expect – and is actually similar to that reported by the age group which includes many recently qualified teachers.

Consider

Why do most people think drug use is more prevalent among young people of school age than it is? There are several reasons. It is easy to be influenced by headlines designed to shock or induce fear or guilt among parents, teachers and young people. News outlets are more likely to report that 15 per cent of 11–15 year olds have ever used drugs, rather than that 85 per cent have never used drugs. Similarly, news articles will seldom mention that of those 15 per cent, most have used illegal drugs only once or twice, which suggests experimentation rather than a risky habit is behind this level of use.

We can be influenced by the perceived behaviour of a small number of individuals who are well known in our peer group or society – even if the reason they are well known is for risky behaviour. This suggests something called the 'availability heuristic' is at work. This means that we use 'rules of thumb' on which to base our estimates of risk (Slovic, 1987). The more high-profile the reports of risk behaviour such as drug misuse, the more likely we are to think it is a frequent occurrence.

This can lead us to make serious miscalculations of our personal risk of harm (see Chapter 7 for more on risk and adolescence). After all, if so many people are using drugs and our personal experience (like Kate's) is that there has been no immediate harmful consequences, we think that the risks must be exaggerated, or that while others are at risk we are somehow immune or more able to manage the risks.

We are also influenced by our own past experience. The annual report 'Smoking, drinking and drug use among young people' shows that drug use among young people has been falling since 2001, when the current survey questions were first used. For example, between 2001 and 2010, 'drug use ever' by 11–15 year olds fell from 29 per cent to 18 per cent, since when it has remained fairly steady. There has also been a decline in the number of times young people report being offered drugs, from 42 per cent in 2001 to 26 per cent in 2014 (Fuller et al., 2014). So if you are a newly qualified teacher, it is likely that that the availability of drugs and drug use among your own peer group at aged 15 was higher than among the current Year 11 group you are currently teaching.

These figures are not the end of the story, of course. Some young people are more likely to use drugs than others. It might not surprise you to find that drug use increases with age (although 76 per cent of Year 11s in 2014 reported they had never used illegal drugs). Those who also smoke and drink alcohol are also more likely to report ever using illegal drugs. Surveys find that boys are more likely than girls to have ever used illegal drugs. Some young people are also more at risk because of other factors: young people who report they have ever truanted or been excluded from school are more likely to report they have used illegal drugs in the last month than those who have not.

What is more surprising is that there is no significant variation by ethnic group or by geographical region, with pupils from London and the South East no more likely than pupils in other parts of the country to report illegal drug use.

So in some ways Kate's story is that of a typical teenager – she wants to be like her friends and do what they are doing, and she was not forced or coerced into using an illegal drug. Like many of her peers she also makes risky assumptions about the possible harms of using drugs, based on limited experience. However, she is not typical of girls (or boys) of her age, most of whom have never used illegal drugs or solvents. We will return to Kate's decision to smoke the spliff later in this chapter.

What all this emphasises is the importance of positive messages for young people about the low prevalence of illegal drug use in their age group and the value of a normative approach – making sure young people know and understand that most young people of their age do not use illegal drugs. Evidence for the effectiveness of this approach has been recorded in well designed studies since the early 1990s (Hansen and Graham, 1991) and is now an established principle of effective practice in drug education.

Despite the strong evidence base, some adults still find the social norms approach challenging. Key to introducing this in your planning is to find out what young people you teach think about the prevalence of drug use. A needs assessment (assessment for learning) need not be complicated (see Chapter 6).

Normative drug quiz

Try out these quiz questions for yourself, with a group of colleagues and then – importantly – with a Year 10 or 11 group. If working with young people you can do this interactively: ask students to stand in designated corners of the classroom according to the answer they think is most likely to be correct. 'I don't know' is an option to reduce the likelihood that they will simply guess. Being able to say 'I don't know' is a very powerful aspect of PSHE education as it is rarely an option in other lessons!

Check out the correct answers at the end of this chapter. The questions and answers are all based on the 2014 report 'Smoking, drinking and drug use by young people' (Fuller et al, 2014).

Question 1: Since 2001, the use of illegal drugs and solvents by 11–15 year olds has:

a) increased
b) decreased
c) stayed the same
d) I don't know

Question 2: Young people aged 11–15 in the North East of England are more likely to report having used illegal drugs or solvents than young people growing up in other parts of England:

a) True
b) False
c) I don't know

Question 3: 16–24 year olds are:

a) More likely
b) Less likely
c) As likely
d) I don't know

to report using illegal drugs in the last year as 15 year olds.

Question 4: Most young people aged 11–24 have never used an illegal drug:

a) True
b) False
c) I don't know

Question 5: Year 7 pupils are:

a) more likely
b) less likely
c) as likely
d) I don't know

to use volatile substances than illegal drugs.

Question 6: Among 15 year old pupils who smoke tobacco regularly:

a) some
b) most
c) none
d) I don't know

have also used illegal drugs in the last month or used alcohol in the last week.

Once you have carried out this small-scale needs assessment, ask yourself: who is the most/least well informed about young people and the substances they use – adults or young people? Does either group generally over estimate young people's drug use? You could also develop your own short quizzes based on the statistics in the same report about the prevalence of smoking and drinking among young people of school age. Chapters 5 and 6 include a number of additional ideas for baseline or needs assessment including 'draw and write' activities.

These baseline needs assessments will help you to establish a useful starting point for your drug education lesson planning. Other ideas for assessment for and of learning in drug education can be found in a briefing paper written by the Drug & Alcohol Education and Prevention Team for teachers and others involved in drug education which, whilst written some time ago, contains a useful summary and assessment ideas (DrugScope, 2006).

Other substances

So far in this chapter we have focussed on young people and illegal drugs, at the expense of other substances more commonly used by young people such as tobacco and alcohol. There is no doubt about the potential harms that a range of substances can cause, including legal drugs such as alcohol and tobacco, misuse of prescription drugs such as painkillers and Ritalin, over the counter drugs such as paracetamol and everyday substances such as caffeine. All these substances affect how people think and feel and so meet our definition of a drug even if, when used appropriately, the benefits outweigh the potential harms. It is worth recalling the mantra that underpinned drug education when it was first introduced into all schools in England in the early 1990s:

All medicines are drugs, but not all drugs are medicines.

When asked (e.g. by Ofsted), young people often complain that drug education in their schools does not pay enough attention to tobacco and alcohol, which are both legal (for adults) and easily available in society. When looked at on a population level, substances which are most prevalent in our society (such as alcohol and tobacco) arguably cause the most harm.

Some facts about alcohol misuse and smoking

In the UK in 2012 there were 1,008,850 hospital admissions related to alcohol consumption where an alcohol related disease, injury or condition was the primary reason for hospital admission or a secondary diagnosis.
In 2012 there were 8,367 alcohol related deaths in the UK and over a million alcohol related admissions to hospital (Alcohol Concern, 2015).

Hidden Harm

- In the UK it is estimated that 1 in 5 children under the age of 1 year live in a family where a parent drinks hazardously. (Turning Point, 2006)

- Around one-third of domestic violence incidents in the UK are linked with alcohol and parental alcohol misuse is a factor in over 50 percent of child protection cases. (Centre for Social Justice, 2013)
- Smoking is the primary cause of preventable illness and premature death, accounting for approximately 100,000 deaths a year in the UK.
- For every death caused by smoking, approximately 20 smokers are suffering from a smoking related disease. In England in 2012–13, around 460,900 NHS hospital admissions were attributable to smoking among adults aged 35 and over, accounting for 5 per cent of all hospital admissions in this age group.
- In the USA the 2010 Surgeon General's report 'How Tobacco Smoke Causes Disease' concludes that 'there is no risk-free level of exposure to tobacco smoke, and there is no safe tobacco product' (CDC, 2010). It is predicted that by the end of the 21st century, tobacco will have killed one billion people worldwide.
- The cost of smoking to the NHS in England alone is estimated to be £2billion every year. (Action on Smoking and Health, 2014)

You could use this information to invite young people to debate whether the law with respect to alcohol and tobacco should be strengthened (*but beware*: do not ask young people to debate if tobacco or alcohol are harmful as this undermines a social norms approach).

Planning for drug education

As we explore elsewhere in this book, effective PSHE education is not 'topic based'. In other words, it should not focus solely on the information or knowledge that we wish young people to gain. Rather it should focus on developing the concepts, skills, attitudes and attributes outlined in Chapter 3, through the context of a range of topics. The drug education component of PSHE education is no different.

There are potentially thousands of different substances you could include in your drug education lessons, so if your approach to designing your drug education was 'I'll do a couple of lessons on cannabis, then one on new psychoactive substances, then something on cocaine and I mustn't forget nitrous oxide, not to mention ecstasy', then not only would you run out of time for anything else but you would fall into the trap of focussing on drug specific knowledge at the expense of skills, attitudes and attributes and provide an ineffective patchwork of learning. The good news is that the principles for effective drug education apply just as much to tobacco, alcohol and other substances as they do to illegal drugs. You could involve the young people in your classes in deciding how much attention should be given to a range of substances when planning schemes of work, as well as using baseline assessment to gauge their needs.

It is clear that drug education, while based on evidence for effective practice, also must meet the needs of young people who have a range of experiences. This is often described as a three-tiered approach: universal, targeted and harm minimisation.

Universal education is what a school offers all young people as a minimum entitlement and is where PSHE education mainly plays its part. This can vary in content and scope according to the age and lifestyle of the young people, so it may focus on preventing tobacco and alcohol use or drinking and driving, as well as on preventing the harms caused by illegal drugs. Universal drug education draws mainly on the principles for effective practice described earlier.

Targeted education should meet the needs of a more vulnerable group of pupils identified as likely to become involved in risky behaviour for a variety of reasons. These interventions are often founded on a deeper understanding of the neurobiological or social psychological factors involved in risk taking and are best when delivered by teachers who have had specific training in the underlying theory and practice. The PreVenture (Castellanos and Conrod, 2006) and Risk-Avert (www.risk-avert.org) programmes are examples of a targeted prevention approach (see Chapter 7).

Harm minimisation education is usually delivered by specialist drug and alcohol practitioners for young people who have an established pattern of drug use which is causing concern to them and their families. Schools can refer young people to these services, which can include smoking cessation groups and rehabilitation. Young people should also have the information they need (and the confidence) to self-refer.

It is most likely that as a recently qualified teacher you will be asked to deliver universal drug education lessons; that is, for all young people in a group or class, a few of whom will be affected by someone else's drug misuse or have begun to experiment with drugs themselves. It is important to remember, however, that the majority of young people in secondary schools will not have used any drugs apart from medicines, so the overall aim of universal drug education is to help young people maintain their healthy behaviour.

Ideally this learning will take place within a PSHE education lesson, although the setting could also be a tutor group session, a science lesson, or as part of a drop down or off timetable event (see Chapter 4 for different approaches to the organisation of PSHE education).

Drug education planning toolkit

Consider how you could use the information in this chapter to develop your own lesson plans, drawing on the evidence-based quality standards outlined above and on existing evaluated resources. Will all lessons that contribute to a young person's drug education refer explicitly to drugs, alcohol or tobacco? What other learning that you might provide through PSHE education would implicitly contribute to this? If possible, look through a complete programme for PSHE education such as the PSHE Association's (2014) national programme of study and highlight not only the explicit references to drug education but also the implicit learning that contributes to it, such as learning focussed on developing strategies for managing risk or peer influence in other contexts.

At the beginning of this chapter we asked you to draw a pen portrait of a young person who has problems with drugs. Take another look at the questions and what you drew or wrote in response. Has your perception changed as a result of what you have read and reflected on in this chapter?

How could you use these (and similar open ended questions) to assess the drug education needs of a group of young people in your school? See Chapter 5 for a guide to doing classroom-based activities which start where young people are.

Remind yourself of the case histories and the quiz questions. How could these be adapted to suit the age and abilities of your the young people you teach?

Useful resources for young people to explore reliable information about drugs include the FRANK website: www.talktofrank.com (accessed 23.3.16).

(Continued)

(Continued)

The PSHE Association reviews resources for teachers https://pshe-association.org.uk/resources (accessed 23.3.16).

Larger, evidence programmes tailored for specific needs can be found at http://cayt.mentor-adepis.org/cayt-impact-studies/ (accessed 23.3.16).

It is important to remember that facts alone are unlikely to influence young people and so your lessons should include discussion of realistic scenarios and opportunities for young people to practise their developing skills in managing a range of situations involving a range of substances.

Inclusive drug education

As well as the traditional three tiers of drug education, in this book we are introducing the idea of *inclusive drug education*. Whenever we talk about inclusive education in schools we are recognising that some young people are more vulnerable than others, even though we may not always know who those young people are. The same should apply when we are planning drug education.

Let's think again about Kate from the case studies above. Kate's situation represents a small but important subgroup of young people in your Year 10 PSHE education group, who have begun to experiment with cannabis. It is very unlikely that Kate's drug use will come to your attention unless it becomes a persistent problem, affecting her attendance at school, her behaviour in school or her achievement, at which point targeted drug education might be appropriate.

It is also unlikely that she will become a frequent drug user, based on the surveys we have seen, so it is important not to over-react to something which may never become problematic, but to provide support which will help her to make healthier decisions in the future. Despite her increased risk of harm, universal drug education may be all Kate ever gets – that means it also needs to be inclusive of her needs, while matching the principles of effective drug education.

For example, it is very important for Kate's wellbeing that she has access to truthful and relevant information about the actual risks of drug use for her age group, challenging some of her assumptions, particularly that using with friends does not make her safe. PSHE education lessons should also provide Kate and her peer group with the opportunity to consider that street or illegal drugs can vary in quality and so they cannot be sure what they are consuming, or its potency.

Kate may be one of the small percentage of young people for whom cannabis can trigger psychosis, or she may become absorbed in the sub-culture associated with cannabis use to the detriment of her studies. There is a small but significant risk of becoming involved with the criminal justice system and so she needs to be aware of the law with respect to drugs and drug use. Importantly, Kate and her peers should be aware of local drug services and have the confidence and competence to ask or tell someone they trust if they feel they are getting into something they can no longer control.

While it is important Kate and her peers know when and how to ask for help, for themselves and for others, it is unlikely that practising refusal skills will be of much benefit for Kate at this stage, although it may be useful reinforcement for others. (Beware falling into the trap of encouraging half the class to practise persuading someone to accept a drug offer – See Chapter 3.)

If we look back at Kate's story it is clear that she chose to smoke cannabis – there was no overt offer and she was not forced or coerced to join in with her friends. It would be more helpful for Kate and her classmates to think about how they manage peer influence rather than peer pressure. This could include understanding how the adolescent brain is hard-wired to seek the approval of peers and, through shared experiences, to establish a new identity for themselves separate from their parents. See Chapters 2 and 7 to help shape lesson plans which address these factors.

Finally, Kate and her classmates should have the opportunity to think about other reasons young people of their age might experiment with illegal drugs. Young people tell us they use a range of drugs to self-medicate for symptoms of anxiety and depression. It is no surprise then that interventions which address the mental and emotional needs of adolescents can have an impact on their drug and alcohol misuse: inclusive drug education could include strategies for managing mental and emotional needs without drugs, such as mindfulness and relaxation, as well as seeking medical help where appropriate. In Chapter 13 we explore the connections between PSHE education, pastoral care and therapeutic interventions for young people attending school.

Everything that inclusive drug education might offer Kate and the minority of her friends who are using cannabis will reinforce the intentions of the majority of young people in the class not to use drugs. It will also provide opportunities for young people to understand more about the way drugs affect people and the services available to support them in a non-stigmatising way, with practical ways to seek help and support if they need it.

Chapter overview

Most young people of school age do not use illegal drugs, but young people who smoke or drink alcohol while of school age are more vulnerable to illegal drug use. Drug education should provide opportunities for young people to develop their knowledge, understanding, attitudes and skills with respect to a range of substances including tobacco and alcohol, over the counter and prescription drugs as well as everyday substances such as caffeine.

Drug education provided in secondary schools should be an integral part of a planned, developmental PSHE education programme. It should be inclusive, reflecting the range of possible experiences of the young people in the group. It should be of high quality, based on the evidence from effective programmes. Like all elements of PSHE education, it should be non-judgemental, reinforce positive social norms and be interactive. Teachers and others working with young people should create a safe learning environment, set relevant objectives based on the needs of the young people, and the learning outcomes should be assessed. Drug education should be supported by policies and a whole school approach which is focussed on the welfare and wellbeing of the young people for whom it is being developed.

Answers to questions on page 196–7

Question 1

Answer is b). The use of illegal drugs among school age children has fallen by approximately half since 2001. This information is generally under-reported.

Question 2

Answer is b). There is little variation in illegal drug use by young people across England. However, young people growing up in London are less likely to report ever having drunk alcohol than other parts of England. Interestingly, the data suggest this is not due to variations in the ethnic mix of young people in London, when compared with other regions.

Question 3

Answer is c). Drug use in the last year among 15 year olds is similar to that reported by 16–24 year olds, when supervision of young people is reduced and opportunities to access illegal drugs is more widespread.

Question 4

Answer is a). Most young people aged 11–24 years have never used illegal drugs. Around 8–9 per cent of adults (aged 16–59 years) have used illicit drugs in the last year.

Question 5

Answer is a). Pupils in Year 7 are 8 times more likely to have used volatile substances than cannabis. This is of great concern since the risk of death from a single use of volatile substance is higher than from cannabis.

Question 6

Answer is b). Around 10 per cent of 15 year olds smoke regularly, of whom only 1 per cent have not also used illegal drugs in the last month or alcohol in the last week. This cluster effect is a common phenomenon. See Chapter 7 for more about the clustering of risky behaviours among young people.

Further reading

Aggleton, P., Ball, A. and Mane, P. (eds) (2006) *Sex, Drugs and Young People: International Perspectives*. London: Routledge.
This powerful book explores how young people have been vilified by theories of adolescence which describe their development in terms of biological determinism, without regard to the social effects of factors such as gender, ethnicity and economic and educational inequality. It explores the need for a positive and inclusive response to young people's health needs, whatever their circumstances.

(Continued)

(Continued)

Bühler, A., and Thrul, J. (2015) *Prevention of Addictive Behaviours.* Luxembourg: Publications Office of the European Union, EMCDDA.
This scholarly work is an overview of addictive behaviours, including tobacco, alcohol and illegal drug misuse and gambling. It examines the evidence for what works in prevention in a range of settings including schools. Researched and written for a German audience, its lessons are of broader relevance to other European countries.

Cohen, J. (2014) *All About Drugs and Young People.* London: Jessica Kingsley.
This book, written by an experienced drug educator, is for parents, carers and all professionals who work with young people. It takes a balanced and non-judgemental approach to helping young people who may use drugs of all kinds.

Coomber, R., McElrath, K., Measham, F. and Moore, K. (2013) *Key Concepts in Drugs and Society.* London: Sage.
A comprehensive overview of the key issues and trends about drugs and society, this book will enable to you to see drug education in its wider historical and political context.

Note: It is important to use the criteria outlined in Chapter 14 to help you select resources for drug education.

References

Action on Smoking and Health (2014) 'Smoking statistics: illness and death – factsheet'. Available at http://ash.org.uk/files/documents/ASH_107.pdf (accessed 13.01.16).

Alcohol and Drug Education Information Service (ADEPIS) (2015) 'Quality standards for alcohol and drug education'. Available at http://mentor-adepis.org/wp-content/uploads/2014/05/Quality-standards-for-alcohol-and-drug-education.pdf (accessed 25.11.15).

Alcohol Concern (2015) 'Statistics on alcohol'. Available at www.alcoholconcern.org.uk/help-and-advice/statistics-on-alcohol/ (accessed 25.11.15).

Castellanos, N. and Conrod, P. (2006) 'Brief interventions targeting personality risk factors for adolescent substance misuse reduce depression, panic and risk-taking behaviours', *Journal of Mental Health*, 15: 1–14.

Centers for Disease Control and Prevention (CDC) (2010) '2010 Surgeon General's Report—How tobacco smoke causes disease: the biology and behavioral basis for smoking-attributable disease'. Available at www.cdc.gov/tobacco/data_statistics/sgr/2010/ (accessed 23.3.16).

Centre for Social Justice (2013) *No Quick Fix: Exposing the Depth of Britain's Drug and Alcohol Problem*. London: Centre for Social Justice.

Council for the Curriculum, Examinations and Assessment (CCEA) (2015) 'Drugs: Guidance for Schools in Northern Ireland'. Available at http://ccea.org.uk/sites/default/files/docs/curriculum/area_of_learning/pdmu/drugs/Drugs_Guidance_for_Schools.pdf (accessed 13.01.16).

Department for Education and Skills (DfES) (2004) 'Drugs: Guidance for Schools'. Available at http://webarchive.nationalarchives.gov.uk/20130401151715/http://www.education.gov.uk/publications/eOrderingDownload/DfES%200092%20200MIG373.pdf (accessed 25.11.15).

Department for Education and Skills (Welsh Government) (DfES) (2013) 'Guidance for substance misuse education'. Available at http://gov.wales/docs/dcells/publications/130703-substance-misuse-en.pdf (accessed 25.11.15).

Department for Education and the Association of Chief Police Officers (DfE/ACPO) (2012) 'Drug advice for schools: advice for local authorities, headteachers, school staff and governing bodies'. Available at www.gov.uk/government/uploads/system/uploads/attachment_data/file/270169/drug_advice_for_schools.pdf (accessed 21.3.16).

DrugScope (2006) 'Assessment in drug education: a briefing paper for teachers and other drug education practitioners'. Available at https://drugscopelegacysite.files.wordpress.com/2015/07/assessmentdrugeducationbriefing.pdf (accessed 25.11.15).

Education Scotland (2015) 'Health and Wellbeing experiences and outcomes: substance misuse'. Available at www.educationscotland.gov.uk/myexperiencesandoutcomes/healthandwellbeing/substancemisuse/index.asp (accessed 25.11.15).

Fuller, E. (ed.) (2014) *Smoking, Alcohol and Other Drug Use by Young People*. London: Health and Social Care Information Centre. Available at www.hscic.gov.uk/catalogue/PUB17879/smok-drin-drug-youn-peop-eng-2014-rep.pdf (accessed 25.11.15).

Hansen, W.B. and Graham, J.W. (1991) 'Preventing alcohol, marijuana, and cigarette use among adolescents: peer pressure resistance training versus establishing conservative norms', *Preventive Medicine*, 20(3): 414–30.

Office for National Statistics (2015) 'Crime in England and Wales, Year ending March 2015'. Available at www.ons.gov.uk/ons/rel/crime-stats/crime-statistics/year-ending-march-2015/index.html (accessed 25.11.15).

PSHE Association (2014) 'PSHE Education Programme of Study (Key Stages 1–4), October. Available at www.pshe-association.org.uk/sites/default/files/PSHE%20Association%20Programme%20of%20Study%20October%202014%20FINAL_0.pdf (accessed 22.3.16).

Slovic, P. (1987) 'Perception of risk', *Science,* 17: 236, 280–5.

Topping, A. (2014) 'London gangs using children as drug mules as they seek to expand the market', *Guardian*, 5 January. Available at www.theguardian.com/society/2014/jan/05/drug-gangs-using-children-as-mules (accessed 25.11.15).

Turning Point (2006) *Bottling It Up: The Next Generation – The Effects of Alcohol Misuse of Children, Parents and Families*. London: Turning Point. Available at www.turning-point.co.uk/media/53899/bottlingitup2011.pdf (accessed 25.11.15).

10

Understanding Relationships and Sex Education (RSE) within PSHE Education

Aim

To understand the nature and purpose of 'relationships and sex education' within PSHE education in secondary schools.

Learning objectives

It is impossible to cover an aspect of PSHE education as large as RSE in one chapter, however, through reading and reflecting on the content of this chapter you will begin to:

- understand the breadth of learning that makes up RSE
- be able to establish a safe learning environment in the classroom
- have strategies for managing pupils' questions
- have a generic methodology that will enable you to begin to teach RSE in a way that is relevant to young people.

Before we start

What comes into your mind when you hear the words 'sex education'?

What if we change that slightly to 'sex and relationships education' (often shortened to SRE)?

How about 'relationships and sex education' (or RSE)?

In some respects the process of developing relationship and sex education programmes reflects in a simplistic way the historical evolution of RSE, from a narrow biological focus, often taught as a one off 'sex education' lesson perhaps as part of science, gradually evolving and broadening into a planned programme of 'relationships and sex education', with the emphasis on relationships, in PSHE education today.

Introduction

Sexual relationships are just one of many types of relationship we may form over the course of our lives. We may have different kinds of relationships with family members, friends, best friends, work colleagues and those people with whom we share intimacy.

Some of the documents we will refer to in this chapter are historical and will use the term 'sex and relationships education' (SRE). The Department for Education rejected calls in 2015 to officially change SRE to RSE; however, we will use the term 'RSE' to reflect how this aspect of the curriculum is continuing to evolve and current usage in many schools and local authorities.

At the time of writing the content and quality of RSE is still inconsistent across England. In 2013 Ofsted reported that:

> lack of high-quality, age-appropriate sex and relationships education in more than a third of schools is a concern as it may leave children and young people vulnerable to inappropriate sexual behaviours and sexual exploitation.

The report went on to state that:

> In secondary schools it was because too much emphasis was placed on 'the mechanics' of reproduction and too little on relationships, sexuality, the influence of pornography on students' understanding of healthy sexual relationships, dealing with emotions and staying safe.

This is naturally a cause for concern for all of us in PSHE education. It is vital that anyone who teaches RSE has a thorough understanding of this central element of PSHE education.

Imagine this scenario

Two young people of about 17 years of age have been 'going steady' for a few months and have engaged in kissing and mutual masturbation or 'heavy petting'. They seem to be 'going further' each time and have been talking to each other about having penetrative sex.

If they go ahead, what responsibilities do they share towards one another and others? And what will they need:

- to know and understand;
- to feel about themselves and each other;
- to be able to say and do

in order to have a healthy, safe and enjoyable experience?

Would this be different if one of them decides at any point 'I am not ready'?

It should be immediately apparent that no 'one-off' lesson can adequately prepare someone for this experience, nor can a narrow 'scientific' focus (essential as the scientific aspect of this is) provide all the learning that will be required.

For this reason we believe the term 'RSE' is more appropriate. Many of the skills that will be needed (e.g. risk assessment and management; negotiation; communication, empathy and assertiveness) will apply to many other opportunities and challenges young people face. For this reason RSE is also best set into the wider context of PSHE education.

Now imagine that there was no school-based sex education. How would young people gain this knowledge and understanding? What sort of messages might these sources provide for young people? How might these messages shape their understanding and expectations? What might be the consequences of accepting these messages?

What is relationships and sex education?

In 2014 three organisations – Brook, the PSHE Association and Sex Education Forum – published 'Sex and Relationships Education for the 21st Century' to supplement the statutory 'Sex and Relationships Education Guidance' produced by the Government (DfEE) in 2000 and which remains the statutory guidance to date. This new document defined SRE in this way:

Sex and relationships education is learning about the emotional, social and physical aspects of growing up, relationships, sex, human sexuality and sexual health. Some aspects are taught in science, and others are taught as part of personal, social, health and economic education (PSHEe).

A comprehensive programme of SRE provides accurate information about the body, reproduction, sex, and sexual health. It also gives children and young people essential skills for building positive, enjoyable, respectful and non-exploitative relationships and staying safe both on and offline.

Why is RSE so important?

Activity

Benefits of RSE to young people and to schools

Make two columns: one headed 'Young person' and the other 'School'. Under the first heading, note down everything that an effective RSE programme provides for each individual young person. Under the second, note down everything an effective RSE programme will provide for the school in terms of fulfilling its duties and responsibilities and other wholeschool outcomes.

'Sex and Relationships Education (SRE) for the 21st Century' (Brook et al., 2014) has this to say about the importance of RSE. Compare it to your two columns above:

High-quality SRE helps create safe school communities in which pupils can grow, learn, and develop positive, healthy behaviour for life. It is essential for the following reasons:

- Children and young people have a right to good quality education, as set out in the United Nations Convention on the Rights of the Child.
- Children and young people want to be prepared for the physical and emotional changes they undergo at puberty, and young people want to learn about relationships. Older pupils frequently say that sex and relationships education was 'too little, too late and too biological'. Ofsted reinforced this in their 2013 Not Yet Good Enough report.
- SRE plays a vital part in meeting schools' safeguarding obligations. Ofsted is clear that schools must have a preventative programme that enables pupils to learn about safety and risks in relationships.
- Schools maintain a statutory obligation under the Children Act (2004) to promote their pupils' wellbeing, and under the Education Act (1996) to

> prepare children and young people for the challenges, opportunities and responsibilities of adult life. A comprehensive SRE programme can have a positive impact on pupils' health and wellbeing and their ability to achieve, and can play a crucial part in meeting these obligations.

The vast majority of parents and carers support schools in the teaching of RSE. Many parents and carers are keen to support their children but are uncertain about what to say or lack understanding about issues such as sexually transmitted infections (STIs) and online safety. (To understand more about the relationship between parents/carers and RSE, see Sex Education Forum, 2011.)

It is important to recognise that 98 per cent of parents and carers are happy for their children to attend RSE lessons and 92 per cent believe it should be compulsory in secondary schools (Durex et al., 2010).

The impact of RSE

There is strong evidence that young people who receive good-quality RSE programmes that start early and are taught either at school or in the community are more likely to first have sex at an older age, to have fewer sexual partners and to use contraception (Kirby, 2007). The National Surveys of Sexual Attitudes and Lifestyles (1991, 2001 and 2012, in Tanton et al., 2015) found that young people who reported school lessons as their main source of sex and relationships education were less likely to report first intercourse before the age of 16 and were more likely to report that a reliable method of contraception was used, that their decision to have sex was autonomous and that both partners were equally willing. Those whose main source of information was school lessons were also less likely to have an unplanned pregnancy.

There is also evidence that children and young people who are taught about preventing sexual abuse at school are more likely than others to tell an adult if they had experienced, or were experiencing sexual abuse (Walsh et al., 2015).

The role of primary schools in teaching RSE

PSHE is part of the vast majority of primary schools' curriculum and relationships, and sex education will almost certainly be part of this programme. As a secondary teacher you will be building on a considerable amount of work being undertaken by our primary colleagues.

Many primary schools use a thematic approach, revisiting a topic such as 'growing and changing' or 'healthy relationships' and RSE will fit naturally into either of these. There is a lot of misunderstanding about RSE in primary schools, with misleading articles in the media that can be at best ill-informed.

Imagine you had to prepare young people to manage their first credit card. They would need to understand compound interest but before this they would need to understand simple interest, percentages, multiplication, addition and a concept of number. Imagine this work 'spiralling backwards down the age range'. You wouldn't talk to 5 year olds about compound interest but you would be hard pushed to teach it to older students without them having experienced a developmental mathematics programme that started with the concept of number in the infant school.

Consider

Think about the 17 year old couple in the exercise above. Think about the feelings, language, skills and responsibilities you identified. How many of these could or would have to be started in Key Stage 1?

Primary schools might cover work on friendship, healthy relationships, respect for one another's feelings, their personal space, good and not so good touches, negotiation, fairness, the process of growing and changing and the responsibilities that come with each change (e.g. if you can now reach the front door handle you need to be careful not to let your younger sibling walk outside).

Preparing children for the physical and emotional changes of puberty is a crucial part of the primary school's safeguarding responsibilities and it is important that this learning happens before children experience these changes. So as many children now begin puberty from the age of about 8 years, most primary schools will ensure this is within the Years 4 and 5 PSHE education and science programmes and includes learning on menstruation, 'wet dreams', changes to skin, hair and body shape, as well as the emotional changes to expect, including mood swings, all of which are a natural part of growing and changing. They will usually place their 'overt work' on conception in Years 5 or 6 depending on their policy and the readiness of their pupils. Primary schools will almost certainly teach how a baby is conceived and possibly some basic work on contraception even if it is only to ensure that pupils understand pregnancy is a choice. It is also likely that they will reassure pupils by ensuring they understand that everyone changes in their own time and the normality of behaviours such as masturbation.

There is one difficulty. The vast majority of primary schools will be working to their own agreed policy, which is the responsibility of their governing body, and which will include the content of their programme. Because of this there can be inconsistencies in the knowledge and understanding of young people in Year 7.

Activity

Visit a primary school and ask if you can see a copy of their RSE (SRE) policy. Ask what is covered in their programme and how it was planned.

Are you surprised by anything?

Does this work support RSE in secondary schools?

The school's policy and the status of RSE (SRE)

Prior to the establishment of academies and free schools all secondary schools were required to provide a programme of SRE. It was the responsibility of governing bodies, ideally in consultation with parents, carers, pupils and local community to create a policy to frame this learning.

As of 2016 the situation is far more complex:

- All state funded schools (including academies) have a statutory duty to publish details of their curriculum for each year group, including PSHE education and RSE, but only in 'maintained secondary schools' (i.e. not in academies, free schools or independent schools) is it compulsory for pupils to have sex education that includes HIV, AIDS and other sexually transmitted infections.
- There are elements of sex education in the statutory science programme of the National Curriculum for Key Stages 1 to 3, but the National Curriculum is not statutory in academies, free schools or independent schools.
- All maintained schools and free schools are statutorily required to have an up-to-date policy for RSE, but academies and independent schools are only advised to have one.

- Parents and carers have the right to withdraw their children from any RSE taught outside of the National Curriculum (i.e. the science programmes of study), but if they choose to withdraw their children from school provision they have a responsibility to provide alternative RSE (in most schools very few parents exercise this right).

In practice, the vast majority of all schools provide a programme of RSE in some form or other and the vast majority of schools will have a policy to determine the content of the programme.

Regardless of the type of school, it is essential that teachers work inside the parameters of their school's policy. This ensures that the programme fulfils the school's commitments, meets parents' and carers' expectations and ensures the professional safety of the teacher.

Before we consider what high-quality relationships and sex education look like in the classroom, we need to consider some other issues. The first is safeguarding.

Activity

Pick a school you are familiar with. Ask to see their RSE or SRE policy. Ask how the policy was constructed. Who was involved? What does it contain? How would it help guide you if you were to teach in RSE in this school? How does safeguarding fit with this policy? Are there any surprises? Do you think anything is missing?

Safeguarding

All schools will have a safeguarding or child protection policy, including protocols to follow in the event of a student being considered vulnerable or at risk and a designated safeguarding lead (DSL) to approach in such an event whose role is to provide support to staff members to carry out their safeguarding duties and liaise closely with other services such as children's social care. Because of the issues covered and the discussions that may arise in PSHE education lessons, you may either directly or indirectly become concerned for a young person's safety or wellbeing. For example, a young person may give you cause for concern during a class or small group discussion, may make a direct approach for support during or following a lesson or ask a hypothetical question about a 'friend'.

It is important to take any concerns very seriously; to listen but not probe for further information and ensure that you notify the school's designated safeguarding lead or 'named person' as soon as possible about your concern and definitely before the pupil leaves the school premises. The golden rule with safeguarding is simple, 'if in doubt, shout', or simply 'if you have the slightest reason to be concerned about a young person's wellbeing, tell the DSL'.

Classroom climate

Establishing a safe classroom climate contributes to safeguarding. The principles of how to do this are explored in Chapter 3, however, the importance of a safe teaching and learning environment is so central to teaching RSE that it bears further consideration here.

Because of the interactive, discussion-rich pedagogy that is used in PSHE education it is essential that learning takes place in a safe classroom atmosphere, and central to this are ground rules or a working agreement. Before teaching any aspect of RSE it is important to revisit and emphasise any relevant groundrules that have been negotiated with the class.

If you need to establish groundrules, a simple technique is to arrange the class in small groups and have them discuss two statements:

- If I wanted to share my ideas and opinions with this class it would help if others …
- If I wanted to share my ideas and opinions with this class it would help if others did not …

If you collect up groups' thoughts then it quickly becomes clear which are common to many groups and what everyone thinks are important ground rules. Those less common requests can be considered and accepted or rejected by the group.

Helpful examples might be: listen; give me time to think; challenge my answers but do not judge me; agree there are no 'stupid' questions.

Examples of what would not be helpful might include: laugh; put me down; make me feel stupid.

Because you are a member of this class, ground rules apply to you as well. However, this also means you have the right to add to them.

Two are particularly important. First, it is essential that young people understand that you cannot guarantee confidentiality. Explain that whilst in principle we can all agree that what is said in the lesson will not be shared with others, there is an exception. If you have a concern about someone's safety or wellbeing you will have to talk to the designated safeguarding lead in order to get them support. Do not be tempted to pretend that you can offer confidentiality when you cannot. You may gain short-term information, but in the longer term you have shown you cannot be trusted. Young people may take a little longer, but they are far more likely to talk to teachers whom they trust to be honest with them.

Second, agree not to make anyone feel they are being 'put on the spot' or being asked or pressurised into sharing personal information. This can be especially helpful if a young person asks you a personal question during the lesson. This may be genuine curiosity or it may be to test how you handle it. Simply refer to this ground rule, explain that we agreed not to do this and move the learning on. This is also important because some pupils may have genuinely difficult questions they may be anxious about asking and will be reassured by the way you manage this (see also 'Creating a safe classroom climate' in Chapter 3).

Consider

Imagine a young person who is in a PSHE education lesson with an RSE focus. They are concerned that, from what everyone else has been saying, they seem to be the only one 'not doing it' and they are steeling themselves to ask a question about how old most young people are when they first have sex.

At that moment the 'class joker' calls out to the teacher 'How old were you when you first had sex then? I bet you were really young!' to which the teacher replies angrily 'If you think I'm going to answer a question like that, you've got another thing coming! Any more like that from you and there'll be trouble!' How likely is the first young person to ask their question now? How else could the teacher have responded?

Answering challenging questions

If you are anxious about what questions may come up during an RSE lesson and whether you will be able to give an appropriate answer in front of 30 pupils, you are certainly not alone. We all share this anxiety!

Consider

Imagine you are teaching RSE to a class of 15 year olds.
    What is the most challenging question you think you might be asked?
    What would you need to think about before you consider answering it?
    If you decline to answer it, how could you do this without appearing to devalue the young person?

It is important to stop and think about this. There is no requirement to answer any young person's question at the time they ask it. This is true of any subject. It is quite appropriate to respect the question 'That is a really interesting question…' and to give yourself some thinking time '…and I need a little time to give you a really good answer.' There may come a time when you need to consult with a more senior colleague. You are answering this question on behalf of the school and asking exactly how the school wants you to respond to a question is legitimate, professional and a lot safer.

Whilst it is important to be sensitive to timing, it can be helpful to ask the young person what *they* think the answer to their question might be. It may be that all you need to say is 'That's right'. Remember there is no rush, give yourself thinking time and if necessary ask a more experienced colleague. We have all done this and at times even the most experienced of us still do!

Many PSHE education leads arrange for a box to be available for young people to anonymously leave their questions before, after or during the lessons. Although it is important to be sensitive, it can be a good idea to invite groups of pupils to research and report back on each other's questions. This can improve their research skills. Critically, they need to report back both their findings and, equally important, convince us of the validity of their source of information. If you are going to try this activity, it is important to type up the questions and use them in the next lesson or write them on the board yourself, as many young people will recognise their friends' or classmates' handwriting and may worry that others will recognise theirs.

Being inclusive

RSE lessons should meet the needs of all pupils, whatever their ability, disability, race, religion, sexual orientation or gender identity. For example, teachers should never create the impression that all intimate relationships are between opposite sexes, or promote a binary view of gender. Schools have a duty under the Equality Act 2010 to ensure that teaching is accessible to all children and young people, including those who are lesbian, gay, bisexual, transgender and questioning their sexual identity (LGBTQ). It is essential that RSE lessons feel inclusive to pupils. Brook et al. (2014) reported:

> Too often, groups of young people say they feel excluded in SRE lessons. For example, lesbian, gay and bisexual pupils (who make up approximately 10 per cent of any school population) often report that their SRE is solely about heterosexual relationships, or that non heterosexual identities were addressed negatively and that it fails to address sexual health issues linked to the range of sexual behaviours and activities that people encounter whatever their sexual orientation. Young people with physical or learning disabilities often report that SRE does not meet their needs, while boys tell us they feel excluded because SRE seems to be aimed more at girls – and they are often anxious about being shown up as being ignorant about sexual matters.

The exact percentage of LGBTQ pupils likely to be in any secondary school class is impossible to determine and really doesn't matter. Based on research you could assume that there are about three young people in your class who recognise that they are experiencing different feelings to those of the majority of their peers. Ask yourself 'How is my lesson planning including these young people? Will every young person in my lesson be able to see themselves in this learning and be able to say, "I can see how this is relevant to me"?'

Young LGBTQ pupils are especially vulnerable. It is essential that they feel included in every aspect of RSE. These lessons may be some of the most important in the curriculum for young people who are questioning their sexual orientation, who may be confused, anxious or completely terrified of the consequences of coming out to their friends or family and be hugely reassured by sensitive RSE.

RSE can also offer opportunities to challenge prejudice. Brook et al. (2014) state:

> Inclusive SRE will foster good relations between pupils, tackle all types of prejudice – including homophobia – and promote understanding and respect, enabling schools to meet the requirements, and live the intended spirit, of the Equality Act 2010.

It is simply a question of thinking about how young people will receive your lesson. For example, young people of all genders can have romantic relationships with young people of all genders and it is therefore best practice not to refer to 'boyfriend' or 'girlfriend' but rather to use the terms 'a person and their partner' or 'a couple'. Every sexual activity can be practised by people of any sexual orientation in some way or another and the qualities of a healthy relationship (e.g. our right to do only things we feel comfortable doing, our right to be treated with kindness and respect, to have our right to give and withhold our consent respected, to reduce our risk of infection and to benefit from the protection of the law) are common to everyone. As Brook et al. (2014) argue:

> All children and young people – whatever their experience, background and identity – are entitled to quality sex and relationships education that helps them build confidence and a positive sense of self, and to stay healthy. All classes include pupils with different abilities and disabilities, experiences and backgrounds, gender and sexual identities. To encourage pupils to participate in lessons, teachers should ensure content, approach, and use of inclusive language reflect the diversity of the school community, and help each and every pupil to feel valued and included in the classroom.

For more information, see Stonewall who have a section specifically for teachers and schools (www.stonewall.org.uk/at_school/).

Faith and culture

This is a large topic, beyond the scope of this chapter and reinforces the importance of being familiar with the school's RSE/SRE policy. Many faith schools separate out the expectations of the school's faith from the understanding, knowledge, skills and values young people need to learn as part of their education.

The Sex Education Forum (2004) has produced a fact sheet that states:

> Children and young people from all faiths and cultures have an entitlement to SRE that can support them on their journey through childhood to adolescence and adulthood. One young woman, aged 15, emphasised the importance of receiving this entitlement: 'I have a faith and I trust my parents to talk to me about values. At school what I need in sex education is to understand about sex and relationships, and understand what different people think.' Teaching SRE effectively means taking into account the many faiths and cultures of the children and young people in Britain today.

The fact sheet identifies three underlying principles:

1. Children and young people have an entitlement to SRE that is relevant to them, supports them in learning about different faiths and cultures and is underpinned by values promoting equality and respect. Children and young people need opportunities to understand the law and health issues in relation to sex, sexuality and sexual health. So, for example,

even if religious doctrine forbids sex before marriage or the use of contraception, young people need to know and understand the legal and health implications of these behaviours as well as different religious perspectives.

2. Valuing diversity and anti-discriminatory practice must be an integral part of the school's ethos, reflected in all areas of the curriculum. In SRE this involves professionals taking responsibility for consulting and involving faith communities in the development of policy and practice.

3. We need to provide a framework and create a safe context within which parents and carers from faith communities, and members of the wider community, understand more about SRE, are able to discuss their views and beliefs, and feel involved with the process of developing SRE.

It is important to recognise that not all pupils will chose to live by the principles of their family's or their school's faith or may have partners who do not share the values of their own faith. This can be addressed by providing a broad and balanced RSE programme while clarifying the expectations of the school's faith.

Working with 'visitors to the classroom'

A rich programme of RSE can benefit from external professionals working alongside a teacher, perhaps bringing expertise (e.g. a school nurse), or helping to establish a relationship between the young people and perhaps a local or national support service. Regardless of who the visitor is, managing the learning remains the responsibility of the teacher. Visitors to the classroom are best thought of as 'living teaching resources' and should be used with the same precision and care as any other resource. Their role is to help your pupils meet your learning objectives. It is important to talk with any visitor prior to the lesson and to be certain they have no personal or alternative agenda that they intend to promote which contradicts the school policy. (See also chapter 14)

Into practice – teaching two key concepts: healthy relationships and consent

What does all this look like in the classroom? We have chosen to illustrate three short learning activities, one teaching about healthy relationships, one focussing on a not so healthy relationship and one exploring 'consent'. All would be part of a far more comprehensive RSE programme and would take place within a lesson that meets the best practice described in Chapter 5.

Example 1

This activity might take place within a lesson with the following intended learning outcomes.

By the end of this learning pupils will be able to:

*   identify the features of a healthy relationship
*   explain what they want and expect from a healthy relationship
*   identify behaviours that are unacceptable in a relationship.

Ask pupils in small groups to discuss:

*   what makes a *good* relationship (this could be any type of relationship) – what are its characteristics, and how do people behave towards each other:
    o   when they feel good;
    o   when they feel bad;
    o   when one of them feels bad?

Take feedback then discuss:

*   How do people feel in a healthy relationship?
*   How should people expect to feel in a close, healthy relationship?
*   How should people *not* feel in a relationship?
*   What might make them feel like that? (*Look for both words and behaviour.*)
*   What might make them feel even worse in a relationship?
*   What could happen that would make them feel that way? (*Look for both words and behaviour.*)

Collect some ideas up and ask whether we can build a consensus for ourselves from how we think people should and should not feel. Gather ideas on the board or on flipchart paper in groups, under the headings:

'We want to feel…'

'We need to be treated…'

'We have a right to…'

'We have a responsibility to…'

If necessary explore the difference between wants, needs, rights and responsibilities in a relationship.

Ask pupils to discuss if it is OK to leave or end a relationship without giving a 'cause' or 'reason'.

Explain that because we can enter into and leave relationships, we don't have to *justify* ending a relationship. If a relationship does not make us feel as we believe a healthy relationship should make us feel, if we are not treated and our rights respected as we would expect in a healthy relationship, if we are uncomfortable or unwilling to meet all our partner's wants and needs, or feel we are unwilling to meet what they perceive as their 'rights', is the relationship one that we should end or leave?

Example 2

This activity might take place within a lesson with the following intended learning outcomes.

By the end of this learning pupils will be able to:

- identify the difference between caring and controlling
- explain what is meant by 'coercive control'.

Ask the young people to think about this scenario:

'That's the fifth time your phone has gone off in five minutes!'

'I know, Sam keeps ringing and texting me. It was nice when we started going out, you know, texting and ringing one another all the time.'

'So what's the problem?'

'Well, Sam keeps wanting to know where I am and who I am with.'

'So just ignore it.'

'I tried that but Sam got really cross with me, actually I got a bit scared, I really got shouted at. Sam really cares about me and just wants to know I am safe. I don't want Sam to worry about me. The other day Sam took my phone and looked at all my calls asking who I was ringing and who was ringing me.'

(Continued)

(Continued)

'So, you coming out tonight? We thought we would all have a friends' night out!'

'No, I'd better not. Sam texted to say I need to stay in tonight in case we don't get a chance to meet up later.'

'That's a real shame, we hardly ever see you since you started going out with Sam!'

Imagine you had overheard this conversation. Explore these questions:

- Why do you think Sam is behaving in this way?
- What could Sam be thinking and feeling?
- How do you think Sam's partner is feeling?
- Why do you think they might be putting up with this?
- Is Sam caring?
- Is Sam controlling? (What do they feel about the words '... *need to stay in tonight in case we get don't a chance to meet up later'*)?
- How else might people try to control others?
- Is this OK?
- How might it feel to experience this type of controlling behaviour?
- Is it ever OK to behave in a way that makes your partner feel scared of you?
- Is it OK to ever feel scared of your partner's behaviour towards you?
- Is it likely that Sam's behaviour will suddenly change?

Ask pupils in small groups to discuss:

- If either of these characters asked for your advice, what would you say?
- If you could talk to Sam, what would you say?
- If a friend of yours told you they were either treating someone else in this way or were being treated like this, what would you say? What could you do?
- If this behaviour continues, what do you think might happen in the future?
- What responsibilities do we have towards our partners?
- If you experienced this behaviour or thought someone you care about is experiencing this type of behaviour, what would you say? What could you do? Whom could you tell?
- When does 'minding our own business' end and 'doing something to help' start?

Did you notice how these sessions are built around questions rather than moving straight into factual content? Are any of the characters definitely male or female? This lesson places the young people in the role of 'adviser' and by structuring learning carefully we can increase their expertise as advisers.

This allows us to add in 'factual content' as it becomes relevant to the ongoing dialogue happening in the classroom. For example, at some point we would want to provide information about school based or local support services along the lines of 'I notice that some us are uncertain what to say or do. Would it help if you knew about…?'

We can then ask young people to build this new information into their discussions, perhaps asking 'How does knowing this help you better advise this character? Would you now say anything differently?'

We could invite young people to undertake their own enquiries into local services and report back to their class.

Consent

Now let's consider 'consent' – one of the fundamental concepts in RSE. Learning about consent goes far beyond simply knowing the 'legal age of consent' and is not only confined to the concept of consent in sexual relationships. This learning is about respecting the rights of others, communication, negotiation and considering the freedom and capacity of others to make choices, all of which are crucial in a range of situations young people will encounter in their lives.

'Consent' is defined in the Home Office (2015) resource 'This is abuse – discussion guide' as:

> A free choice to give permission made by someone feeling comfortable in giving that permission.

Imagine a young person in two 'critical moments': first, the moment when they need, want or have to gain another's consent; and second, the moment when they have to either give or not give their consent to someone else. In both situations they will need:

- an understanding of the concept of 'consent' including:
  - that it is the person seeking consent who is responsible (ethically and legally) for ensuring that consent is given by another person, and for ensuring that person has the freedom and capacity to give their consent
  - that everyone has the right to give or not give their consent
  - that if the person seeking consent is not completely certain that the other person's consent is clear, informed, willing and active, they must assume that consent has not been given

- that if consent is not clearly given, or is given and then subsequently retracted, this decision must always be respected
- that consent is an ongoing process – since people can change their minds, or consent to one thing but not to something else, the person seeking consent must keep assessing whether consent is clear, informed, willing and active.

- strategies and skills that enable them to seek someone's consent, give or not give their consent to others
- the language that allows them either to seek someone's consent, or to give or not give their consent to others. (PSHE, 2015a)

In the second situation, in addition to the above they will also need:

- a detailed understanding of exactly what they are consenting to and the likelihood and severity of the consequences of giving this consent
- to understand how they feel about this decision, their beliefs and their values
- a feeling of 'self worth' that will ensure they know their giving or not giving of consent is worthy of respect and an understanding that a person is never to blame if their decision not to give consent or to withdraw consent is not respected.

Activity

Ask teachers in a school you are familiar with if you can undertake a quick piece of research with a small group of pupils (perhaps 10 young people in Years 8 or 9).

Ask the young people to imagine an alien has just arrived on Earth. They have heard about something called 'consent' but they don't know what it means. How would the young people explain it to them? The alien asks how people know that someone is giving consent. How would they explain how we know someone's 'consent' is real and active?

What did the young people tell you? Do you feel they have a good understanding of consent? Was anything confused, worrying or missing? If you now had to teach these young people about consent, how would you focus your work?

Consent is not just something you 'academically understand'; seeking, giving and not giving consent is something you 'do', requiring a language, skills, strategies and energy. There is a world of difference between *knowing* your rights and responsibilities and *exercising* your rights and responsibilities.

Perhaps the most critical learning is that it is the responsibility of the person seeking consent to ensure that the giving of consent is willing and active, feely given and by someone who has the capacity to understand what they are consenting to. No one need justify not giving or later withdrawing their consent.

Example 3

This activity might take place within a lesson with the following intended learning outcomes.

By the end of this learning pupils will be able to explain:

- that no one has the right to threaten someone into giving their 'consent'
- why such agreement is not consent.

Explain to the class that in this session it is not clear exactly what it is that someone is being pressurised to do. It could be virtually anything. That isn't the point. The issue is understanding that saying 'yes' while under duress in any situation is not consent and actually means 'no'. Putting someone under duress to say yes is wrong and could lead to a very serious offence.

Share the following dialogue with the class:

'Look... everyone does it.'

'No... I don't want to.'

'That's not normal, you're not normal!'

'I just don't want to! I don't like it!'

'I'll tell all our friends there is something wrong with you!'

'Why would you do that?'

'You want everyone round here to think you're weird?'

'Please don't get angry.'

'If I am it's your fault that I am!'

'Alright! I will!'

(Continued)

(Continued)

'So, you are saying yes then?'

'Yes, yes, alright ...I will...'

In pairs or groups ask the young people to imagine they have overheard this conversation and explore these questions:

- What do you think the two people are feeling?
- Would you describe this as a healthy relationship? Why? Why not?
- What would you be feeling when you hear this conversation?
- If the person under pressure to say 'yes' asked for your advice, what would you say?
- If you thought a friend of yours or someone you cared about was experiencing something like this, what would you say or do?

If using this to explore unwanted sexual advances, ask:

- Does it matter what age these people are?
- If the person under pressure to say 'yes' needed to get help from someone now or later (perhaps the police), does it matter that they said 'yes'?

End the session by reinforcing that 'no means no' but sometimes people may be too frightened to say anything, so the lack of a 'no' also means 'no', as might a change in body language (e.g. 'freezing', becoming very quiet, looking worried or scared). This could be a good opportunity to work with a local police officer to reinforce that a 'yes' given while under any form of duress or whilst not having the capacity or freedom to consent is not consent. This is an abuse of power. Depending on what happens next, a serious crime (sexual assault or rape) may be committed. It is not the fault of the victim of this crime in anyway whatsoever, and they will be taken seriously regardless of saying 'yes'.

The PSHE Association has produced comprehensive guidance including detailed lesson plans to support the teaching of consent in secondary schools (see PSHE, 2015a).

The government's discussion guide (Home Office, 2015) also contains valuable material on teaching about consent.

Pornography

There is concern about young people's increasing access and exposure to pornography and the impact this may have on their understanding of healthy relationships. A mature adult may be able to separate the fantasy of pornography from the 'real world', however, a young person with limited experience may view pornography as a genuine reflection of a normal or healthy relationship. A survey by the NSPCC (2015) found that:

- 1 in 5 children aged 12–13 think that watching porn is normal behaviour
- nearly 1 in 10 children aged 12–13 are worried they might be addicted to porn
- around 1 in 5 of those surveyed said they'd seen pornographic images that had shocked or upset them
- 12 per cent admitted to making or being part of a sexually explicit video.

The guidance document produced by Brook et al. (2014), referred to throughout this chapter, gives a clear and comprehensive overview of how best to approach teaching about the effects of pornography. We have therefore chosen to quote it at length without further expansion:

> It is helpful to address the issues surrounding pornography and there is widespread support from parents who recognise the need for this. Teaching should emphasise that pornography is not the best way to learn about sex because it does not reflect real life, and can therefore be worrying, confusing and frightening for young people. Pupils must also learn that some pornography – child abuse images, for example – is illegal for any age.

> At secondary level, discussion about pornography can be included in lessons that focus on negotiation and assertiveness skills, the importance of communication in relationships and analysing the stereotyping in some media images. Teaching can focus on the role of peer influence in young people's lives, the importance of not pressuring or coercing a partner to look at pornography or imitate behaviours in it and the skills required to resist unwanted pressure.

> …SRE should enable all young people to understand pornography's influence on gender expectations of sex. It should build on earlier learning about relationships, body image, consent and gender, which begins in primary school

with discussions about the importance of loving and respectful relationships. Pupils should understand that pornography shows a distorted image of sex and relationships, including 'perfect' bodies and exaggerated sexual prowess. SRE provides opportunities to discuss body image and understand how pornographic pictures and videos are routinely edited and 'photoshopped'. Pornographic images must never be shown to pupils, and there is no need for teachers to look at pornography to plan their teaching.

Pornography can depict a lack of communication about choices, sexual consent and contraception, and often shows violent and oppressive behaviours towards women, which can be frightening and confusing, and make young people feel pressured to behave in particular ways.

Sexting

'Sexting' is a term for the sending of sexually explicit images or text; young people will also use terms such as 'nudes', 'selfies' or 'fan pics', but terminology can change quickly.

It is important that young people understand the possible immediate and long-term and even permanent consequences of sharing such data, especially if recipients share them with others. Work on sexting fits naturally into contexts such as:

- **Personal privacy**: Understanding the need and being able to control how much of your life you want to share and with whom; being able to make clear these personal boundaries and having the skills to establish and maintain them.
- **Personal safety**: Understanding that sharing personal data and images can be risky; being able to assess accurately those risks and having the skills to manage them.
- **Relationships**: Being able to negotiate within relationships; having the language and skills required to seek, give and not give consent in relation to sending or requesting images and data; understanding the responsibility to protect other people's data and images even if a relationship has ended.
- **Abuse**: Recognising that sharing images of or data concerning other people without their consent could constitute abuse and could be an offense. (The passing of sexually explicit images of under 18 year olds is a serious criminal offence.)

Sexting is a topic that lends itself to being team taught with colleagues in computing as part of work on online safety. As the world becomes ever more connected, the importance of this work will only increase.

Chapter overview

This chapter has provided a broad overview of the nature and scope of RSE, explored many of the key issues and has illustrated some 'ways in' to this vital learning. It has considered the important foundation offered by primary schools, the importance of working within school policy and the constructive use of visitors to the classroom. It has also considered the critical concept of consent, the contribution RSE makes to safeguarding and the importance of being sensitive to young people who may indicate they are at risk.

Further reading

Boddington, N., King A. and McWhirter, J. (2014) Understanding Personal, Social, Health and Economic Education in the Primary School (Ch. 9). London: Sage.
This will provide an understanding of the nature of RSE in primary schools and how this work lays the foundation for RSE in the secondary school.

Brook, PSHE Association and Sex Education Forum (2014) 'Sex and relationships education for the 21st Century'. Available at: www.sex educationforum.org.uk/media/17706/sreadvice.pdf (accessed 19.1.16).
This provides an overview of RSE and builds on and updates earlier the guidance to schools provided by the DfEE in July 2000.

PSHE Association (2015) 'Teaching about consent in PSHE education in Key Stages 3 and 4'. Available at www.pshe-association.org.uk/ curriculum-and-resources/resources/guidance-teaching-about-consent-pshe-education-key (accessed 14.4.16).
This is a comprehensive guide including lesson plans to support schools teaching about the key concept of consent with an emphasis on consent in sexual relationships.

Sex Education Forum (2016) Sex Education Supplement, the SEF's termly e-magazine. Available at www.sexeducationforum.org.uk/ resources/sex-educational-supplement.aspx (accessed 23.3.16).
These e-magazines help to keep teachers up to date with developments in RSE.

References

Brook, PSHE Association and Sex Education Forum (2014) 'Sex and relationships education (SRE) for the 21st Century'. Available at www.pshe-association.org.uk/uploads/media/17/7910.pdf (accessed 19.8.15).

Department for Education and Employment (DfEE) (2000) 'Sex and relationships education guidance'. Available at http://webarchive.nationalarchives.gov.uk/20130401151715/https://www.education.gov.uk/publications/eordering-download/dfes-0116-2000%20sre.pdf (accessed 23.3.16).

Durex, NAHT, NCPTA, NGA (2010) 'Sex and relationship education: views from teachers, parents and governors key findings'. Available from www.mumsnet.com/campaigns/mumsnet-sex-education-survey (accessed 20.8.15).

Home Office (2015) 'This is abuse'. Available at www.gov.uk/government/uploads/system/uploads/attachment_data/file/443659/Discussion_Guide_-_This_is_Abuse_update_July15_v2_Final.pdf (accessed 20.8.15).

Kirby, D. (2007) *Emerging Answers: Research Findings on Programs to Reduce Teen Pregnancy and Sexually Transmitted Diseases*. Washington, DC: National Campaign to Prevent Teen and Unplanned Pregnancy.

NSPCC (2015) 'On-line porn: evidence of its impact on young people'. Available at www.nspcc.org.uk/fighting-for-childhood/news-opinion/online-porn-evidence-impact-young-people/ (accessed 16.1.16).

PSHE Association (2015a) 'Teaching about consent at key stages 3 and 4'. Available at www.pshe-association.org.uk/curriculum-and-resources/resources/guidance-teaching-about-consent-pshe-education-key (accessed on 26.4.2016).

PSHE Association (2015b) 'Preparing to teach about mental health and emotional wellbeing'. Available at https://pshe-association.org.uk/resources_search_details.aspx?ResourceId=570&Keyword=&SubjectID=0&LevelID=0&ResourceTypeID=3&SuggestedUseID=0 (accessed 24.1.16).

Ofsted (2013) 'Not yet good enough: personal, social, health and economic education in schools'. Available at www.gov.uk/government/publications/not-yet-good-enough-personal-social-health-and-economic-education (accessed 19.8.15).

Sex Education Forum (2004) 'Faith values and sex education'. London: National Children's Bureau. Available at www.ncb.org.uk/media/581516/faith02_sef_2005.pdf (accessed 19.8.15).

Sex Education Forum (2011) 'Parents and SRE: a sex education forum evidence briefing'. London: National Children's Bureau. Available at www.ncb.org.uk/media/333401/parents___sre.pdf (accessed 20.8.15).

Tanton, C., Jones, K.G., Macdowall, W., Clifton, S., Mitchell, K.R., Datta, J., Lewis, R., Field, N., Sonnenberg, P., Stevens, A., Wellings, K., Johnson, A.M. and Mercer, C.H. (2015) 'Patterns and trends in sources of information about sex among young people in Britain: evidence from three national surveys of sexual attitudes and lifestyles', *BMJ Open*, 5(3).

Walsh, K., Zui, K., Woolfenden, S. and Shlonsky, A. (2015) *School-based Education Programmes for the Prevention of Child Sexual Abuse*. New York: Wiley Online Library, Cochrane Library.

11

Economic Wellbeing and PSHE Education

Aim

To provide an introduction to teaching economic wellbeing as an integral part of a PSHE education programme.

Learning objectives

Through reading and reflecting on the content of this chapter you will begin to:

- understand the place of economic wellbeing in PSHE education
- understand some routes into this area of the curriculum.

Before we start

What sorts of issues come into your head when you think about 'economic wellbeing'?

Introduction

PSHE education has had a lot of different names during its evolution and the most recent was introduced in the National Curriculum in 2008 with the addition of economic wellbeing and financial capability as one of the two programmes of study, the other being personal wellbeing. Personal, social and health education (PSHE) evolved to become personal, social, health and economic education (PSHE education). This was intended to complement work undertaken as part of mathematics in the National Curriculum.

More recently, in 2013, the personal finance education element of 'economic wellbeing and financial capability' was included in the statutory citizenship programme of study within the National Curriculum and within the mathematics programme of study, therefore becoming statutory for local authority secondary schools. At that time both the non-statutory National Curriculum programmes of study for PSHE education (including the programme of study for 'economic wellbeing and financial capability') were archived, although the subject continued to be called PSHE education, retaining the 'economic' element, and the current national programme of study produced by the PSHE Association, which is widely used across the country and signposted by the current Department for Education, contains elements of economic wellbeing and careers education within its core themes.

The revised programme of study for citizenship states that young people in Key Stage 3 should learn about:

- the functions and uses of money, the importance and practice of budgeting, and managing risk.

Students in key stage 4 should learn about:

- income and expenditure, credit and debt, insurance, savings and pensions, financial products and services, and how public money is raised and spent.

This complements learning outcomes in mathematics where in Key Stage 3 young people should:

- develop their use of formal mathematical knowledge to interpret and solve problems in financial mathematics
- use standard units of money including decimal qualities
- solve problems involving percentage change, including percentage increase, decrease and original value problems and simple interest in financial mathematics
- use compound units such as unit pricing to solve problems.

And young people in Key Stage 4 should:

- develop their use of formal mathematical knowledge to interpret and solve problems, including in financial contexts.

At first sight this looks very thorough, so perhaps it's enough to 'leave finance to citizenship and maths'? Let's look a little deeper.

Consider

The Personal Finance Education Group (pfeg – part of Young Enterprise) is one of the leading organisations providing support for this area of the curriculum, sets out four core themes for personal finance education:

1. How to manage money.
2. Becoming a critical consumer.
3. Managing risks and emotions associated with money.
4. Understanding the important role money plays in our lives.

Do you feel the National Curriculum requirements for citizenship and mathematics would adequately cover these? What might be missing?

The relationship between personal wellbeing and economic wellbeing

The division between our personal and social wellbeing and our economic wellbeing is artificial; each can profoundly affect the other. For example, an unintended pregnancy, a serious accident, the inability to repay debt or developing drug dependence are all likely to have significant impacts on both. While many products are marketed on the basis of possible benefits to our personal wellbeing (e.g. mobile phones – and especially the benefits of their constant upgrading), others target our social wellbeing (e.g. fashion labels or fragrance).

Our sense of personal identity, especially a poor sense of self-worth, may limit our future career aspirations regardless of our success in gaining academic qualifications. Equally our determination to achieve may help us overcome significant financial obstacles. Financial education, careers education, work related learning and enterprise education all support one another and contribute to our personal, social and economic wellbeing but they are not the same thing. For example, an outstanding careers education programme may have little impact on a young person's immediate financial capability.

Let's consider some terms

Economic wellbeing is a huge concept. It collects all the factors that together improve our overall wellbeing. It may include the income from our employment but this may not be simply the size of that income. It may also include the security of our employment and hence our confidence in that income continuing. It may include the extent to which we have sufficient savings to give us the confidence that we can cope with any sudden change to our circumstance or our willingness to take a risk. It may include the extent to which we feel confident that we can take out or continue to service our debts. It may include the extent to which worries over someone else's economic situation (e.g. a parent or partner) affects our wellbeing.

Financial capability covers all the skills we need to manage our finances, for example our ability to budget by balancing our income with our expenditure. Financial capability allows us to be informed consumers of financial products and services, such as which bank account offers the best security and return on our investment, how should we invest for retirement, are we paying the right amount of tax or should we take out some form of insurance?

It would include concepts like 'unit price', an essential piece of information if you are comparing price of product in a supermarket, and 'true cost', an essential consideration if you are taking out a loan or buying product that has additional running costs. (For example, recognising a cheap computer printer may have expensive replacement ink cartridges, or having the skills to navigate the maze of mobile phone tariffs to find one that offers the best value for money and one that is affordable.)

Careers education is not simply making young people aware of the careers options available to them but also helping them match their interests, abilities and personalities to possible academic and career pathways. It includes developing an understanding that a person's career is not only about the job they do but that it is their pathway through life, education and work and it focuses on developing the transferable skills and attributes that employers value. Increasingly this is provided through a combination of one-to-one careers guidance underpinned by work in PSHE education. This underpinning work might include developing the more generic skills and attributes of managing change, a sense of personal identity and resilience as the nature of work continues to evolve, the transferable skills referred to above, such as communication, negotiation, team working and critical thinking, as well as the skills specific to securing a chosen career or educational pathway such as interview and presentation skills. The more focused work, often undertaken one to one, might involve helping to map out an academic strategy for entering a specific career. Since 2011 it has been schools' responsibility to provide independent and impartial careers guidance for pupils from Year 8 to Year 13; however, there is no statutory requirement to provide wider careers education beyond that contained within 'Careers guidance and inspiration in schools: statutory guidance for governing bodies, school leaders and school staff' (DfE, 2015a) which states:

> [Schools should]provide access to a range of activities that inspire young people, including employer talks, careers fairs, motivational speakers, colleges and university visits, coaches and mentors.

> Schools should create a learning environment which allows and encourages pupils to tackle real life challenges which require them to manage risk and to develop their decision making, team building and problem solving skills.

Employability

Before we look at 'work related learning' it is important to consider something a little deeper. We might think of 'work related learning' as being learning *about* the world of work, but this is slightly different from the broader contribution PSHE education makes to 'employability' or the broader skills necessary for entering the world of work. The importance of the skills and attributes associated with employability are widely recognised by those in education and business, as it has the potential of PSHE education to develop them:

> PSHE education provides an opportunity to provide or enhance skills such as perseverance, conflict resolution, emotional intelligence, self-management, self-respect, team work, locus of control, time and stress management. (DfE, 2015a)

> From an individual's perspective, our latest research shows that having a developed set of soft skills can increase an individual's lifetime earnings by up to 15%, once again demonstrating the vital nature of acquiring, nurturing and recognising these skills. (Forte, 2015)

> Business is clear that developing the right attitudes and attributes in people – such as resilience, respect, enthusiasm and creativity – is just as important as academic or technical skills. (Carberry, 2015)

The development of the transferable skills, sometimes referred to as 'soft skills', both explicitly and through the pedagogy of the subject lies at the core of the relationship between PSHE education and future employability.

Work related learning (often referred to as WRL) is no longer a statutory part of the curriculum, however, the term continues to be used in some schools and is useful when thinking about PSHE education's role in building employability. It combines learning about the world of work, the place and function of commerce and industry in a global economy and more specific concepts such as 'customer service', 'health and safety', unions and the rights of an employee. This area of the curriculum can also link to others such as environmental awareness and citizenship. For example, understanding dilemmas such as purchasing cheap clothing may involve poor working conditions for employees in developing countries, whilst boycotting such products may leave these people without any work at all. It may also cover issues such as 'air miles', the environmental impact of transportation and understanding concepts such as 'fair trade'.

Work related learning might involve undertaking 'work experience', which is often confused with 'career tasting'. Career tasting provides a short-term placement for a pupil in a career in which they have expressed an interest. This is very rare and usually offered to a very small number of older pupils and often during vacation periods. Work experience is just that, offering an experience of being in a working environment, experiencing its different relationships, responsibilities and routines. At the time of writing a decreasing number of schools are offering work experience placements for all of their pupils as part of the curriculum.

You may encounter WISE, the British campaign to promote women in science, technology and engineering (see www.wisecampaign.org.uk, accessed 2.12.15). Careers in both science and engineering attract a disproportionate amount of males, and WISE events challenge stereotypes around these areas of employment and provide positive female role models drawn from these employment sectors. WISE events have far more impact if they are set within a wider PSHE education programme than if they are isolated events.

Careers education or work related learning could be the context for learning the skills of crafting applications, a curriculum vitae and preparing for interviews. Many schools provide opportunities for young people to role play mock interviews, frequently with external representatives from local commerce or industry. These contexts may also cover issues such as ensuring that young people's online presence such as email addresses and social media profiles will maximise rather than hinder their chances of being a serious contender for a job or place in further or higher education.

Enterprise education is providing young people with the skills of creating their own products and business, sometimes referred to as 'entrepreneurship'. These activities are often referred to as 'mini-enterprise projects' and supported by local commerce and industry. Once again these are far more effective if they are underpinned by a broader curriculum that encourages creativity, problem solving and risk management.

PSHE education can be the setting for all of this work or contribute to it as part of a wider cross-curricular approach.

The relationship between personal finance education and economic wellbeing within PSHE education

As stated earlier in this chapter, personal finance education now officially sits within the citizenship and mathematics programmes of study; however, in practice it is almost impossible to separate this out from the more personal aspects of economic wellbeing that remain the domain of PSHE education. We have therefore intentionally included a consideration of how personal finance education can be incorporated within the economic wellbeing elements of PSHE education as many schools will still teach it within PSHE education and because to us, this makes sense!

How is money changing?

The physical nature of money has changed dramatically since 1966 when the first bank-based credit cards were introduced. Since then money has gradually become increasingly 'abstract'.

We have moved from paying predominantly with physical money, through cheques, credit and debit cards. With the arrival of touchless technology, many of us increasingly use our smartphones or wearable technology such as 'smart watches' when paying (for now) for low cost items. It's possible to make regular payments for services and products online and again 'money' (or the money's value) is exchanged electronically. It is easy to see a near future where physical 'cash' has been replaced by an entirely electronic currency, for example 'bitcoins'.

This shift in the nature of money and spending brings with it new risks. Here is one of the places where personal finance education, PSHE education and computing link up. As money increasingly shifts to an electronic form, young people need to understand new rules and habits for keeping their money safe from fraud and develop additional strategies for managing financial risk in a digital world.

Consider

Does it feel different to pay for something electronically, perhaps with a credit or debit card, online or using your phone rather than handing over physical money?

Piaget and Inhelder (1973) argue that young people gradually move from 'concrete operations' to 'abstract thinking'. Some people struggle with this development, staying largely in 'concrete operations'. Financial transactions are rapidly moving from a 'concrete operation', the physical exchange of money, to an 'abstract operation', where the transaction is 'virtual'.

How might this create problems for some people? Does this create additional or different problems for young people learning to manage their own economic wellbeing when they are growing up as 'digital natives'?

At the same time as technology has made the process of spending increasingly simple, companies are becoming increasingly sophisticated in their marketing strategies. Turn on the television and the chances are that you will see advertising for quick loans, products that you can buy now and pay for later or products for which you can spread the payments over a period. But have you also noticed the interest payments? At the time of writing one company is offering computer games consoles through an instalment plan, with no credit checks, that will actually cost the purchaser double the cash price. Does this mean people with the least money will ultimately pay the most?

Then there is the rise in online gambling, either passively in the form of lotteries or more actively through online betting agencies or online gaming such as casinos or bingo. The chances of winning the UK national lottery currently stand at 14 million to one, and even some of the smaller lotteries are still close to a million to one. (To put this in perspective, the chances of being struck by lightning in the UK are 300,000 to one.) Although it is not possible to go into detail here, gambling education is often covered as part of a comprehensive PSHE education programme.

But do the odds of winning at least something in a lottery really feel this small? The advertising industry has known for a long time that many of our purchases are not based on reason but on emotion. Witness how many advertisements provide virtually no factual information, instead selling their products to the emotions which the lifestyle associated with their product may inspire. In the case of lotteries, advertising would make it seem that all you need do is play. It could be you, but it is a much (much) safer bet that it won't be.

Pressures to spend may come at us in different ways: the direct pressure created by the increasingly sophisticated persuasion techniques and language used by sales staff; the indirect pressure of advertising; and the more subtle pressures we may place on ourselves to buy products and brands that help us feel we are more likely to 'fit in' with our peers.

Advertising has changed over the last few years. From the blanket advertising of posters, radio and television, advertising has evolved to become more tailored and personal. By gathering and using data that most of us freely provide through our online behaviour and technologies such as loyalty cards, companies provide adverts and offers that are increasingly bespoke being sent and seen only by you and matched to your interests and previous purchasing history.

Understanding how these technologies are employed and how they influence us are part of economic wellbeing education.

The relationship between mathematics and PSHE education

Let's start to tease apart the relationship between the 'hard learning of finance', the mathematics and what we might call the 'softer learning' explored through PSHE education.

Consider

Imagine you have been given £1,000 and been offered three investment opportunities. Over a period of a year:

- the first will provide a 25 per cent profit
- the second will provide a 15 per cent profit
- the third will provide 6 per cent profit.

Which will you pick? Mathematically it is obvious, but what if you now know

(Continued)

> *(Continued)*
>
> - the first will invest your money in the armaments industry
> - the second will invest your money in a major clothing manufacturer which has a poor reputation for the treatment of its workforce and whose factories are all in the less economically developed countries
> - the third will invest your money in a company building affordable housing.
>
> So which would you pick?
>   Or perhaps you will just spend the money?

In mathematics young people will learn to calculate interest and especially compound interest, both of which are vital skills. However, it is unlikely that mathematics teachers will have the curriculum time to consider the broader question of values. For example, it is not a simple matter to decide not to invest in clothing manufacturers in developing countries. What if those jobs did not exist at all?

Let's use the concept of 'debt' to look a bit further.

Consider

- Can there be 'good debt'? Can you think of some examples?
- Can there be 'bad debt'? Can you think of some examples?

Would you consider taking out a student loan to be a good debt? Or taking out a loan to purchase transportation to a place of employment? How about taking out a mortgage to buy property? What makes a debt a 'good debt'? Would you consider taking out a loan to pay for a holiday a good debt?

There is no simple answer to these questions. It isn't simply a question of 'good' or 'bad', and our guess is that you found yourself thinking 'it all depends'. The important issue is that we stop and think and have some criteria for making a judgement. Spontaneously agreeing to a loan can be a very bad idea.

If we do decide to take out a loan we first need the skills to calculate if we can afford to repay it. This may mean giving up other things in our lives, so we have to decide if this is acceptable. Is what we gain worth what we might lose?

If a debt requires payment over a period of time, we need to consider if we will have the financial stability to maintain the payments and what will happen if we can't. Is this risk acceptable?

If we decide that it is, we then need to consider the different sources of finance available to us. Whilst interest rates may be one determinant, another is the consequence of not paying on time. With a bank there is likely to be room to negotiate but what about a 'loan shark'?

Failing to manage debt is a serious problem for many individuals and families and losing control of debt can be a terrifying experience. This can happen very easily with the very high interest payments offered especially by short-term (or 'payday') loans that are intended to provide instant money for short periods.

Because debt can be so problematic for some families, teaching about debt should be considered a 'sensitive issue'. It is likely that some of your young people will have first-hand experience of the impact of debt. It is vital therefore to be sensitive in how we explore this issue. It is easy to accidently appear judgemental of those who lose control of their finances and leave a young person vulnerable or upset.

Activity

Use the internet to find a company offering short-term loans (sometimes called 'pay-day loans'). Locate their 'APR', the annual percentage rate of charge: the interest rate that will determine how much the loan will cost to repay.

Now find an interest rate calculator – there are lots available online. Imagine someone has taken out a loan for £200 from such a company to pay for an emergency. Imagine for some reason, perhaps loss of employment or an accident, they are unable to pay it back.

Find out how much they would owe in 1 year, 2 years and 3 years.

Now compare this to getting the same loan from a bank.

At the time of writing it would not be unexpected to see an APR of 1,500 per cent from a short-term loan agency compared to an APR

(Continued)

(Continued)

of 4.2 per cent from a bank. Of course, the difference is that it will be far easier to meet the requirements of a short-term loan agency. Many will willingly offer loans to people with a poor credit history or indeed young adults with no credit history.

This raises a number of possible questions:

- Is it right that people who may be at the greatest risk of defaulting on a loan can find it easy to get a loan, provided they can accept the risk of getting even deeper into debt?
- Is it right that a company offering a loan to people with a high risk of default should protect their money by offering a high interest rate to offset any money they cannot get back?
- Should these companies be made illegal?
- Should we legislate to prevent adults from making their own choices about their use of loans?

What do you think?

All of the exercises above are examples of activities that could be part of the economic wellbeing elements of a PSHE education programme. They combine raising young people's awareness and deepening their understanding, with a consideration of both the practical and ethical complexities. Financial scenarios also provide the ideal context through which to focus on and rehearse risk assessment and management skills in PSHE education lessons. It is unlikely that mathematics alone would cover this range of learning.

Activity

Look at the scenarios below (adapted from Boddington and King, 2009). How might you use them to explore different aspects of economic wellbeing and especially financial capability?

Scenario 1

'I want it, I want it, I want it, I want it,' Emma said, looking through the shop window.

'So, I'm guessing you want it, then,' Parama replied.

'I want it, I want it, I really, really, really, REALLY want it!' Emma was almost jumping up and down. She could be a bit embarrassing, especially in front of all the other shoppers on a Saturday morning. Parama looked away and pretended they weren't together.

'Only snag is: you ... can't ... afford ... it ... because ... you spent all your money already!' Parama said slowly and with some exasperation.

Parama walked around town just looking at what was available, then made up her mind before going back to the things she really liked. If there were more choices than she could afford, she would pick just one. Actually, she hated doing that and always worried she had picked the wrong thing, but usually it worked out OK. She tended to buy one good item.

Emma was so different. She would buy the first thing she saw, end up with loads of things then see the 'one thing she really wanted' when all her money had gone.

'I have GOT to have it! Parama, will you lend me some money?' Emma said, looking nervous and biting her bottom lip. 'I'll pay you back, I will, honest!'

Scenario 2

'Of course you can afford it, you have all your birthday money left!' Josh said to Avnish.

'Well, yes I do have enough money ...' Avnish replied.

'So get it, then!' Josh said.

'But I have to put some money away for the holiday, I owe Hannah some for a DVD and I want to get Mum a birthday present, so no, I don't think I can afford it,' Avnish said sadly.

Scenario 3

'Look, it says "Buy now, pay later"!' Emma said. She and Parama were being dragged round the furniture shop with Parama's mum and dad.

'Yes,' agreed Parama's mum Riya, 'but you have to be very careful. Look at the interest rate. You can buy it now, for the price on the

(Continued)

(Continued)

label, or you can have it now and pay for it monthly over two years. Notice that they don't tell you the monthly repayments or the final cost. Let's check it out.'

The sales assistant came over and did a quiet calculation and gave Riya the figure and walked away.

'Look,' Riya said, 'you have to pay this much back each month,' showing Parama and Emma the figure.

'Cool,' Emma said, 'that's not much.'

'But wait,' Riya said, 'now multiply that by 24 to get the total amount.'

Emma concentrated hard.

Parama told her the answer.

'Wait a minute,' Riya said. 'That's much more expensive!'

'Exactly. If you take out a loan it almost always is!'

'But we're in a furniture shop, not a bank!' Emma said.

'Ah, but that's where you are still probably borrowing from,' Riya replied. 'If you take out credit on this sofa, the shop will get its money from a bank or a credit company and then we owe the money to them. Basically you have taken out a loan! Now, what we have to do is ask ourselves some questions: Do we really want it? Do we want to pay the full price now? Do we want to pay less a month over two years but end up paying more in total?'

'I think there's another question,' Parama said. 'In two years' time will we still want to be paying for a two-year-old piece of furniture?'

'Who knows what the future will bring?' Riya said. 'That's what you have to risk with a loan, that everything will still be OK and that you can afford to keep paying all the monthly repayments.'

'I think it's all far too complicated!' Emma sighed. 'I think I would just buy it and enjoy it!'

'With that way of thinking, sales people will love you. I think you're going to make a lot of people you don't know very rich one day,' Riya sighed.

Scenarios or case studies like these can pin down moments when someone needs to make a choice. Questions that can help explore the financial implications of any financial issue (including those above) might include:

- When we ask ourselves 'can I afford this?', what do we mean?
- Does 'afford' simply mean 'I can pay for it'?
- How are these people feeling?
- Is it OK to ask a friend if you can borrow money?
- If a friend asks you for a loan is it OK to refuse?
- What thoughts or feelings might be driving them forward? What thoughts or feelings might be holding them back?
- Is anyone under pressure?
- What might be the financial cost or gain? Now? In the future?
- Is it worth the financial cost?
- Will the cost be a 'one off' or will someone need to keep paying?
- Who will pay? Is this fair?
- If there is a financial cost might someone need to go without something? Now? In the future? Is this OK? Is this fair?
- Where might the money come from? How will people get it?
- Will they need to earn it? Borrow it? Sell something to pay for it?
- If money has to be borrowed will there be interest to repay? How much and for how long? What will be the 'true cost' of paying back the loan?
- What are the consequences if the loan can't be repaid to the lender?
- Could this benefit someone's long-term financial wellbeing?
- Imagine you could speak confidentially to different characters – imagine they asked you for your advice – what would you say?
- Imagine they asked you why you think they should follow your advice – how would you convince them?

Activity

Using some of the ideas in this chapter if you wish, and the guidance on planning PSHE education lessons in Chapter 5, draft a lesson for a Year 10 class that has the following learning objectives and intended learning outcomes.

Learning objectives: We are learning about credit ratings and debt.

(Continued)

(Continued)

Learning outcomes: We will be able to:

- identify and discuss why someone might get into debt
- identify and analyse the range of risks faced by someone who gets into debt
- explain the term 'credit rating' and evaluate how a person's credit rating can affect their life.

Chapter overview

In this chapter we have considered the relationship between economic and personal wellbeing, the elements of a PSHE education programme that can be said to constitute education for 'economic wellbeing' and the changing status of personal finance education. We have discussed the relationship between the different curriculum areas that contribute to a young person's economic education and have suggested some scenarios that could be used in the PSHE education classroom as a means to explore different aspects of personal finance education.

Further reading

Department for Education (2015) 'Careers guidance and inspiration in schools. Statutory guidance for governing bodies, school leaders and school staff'. Available at www.gov.uk/government/uploads/system/uploads/attachment_data/file/440795/Careers_Guidance_Schools_Guidance.pdf (accessed 29.3.16).
This document outlines the responsibilities placed on schools to provide careers guidance for their pupils.

Personal Finance Education Group (2015) 'A practical guide to financial education within PSHE education'. Available from www.pfeg.org/resources (accessed 9.12.15).

This resource will help you understand the connections between PSHE education and financial education.

Personal Finance Education Group (2015) 'A practical guide to financial education within careers education'. Available from www.pfeg.org/resources (accessed 9.12.15).
This resource will help you understand the connections between careers education and financial education.

References

Boddington, N. and King A. (2009) *Real Health for Real Lives 13–14*. Cheltenham: Nelson Thornes.

Carberry, N. (2015) Campaign puts £88bn economic value on 'soft skills', the CBI's director for employment and skills reported by the BBC. Available at www.bbc.co.uk/news/education-30802474 (accessed 14.4.16).

Department for Education (2015a) 'Careers guidance and inspiration in schools: statutory guidance for governing bodies, school leaders and school staff'. Available at www.gov.uk/government/uploads/system/uploads/attachment_data/file/440795/Careers_Guidance_Schools_Guidance.pdf (accessed 29.3.16).

Department for Education (2015b) 'PSHE education: a review of impact and effective practice. Available at www.gov.uk/government/uploads/system/uploads/attachment_data/file/412291/Personal_Social_Health_and_Economic__PSHE__Education_12_3.pdf (accessed 29.3.16).

Forte, R. (2015) 'Backing soft skills: a plan for recognising, developing and measuring soft skills at every stage of education and work'. Findings and recommendations from a public consultation launched by McDonald's UK.

Piaget, J. and Inhelder, B. (1973) *Memory and Intelligence*. London: Routledge and Kegan Paul.

Part Three

In this part we look at the relationship between PSHE education as a subject and the pastoral care offered by the school. We also consider how, like any other subject, PSHE education is taught within the school's policy framework, which shapes and directs learning. We end this part by offering practical guidance and key questions you should ask when selecting from the wide range of teaching resources that are available for PSHE education.

12

PSHE Education and School Policy Matters

Aim

By the end of this chapter you will have an understanding of the concept of policy as it relates to PSHE education.

Learning objectives

Through reading and reflecting on the content of this chapter you will begin to:

- understand the way policies shape learning within PSHE education
- understand how teaching in PSHE education can generate data to allow 'student voice' to inform the construction or review of school policy.

Before we start

Consider

- What do you understand by the term 'school policy'?
- When were you last asked to look at a school policy before thinking about teaching?
- How do you think a school policy can support the teaching of PSHE education?

Introduction

There are two 'directions' that we need to consider when thinking about PSHE education and policy; we might think of them as 'upwards' and 'downwards':

- **Upwards**: The national policies that will impact on and help shape practice.
- **Downwards**: The internal school policies that define how an individual school responds to these national policies, the school's own aims and objectives and the needs of its students.

PSHE education is shaped and supported by a number of school policies including the school behaviour policy, sex education policy (or as we refer to it, RSE), drug policy, equality policy and child protection policy. This chapter reflects on how an understanding of the way policies are developed and implemented by schools can contribute to the effectiveness of PSHE education.

This chapter will consider a school's PSHE education policy and how it fits into a school's wider policy framework. The best policies are produced collaboratively by the people who will be affected by them and should be consulted on widely. This consultation should include students and parents/carers where appropriate. The reality is that the process of drafting a policy can be more powerful than the final product. The discussions, debates and analysis of both school and local data used to formulate the policy can both inform and bring clarity to all those involved in its construction. The wider the collaboration, the greater the sense of ownership and chance the policy has of being effective.

What is a policy?

A policy is primarily a tool to help inform decision making. If you need to show someone how an aspect of the school works, if you need to make a decision about something concerning a student or perhaps about the appropriateness of a lesson or resource, or pretty much any aspect of school life, there will be a policy to which you can refer. Some are statutory and will be found in all schools, such as the child protection policy. Others are not statutory, so you may not find them in all schools and this group includes the PSHE education policy. We believe there are compelling reasons for schools to have a policy for PSHE education, however, not just for relationships and sex education (all maintained schools are required to have a 'sex education' policy).

Consider

As you read through this chapter, consider the advantages for you as a teacher of having a school PSHE education policy and the potential challenges of teaching in a school that does not have one.

A policy is only useful if it leads to an outcome that is in the best interests of those for whom it is intended, whether that be students or staff. A school may have a drug policy which staff are expected to follow with respect to students and there may be a parallel policy with respect to staff, perhaps as part of the human resources policy. Policy is a powerful tool to guide practice but it should still be subject to appropriate review and, if necessary, revision. Most schools review their policies on a two-year cycle.

A school policy serves two main purposes:

- To people unfamiliar with the school, it publicly defines 'what we believe and how we do things here'.
- For people working in the school, it offers a clear framework for teaching, protocols to follow should an incident occur or a student indicate that they need support, and a 'tool' that helps to shape decision making.

Consider

- Ask to see a school's PSHE education policy. How is it constructed?
- Does it make reference to the school's overall aims or mission?
- How useful is it in helping to guide teachers' practice in this school?
- Does it offer any form of protection, perhaps with regard to teaching more sensitive issues?

The policy framework

The policy framework within which the PSHE education policy will reside begins with the school's overall mission statement or what the school considers to be its overall purpose. Mission statements can sometimes feel like 'advertising slogans', but if they are produced through a genuine consultation and open dialogue they can be the product of a valuable process that focuses the school community towards a common purpose.

Many schools follow this by constructing more detailed overarching aims and objectives that start to 'ground' the mission statement into the outcomes the school intends for its students.

This will be influenced by the statutory duties placed on schools such as 'to provide a balanced and broadly based curriculum and to promote student wellbeing' and any relevant National Curriculum requirements.

Individual school policies such as the PSHE education policy come next, and it needs to be part of a suite of policies that include child protection (or safeguarding), equality, relationships (including anti-bullying and behaviour) and confidentiality. It is important that specific policies reflect the values set out in the school's stated aims, objectives and mission statement.

A policy is not a scheme of work or curriculum and does not have to duplicate it. The scheme of work and PSHE education lesson plans detail how the aims of the policy will be realised for students. In this way, all three form a suite of documents, which underpin PSHE education delivery in schools.

The curriculum elements of the school's approach to drug education and sex and relationships education logically become appendices in many schools to the overall PSHE education policy, but curriculum planning should always have regard to the wider policy elements such as managing drug incidents or involving visitors in the classroom. These do not need to be separate documents, but it is essential that the school's approach to teaching these areas of learning within PSHE education is set out clearly and comprehensively. For 'maintained schools' an SRE policy is a statutory requirement and like many statutory policies its production is the responsibility of the school's governing body, although it can delegate responsibility to a committee of the governing body or the headteacher.

Having said that, there is no need for a PSHE education policy to provide detail of the schemes of work; many schools do provide details of the content of their RSE programme within their sex and relationships policy either as a stand-alone document or detailed appendix. This provides clarity for parents and young people and, once approved by the school's governing body, protection for teachers. For this reason most schools, including academies, free schools and independent schools, have such a policy whether it is a statutory requirement or not.

The interaction between PSHE education and other subjects

It is important that learning in PSHE education is linked to broader school policies and the curriculum in relevant subjects. A commitment to equality, for example, must run through the life of the school rather than being seen as a 'topic' which can be covered in PSHE alone. Similarly, while students may receive factual learning about the biology of reproduction or the effects drugs have on their bodies through the science curriculum, PSHE education is where students have the opportunity to consider what this knowledge and understanding means to them and to develop the skills and strategies they will need to apply this knowledge in their real lives. Other linked subjects include citizenship, religious education and computing.

Meeting legislative requirements through PSHE education

Not only do we have to consider the structure of the school's internal policy framework, there are also national statutory duties with which we need to comply.

As we stated in Chapter 1, under the Education Act 2002/Academies Act 2010 all schools must provide a balanced and broadly based curriculum which:

- promotes the spiritual, moral, cultural, mental and physical development of students at the school and of society
- prepares students at the school for the opportunities, responsibilities
and experiences of later life.

The Education and Inspections Act 2006 placed a duty on governing bodies
'to promote the wellbeing of students at the school'. The duty came into
effect in September 2007. Since that date, an equivalent requirement has
been placed on new academies through their funding agreements.

Schools also have wider responsibilities under the Equality Act 2010 and
should ensure that their school strives to do the best for all students, irre-
spective of 'disability, educational needs, race, nationality, ethnic or national
origin, sex, gender identity, pregnancy, maternity, religion or sexual orientation or whether they are looked after children.'

This means that PSHE education, as reflected in the policy, must be sensitive to the different needs of individual students and may need to evolve
over time as the student population changes. At all times the overarching
principle is to ensure the present and future wellbeing of students and to
meet their learning needs. It is also crucial for lessons to help young people
to realise the nature and consequences of discrimination, teasing, bullying
and aggressive behaviours (including cyber bullying), use of prejudice-
based language and how to respond and ask for help.

It is important to remember that 'equality' means providing learning in
ways that enable all young people equal opportunities to access the learning and meet their diverse needs. In order to do this it is important that we
understand these needs.

But what if I disagree with my school's PSHE education policy?

Consider

Imagine a teacher new to a school has read their school's policy on
either PSHE education or SRE. Imagine there are parts of it that they
disagree with or that conflict with their own values or beliefs. Should
this affect how they teach PSHE education?

This may happen in PSHE education where teachers' own personal or
religious values may conflict with school policy, for example in some
aspects of RSE (see Chapter 9). The simple answer is that as an employee

of the school you have a professional responsibility to follow the school's stated policy in PSHE education and other related policies.

The school has publicly stated that the young people are entitled to this learning and the parents have a right to expect that they receive it. We are all entitled to hold our own personal values and beliefs and this right is one of the outcomes of PSHE education. However, in this instance you are 'a member of staff' with a shared responsibility to promote the values and beliefs enshrined in the school policy. While a teacher may openly state their personal point of view, you should not promote that position to young people to the exclusion of other points of view. This would deny students access to breadth of learning and the balance of argument they need to exercise their right to arrive at their own position. It is important to remember that schools have a statutory requirement to *provide a curriculum which is balanced and broadly based.*[1]

A refusal to teach about same sex relationships and same sex marriage as being equal to heterosexual relationships and marriage would also almost certainly breach the Equality Act and would deny a minority of young people their right to learning essential to their wellbeing as well as undermine a school's work to ensure an inclusive community.

In the real world most schools will want to be supportive of their staff's sincerely held beliefs and may be willing to negotiate a compromise. However, they are under no obligation to do so. This is one of those occasions when it to best to have read your school's policies about any issue you may feel will cause you difficulties long before a problem arises so that a constructive professional dialogue can take place.

There is nothing to stop any teacher from making a professional representation to a working group during a time of policy review and most schools will welcome an informed contribution to such a review. Ultimately schools are not democracies. The senior management and governing body will have the final sign off of policy; they also share accountability.

Using policies as teaching resources

The analysis of a school's policy can offer a useful teaching resource. For example, imagine asking young people to discuss their school's drug education or behaviour policy. Do they agree with the position

---

[1] Section 78 of the 2002 Education Act applies to all maintained schools. Academies are also required to offer a broad and balanced curriculum in accordance with Section 1 of the 2010 Academies Act.

taken by the school? Is there anything they would wish to challenge or something they would wish to add? Such discussion helps to make a policy more transparent for young people and if the lesson coincides with the time the school is reviewing its policy, can offer an opportunity for 'student voice' to contribute to any review.

Activity

Imagine this as a workshop activity, perhaps involving young people working in groups of four. Invite each person to write privately three things they would want included in their school's sex education policy. Now shuffle them so no one knows whose is whose then open them all up. Group them under three headings:

- We can all agree with these.
- We could agree with these if they were slightly reworded.
- We can't all agree with these.

Record what's agreed, discuss, reword and agree where possible and park what is contested for more thought – at least there is a draft start and some options for more structured debate at another stage when people are better informed.

In this way learning about the process of consultation, having the opportunity to consider their own viewpoints on an issue and having the opportunity to feed back to the school leadership team can all be contained in one lesson. In this way PSHE education can transcend simply being a lesson; if the school is receptive, the product of learning in PSHE education can be a genuine part of a more democratic process of school development.

Chapter overview

In this chapter we have explored the nature of school policies and considered the role of the PSHE education policy in shaping PSHE education, providing parameters for all involved, guiding and protecting teachers. We have thought about the potential of policy review to increase student voice, using the policy as a stimulus for engagement with the aspect of school life or the curriculum that the policy covers.

Further reading

PSHE Association (2015) 'Creating a school personal social health and economic (PSHE) education policy'. Available at https://pshe-association.org.uk/uploads/media/27/7460.pdf (accessed 19.1.16).
This document provides comprehensive guidance and a structure to help schools formulate their PSHE education policy.

References

Department for Education (2006) *Education and Inspections Act 2006*. London: The Stationery Office.
Department for Education (2014) *The Equality Act 2010: Departmental Advice for School Leaders, School Staff, Governing Bodies and Local Authorities and Schools*. London: The Stationery Office.

13

Understanding the Relationship Between PSHE Education, Pastoral Care and Therapeutic Interventions

Aim

To review the different roles that PSHE education, pastoral care and therapeutic interventions may play in the personal development of young people in secondary education.

Learning objectives

Through reading and reflecting on the content of this chapter you will begin to:

- know the boundaries of and overlaps between different approaches to personal development for young people of secondary school age
- understand the role of form tutor in recognising the range of needs young people may have with respect to personal development
- understand how schools identify and support therapeutic support for pupils whose personal development is challenged in some way.

Before we start

Most of us who become teachers can recall a teacher from their past who inspired or helped us – a teacher we would like to emulate. That teacher could have been a subject teacher, a form tutor or perhaps even a head teacher. Perhaps you can also remember a teacher you did not find inspiring or understanding – those people can also shape the kind of teacher we become. What would you say to the teachers you recall, now you are becoming a teacher yourself? How did they contribute to your personal development?

Consider

What proportion of *your* day do you spend focusing on the personal development of young people? As a beginning teacher you may be a form tutor and you may contribute to the PSHE education programme. You may be involved in school trips and visits which have a personal development element. How well has your training prepared you for this aspect of your professional life?

Introduction

Children spend the bulk of their education in secondary schools where the care for the whole child including academic achievement, personal development and wellbeing is the responsibility of a large number of different people with different roles and can involve liaison with family members and external agencies.

It's useful at this point to recap what we mean by PSHE education:

> PSHE education is a planned programme of learning through which children and young people acquire the knowledge, understanding and skills they need to manage their lives. As part of a whole school approach, PSHE develops the qualities and attributes pupils need to thrive as individuals, family members and members of society. (PSHE Association, 2015)

Based on this definition, PSHE education clearly supports the personal development of young people but is not the only way in which schools contribute to this important goal.

In Chapter 11 we looked at school policy and how it supports and reinforces specific aspects of the PSHE education curriculum. This chapter explores the similarities and differences between PSHE education, pastoral care and some therapeutic interventions and how they all support the overall development of young people including those who are more vulnerable to poor outcomes.

Boundaries

Some teachers who are new to PSHE education are unclear about the boundaries between PSHE, their pastoral role and what might be seen as a quasi-therapeutic approach to mental and emotional wellbeing. Perhaps one way to sort out any confusion between pastoral, therapeutic and curriculum responsibilities is to think about the relationship you would have with a student in each role.

In PSHE education your responsibility is to plan and implement a curriculum which inevitably touches on some of the most personal aspects of a student's life. We have seen how students need to feel safe and supported in the classroom if they are to discuss some of the sensitive issues which PSHE education includes – gender identity, personal relationships, body image, diet and other lifestyle issues. Nevertheless, one of the techniques we encourage you to use is 'distancing', so that students begin by considering how a topic affects someone else (using a fictitious case study) rather than themselves. We also emphasise the importance of drawing on personal experience and building in time for personal reflection, so that students can think about how what they are learning applies in their own lives.

As a PSHE teacher your focus is on ensuring that all students, no matter their prior learning or circumstances, can access the knowledge, understanding and skills they need and to have the confidence to act on their intentions. You may be aware that students have particular concerns or needs, but while you should make sure that students are aware of services which can help them, it would be inappropriate to give personalised advice to individual students in a PSHE education lesson.

As a tutor answering to a year head or learning manager your pastoral responsibilities include enabling every young person in your class to be ready to learn. This might mean helping them to manage friendship issues, dealing with disruptive behaviour or supporting them during a difficult time at home. Your support will be individual and specific to each young person's needs. You might liaise with another member of staff, with family members or with student support staff, or with an external agency such as a social worker or specialist service. In this situation it is likely that your role will be directive; that is, that you will be encouraging a student to follow specific advice which will help them resolve the particular concern.

In contrast, therapeutic interventions, including counselling, are often described as non-directive. A therapist will develop a relationship with a young person in which their feelings and thoughts are accepted – although the aim might be to reduce any associated harmful behaviour. Key to the success of therapeutic interventions is trust, and this relies on the development of a relationship in which there is unconditional positive regard of the therapist for the young person, as well as empathy and congruence (sometimes described as authenticity).

Trust also depends to a large extent on the expectation of confidentiality. While professionals working with young people cannot promise confidentiality, this means that a therapist is unlikely to share with teaching staff the content of the discussions they have with a young person.[1] The therapist's prime concern is not what the young person is learning, or whether they are ready and able to learn, but for their mental and emotional wellbeing as an end in itself. However, they will recognise that a young person who is more able to learn and achieve their academic potential is a legitimate and beneficial outcome of their work with the young person.

Consider

How do these same relationships appear from the point of view of a young person? In one context it might be inappropriate for a young person to talk to you about the personal implications for them of the topic under discussion, while in another it might be openly acknowledged as causing concern to themselves and others. In a therapeutic setting the young person themselves will decide what will be discussed, and when.

---

[1] Counsellors are bound to report anything that suggests a child or vulnerable adult is at significant risk of harm. However, they will balance the right of the young person to confidentiality with the possible outcomes of disclosure and involve the young person as much as possible in deciding what is disclosed, how and to whom. A Service Level Agreement or Memorandum of Understanding between schools and services should set out the procedures to follow (BACP, 2015).

Consider

Is it possible for one adult to manage three different relationships with the same young person? PSHE teacher and counsellor seem to be at opposite ends of a continuum, with the pastoral role of the form tutor or year head somewhere in the middle.

The complexity of these different relationships is one reason why we recommend PSHE education is not delivered solely through the tutorial system (see Chapter 4). The following example brings this challenge into sharp focus – where the way pastoral and curriculum priorities are managed can make a real difference to the outcomes for a young person.

Example

Malina is in your Year 11 form. Recently, she has lost a lot of weight due to an eating disorder. This includes a very restricted diet, making herself sick after meals and excessive exercise. She often feels cold and dizzy and is not concentrating in lessons because she is hungry and so thinking obsessively about food all the time. She avoids eating at school because her friends are constantly discussing 'being on a diet' while eating what Malina regards as unhealthily. Although Malina's friends are concerned about her obvious weight loss, none of them has commented on it, which makes her feel that she is still not thin enough. Malina's parents are concerned and are in contact with the year head. Malina has been referred for an assessment at an eating disorders clinic.

   The year head has brought this to your attention as the PSHE programme for next term includes body image and is delivered by form tutors.

   Can you, as Malina's form tutor, wear two or more hats at once: being responsible for the learning of a whole class of students while recognising the specific needs of Malina and her friends? What model of organisation would offer the best of all worlds for this vulnerable young person?

The role of the form tutor in personal development

The role of the form tutor is clearly complex, bridging as it does the divide between PSHE education and therapeutic approaches, contributing to both academic and personal development.

Consider

Think back to your secondary school. Can you write a job description for the role your form tutor fulfilled?

How important do you consider your form tutors were in your personal development?

The role and 'status' of the form tutor can vary depending on the organisation of the school. Some schools place the form tutor at the very centre of the young person's learning, having oversight of their academic progress, acting as a mentor or coach and liaising with other colleagues to monitor their students' work. (In independent schools this role could be fulfilled by house master or mistress.) Occasionally tutors may find themselves acting as an advocate representing less articulate members of their form who may be experiencing difficulties.

In other schools the form tutor can be little more than an administrator ensuring that the organisational arrangements of the school are carried out effectively (e.g. registration, room changes, chasing missing homework, distribution of reports and the day-to-day management of the form).

At either extreme we can see a distinct difference between a subject teacher's role and that of the tutor: a subject teacher can recognise when a young person is having difficulties with their subject; the tutor can identify when a young person is having difficulties in *every* subject. Although a little simplistic, you might consider the relationship between subject specialists and young people usually to be focused on learning in their academic subject; the relationship between the tutor and student usually to be focused on the young person.

The role of the tutor also depends on the structure and organisation of a school. In some schools the form tutor goes through the school with the students, forming a lasting connection with them as they progress through their education. This can be of real benefit if the relationship is positive but can be problematic if the relationship is less so. In others the tutor remains within a single year group, specialising in the needs associated with that group, such as transfer from primary school or preparation for external examinations. Other schools operate a house system to promote integration across different year groups. Vertical tutor groups offer a form of crossover between these models where students from Year 7–11 mix.

Form tutors usually work under the leadership of either their head of year, head of house or learning manager, depending on the structure of the school. Some schools also employ a pastoral support team who, whilst not necessarily teachers, may be trained in counselling and coaching and who are available to work directly with students who require pastoral support.

Crucially tutors may also be responsible for teaching the PSHE education programme, and if this model is chosen it will sometimes be referred to as the 'tutorial programme' (see Chapter 4).

At some level, however, all form tutors have a responsibility for personal development of the young people in their tutor group or house, which is often described as 'pastoral care'.

Pastoral care

Consider

The PSHE Association has provided a useful definition of PSHE education. How would you define pastoral care in schools?

Most writers on the subject (excluding those which relate to the role of a priest or other religious leader!) tend to describe pastoral care as a form of counselling on the one hand or as PSHE education on the other.

Michael Marland was primarily concerned with the way pastoral care was organised in a secondary school and wrote what is arguably the first book for schools with pastoral care in the title: *Pastoral Care: Organising the Care and Guidance of the Individual* (1974). The subtitle to his book perhaps gives us a definition we can work with. He saw pastoral care as encompassing both PSHE education *and* counselling, writing about the 'pastoral curriculum' which includes many of the topics we might expect to see as part of PSHE education (sex and drug education) and careers (preparation for the world of work). He also described counselling (provided by the school) as 'an additional tool for the pastoral system'.

Missing from Marland's model are the responsibilities of schools for the behaviour and safety of students. It is interesting that while in England Ofsted makes no mention of pastoral care, there is a clear emphasis on these two elements (Ofsted, 2015). If we combine Marland's view from the 1970s with the view of Ofsted 40 years on, pastoral care in secondary schools in England could be summarised as shown in Figure 13.1.

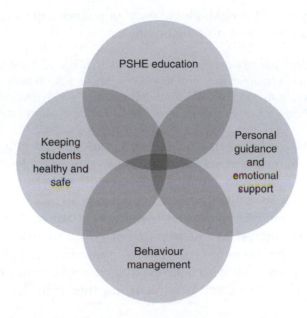

Figure 13.1 Pastoral care in English secondary schools, 2016

Consider

Think back to your experience as a student at secondary school. How did your school organise the 'care and guidance' of students? Were you aware of your tutor, year head and/or senior teachers all playing a part in supporting you or other students? Perhaps you went to a boarding school. How was pastoral care organised in this setting?

Is there anything you would add to or change to Figure 13.1 based on your experiences then and now?

However your school has shaped the role of the tutor, the pastoral relationship between teachers and young people can be very powerful. Bowlby, who first wrote about attachment of infants to their mothers, also argued that:

> human beings of all ages are happiest and able to deploy their talents to best advantage when they are confident that standing behind them, there are one or more trusted persons who will come to their aid should difficulties arise. (1979: 103)

One of the key areas YoungMinds (www.youngminds.org.uk) identifies that helps build resilience is that of 'belonging':

> When a student has good relationships in their life, and they belong to a group that accept them as they are, this helps create a good sense of self and identity. Tutors can help by trying to encourage good relationships with friends, teachers and other members of staff. (Taylor et al., no date)

Good relationships between teachers and students can help young people to engage more effectively with schools, can be protective and help young people feel able to ask for support that can help remove barriers to learning such as bullying. Teachers can also act as role models. Werner (1995) found, in her Kauai Longitudinal Study, that role models helped protect high-risk children from several risks they faced. Regardless of the source (e.g. family member, neighbour, school teacher), having an adult who demonstrates positive behaviour and support towards a young person is a recurring theme in the development of resilience.

If a young person has one adult in school with whom they have a pastoral relationship, that is beneficial, but research into resilience also suggests that it is connectedness to the whole school which offers the most protection to young people, especially those who are vulnerable in some way.

McLaughlin and Clarke (2010) reviewed the evidence for the impact of school experience on mental health of young people and looked at the relationships with teachers as well as with other students. It became clear that another important role for a form tutor is to help young people to develop and sustain interpersonal relationships. While this may be a focus for tutors of students who have just started secondary school, it continues to be an important factor as young people's identities grow and change throughout their years at secondary school.

Research in the UK and the USA indicates that the individual factors that are related to academic success in school are the same as those which promote emotional wellbeing. According to McLaughlin and Clarke (2010) these are: persistence; having positive goals; feeling part of a social group; being engaged in something worthwhile; having a sense of competence and of safety; developing a capacity for problem solving; and a sense of self-efficacy – that they can achieve what they set out to do. Among early adolescents a sense of fairness is also paramount in their relationships with teachers. These attributes arguably don't just emerge from trying to shape or change the behaviour of individual students, but from the sense of connectedness they (and to some extent their parents and carers) feel towards the school.

Consider

The Centre for Disease Control and Prevention (CDC) in the USA has summarized the strategies that contribute, in practice, to school connectedness (CDC, 2009):

1. Create decision-making processes that facilitate student, family, and community engagement; academic achievement; and staff empowerment.
2. Provide education and opportunities to enable families to be actively involved in their children's academic and school life.
3. Provide students with the academic, emotional, and social skills necessary to be actively engaged in school.
4. Use effective classroom management and teaching methods to foster a positive learning environment.
5. Provide professional development and support for teachers and other school staff to enable them to meet the diverse cognitive, emotional, and social needs of children and adolescents.
6. Create trusting and caring relationships that promote open communication among administrators, teachers, staff, students, families, and communities.

There are many similarities between the strategies that promote school connectedness and those underpinning the Healthy Schools approach (Stewart et al., 2004; Stewart-Brown, 2006).

Therapeutic interventions – what can a school do?

In Chapter 2 we explored not just how cognition changes during development but also the impact of puberty on identity. Erikson's idea of a psychosocial crisis in adolescence provides therapists who work with secondary school age students with a useful framework (Erikson, 1968; Kroger and Marcia, 2011). They recognise that to some extent it is normal for young people to be anxious and to be in conflict with authority figures as they actively redefine their relationship with their parents and move towards a settled adult identity. Coleman's focal theory of adolescence also reminds us that most young people are active agents in managing their mental and emotional wellbeing (Coleman, 2011).

However, for some young people their levels of anxiety and conflict become a cause for concern for themselves and for others. There is some evidence that mental and emotional wellbeing of young people in the UK is worse than it was in the past. A study by UNICEF (2013) found that young people in the UK scored very low in measures of wellbeing when compared with other relatively wealthy countries. The proposed reasons for this have been the subject of debate but include:

- increasing social and economic inequality
- changing family structures and greater economic dependence on parents for a longer period
- increasing expectations of academic achievement
- changing patterns of youth employment
- impact of difference in youth culture
- changes in the nature of peer relationships and how young people spend their leisure time, including spending less time with adults
- greater availability of alcohol and other drugs
- social change affecting young men and their relationships.

(based on Holliday, 2014)

These different pressures can lead to some young people feeling worthless or powerless and out of control. This can manifest in withdrawal and depression, self-harm and eating disorders. Young people who have experienced serious neglect, physical or sexual abuse or witnessed the abuse of others can develop post traumatic stress disorder (PTSD). It is no surprise that some young people attempt to self-medicate for these disorders, for example with drugs and alcohol, or seek comfort through inappropriate sexual relationships.

As a form tutor you may be the first to be aware of the impact of mental and emotional problems for a young person. It is important not to jump to conclusions but to follow up your concerns by talking to a more senior member of staff who will be able to support the young person and put an appropriate response in place.

Young people with an eating disorder or other specific mental health need require specialist support, usually through the Child and Adolescent Mental Health Services (CAMHS) or a specialist eating disorder team. Young people may spend a period of time in hospital if they are experiencing a crisis. There is not scope to go into depth about the range of therapeutic interventions in this chapter, but those that are used most often, and most effectively, depend on the therapist's understanding of the developmental stage of the young people they are working with. For example, cognitive behaviour therapy (CBT) is often used to help people with anxiety disorders such as panic attacks, phobias and obsessive compulsive disorder (Holliday, 2014). As the name implies, CBT is based on the understanding that a person's thinking has become distorted or even disordered.

Case study: Leanna's story

Leanna was learning to drive. After each lesson her parents asked her how it went. Her reply was always about the mistakes she had made, how 'bad' a driver she was and how she would never pass her test. She was becoming anxious before each lesson and was even finding excuses to cancel lessons. Her driving instructor was unaware of this and was actually pleased with her progress. Leanna's parents decided to change their approach and began to ask her to tell them what went well in the lesson and then what they could help her to practise between lessons with her driving instructor.

Leanna's parents recognised her tendency to recall only the negative aspects of an event and helped her overcome her anxiety by encouraging her to recall the positive elements of the lesson and by giving her practical support and encouragement to deal constructively with the negative elements. In some respects this mirrors how a cognitive behavioural therapist might work, which is to redirect negative thought processes to more positive ways of thinking which enable growth and change.

Being able to use CBT depends to some extent on the stage of cognitive development of the young person, in particular they need to be able to:

- monitor affective states
- reflect on automatic thoughts
- distinguish between thoughts and feelings
- engage in thought appraisal and cognitive restructuring.

(Holliday, 2014)

Most therapists agree that young people aged 12 years and above would be able to benefit from CBT and related approaches.

Some approaches to mental health used in schools

Mindfulness

Mindfulness is an approach that is increasingly used in secondary schools to support students' emotional wellbeing. It is based on Buddhist practices of meditation, and in experienced practitioners has been shown to affect parts of the brain associated with emotion, decision making and attention (Taren et al., 2013; Fox et al., 2014), all of which are developing rapidly in adolescents. There is also evidence that mindfulness based cognitive therapy can help people with mental illness such as depression (NICE, 2004).

Consider

According to the Mindfulness Centre at the University of Oxford, mindfulness is

an integrative, mind-body based training that enables people to change the way they think and feel about their experiences, especially stressful experiences. Mindfulness

- helps people to pay attention to thoughts, feelings and body sensations, to become directly aware of them, and better able to manage them
- has deep roots in ancient meditation practices and also draws on recent scientific advances
- is of potential value to everybody to help find peace in a frantic world.

People who have learned mindfulness

- experience long-lasting physical and psychological stress reduction
- discover positive changes in wellbeing
- are less likely to get stuck in depression and exhaustion, and are better able to control addictive behaviour.

Solution focussed approaches

Some schools have adopted 'solution focussed approaches', which enable those responsible for pastoral care to have constructive conversations with young people. Solution focussed approaches borrow some of the ideas of counselling without crossing over into therapy, which requires years of training, practice and clinical supervision (where a therapist discusses their work with clients with a more experienced therapist).

HandsOnScotland has some advice on how to use these and other approaches with young people:

Solution-focused questions are designed to help people explore their strengths and resources rather than concentrate on their problems and deficits. The questions can help a young person identify what their goals or preferred future will look like when they have overcome their problems or challenges. They help the young person notice things in their lives that are going well or parts of their goals that are already happening. The techniques are very appropriate to older children and adolescents and can be easily learned and are usually safe to practice. (HandsOn Scotland, 2016)

We recommend that interventions like mindfulness or solution focussed approaches should only be used as part of a whole school approach and not attempted by an individual teacher without the support of their manager.

Young people with a specific mental health need such as anxiety or an eating disorder require specialist support, usually through CAMHS or a specialist team. As well as these services available in the community, however, many secondary schools offer counselling and other therapeutic services such as art or drama therapy on site, and many young people find these short interventions helpful. Young people can be assessed by a member of the pastoral support team and referred, or can self-refer; in some circumstances an external agency such as social services may refer a young person for counselling and ask for this to be delivered on school premises if the young person is comfortable with that arrangement.

Relationships between therapeutic services and schools

There is a range of ways in which schools provide counselling and other forms of therapy. Some employ trained counsellors directly, others act as a host for an external agency whose staff operate on a peripatetic basis by providing a room which a therapist can book and use with students. In some cases schools employ an agency to provide a service in their school. No matter what the financial arrangements, the more school staff and therapeutic services work in partnership, the better the outcomes for young people are likely to be.

Case study: Jack's story

Jack is 14 and has been in foster care since he was a baby. Jack's mother is addicted to class A drugs and he has only infrequent contact with her. He does not know his birth father. Since Jack was 11 he has been fostered by his aunt who also has two younger children of her own. Because Jack is in the care of the local authority there are regular personal education plan meetings with his social worker, head of year and his carers. Recently Jack's behaviour at school and at home has become a cause for concern. Jack has had several short periods of in-school suspension and one temporary exclusion for fighting. Jack's aunt says she is beginning to be afraid of his temper especially now he is so big and strong. She also describes how the relationship between Jack and her own children has 'turned nasty'. However, she does not want her relationship with Jack to break down as she knows this will only lead to worse outcomes for him in the long run.

Jack's school 'buys in' a counselling service provided by a national children's charity. The counselling service manager attends regular inclusion panel meetings with the pastoral care team to discuss the social, emotional and learning needs of individual students. Together they discuss not only what they can offer, but also how best to approach to Jack and his foster family so that they feel supported. They decide to offer Jack eight sessions with the counselling service. Jack's foster carers are also offered a place on a parenting teenagers course, which the school has hosted for several years.

The work the counsellor does with Jack is confidential. However, his needs continue to be discussed in inclusion panel meetings. Teachers are made aware of the overall approach counsellors are using to help Jack manage his anger and feedback to the year head how Jack is coping in lessons and form time.

Jack's story is an example of really good practice of a school working in partnership with another organisation to support a vulnerable student and his family. Although initially Jack felt he had been sent to the counsellor because of his 'bad behaviour' he soon found that having someone he could confide in about his feelings was really helpful. He built up a good rapport with his counsellor who acknowledged his hurt, angry feelings and helped him to develop strategies for 'cooling off' when he felt his temper was getting the better of him.

Jack's aunt found that the parenting course provided some useful strategies for improving their relationship. It was also a really good opportunity for her to talk about Jack's situation in a supportive setting and see that while some of Jack's behaviour was related to his circumstances, some was what she described as NFA – normal for adolescents!

The postscript to this story is that as Jack felt more confident to express his feelings verbally, he settled down in lessons, had no more suspensions or exclusions and got seven good GCSEs. He is now attending the local further education college.

Our experience of schools suggests that this example of good practice is not universal. Some counsellors see their work as separate from the aims of the school, while some schools see the emotional wellbeing of students as the responsibility of the service they purchase to address this. In both instances teachers can feel frustrated by a lack of feedback from counsellors, which they believe could help them support a young person in the classroom.

Ultimately creating the kind of environment in a school in which professionals can share appropriate information about students and reach out to their families without breaching confidentiality is led by senior managers. Inclusion or pastoral meetings between professionals with complementary responsibilities can help bridge the divide. The Department for Education has recently published guidance for schools on counselling services in schools (DfE, 2015).

Chapter overview

In this chapter we have looked at the connections, and boundaries, between PSHE education, the pastoral role of the form tutor and therapeutic interventions. While in some schools these elements are well defined and distinct, in others there may be grey areas. It is clear, however, that secondary schools, their staff and the agencies with which they interact have a powerful contribution to make to the overall development of young people, not just to their academic success.

Further reading

Marland, M. and Rogers, R. (2004) *How to be a Successful Form Tutor*. London: Continuum.

Although slightly outdated in its references to the National Curriculum and other policy areas, this book still provides food for thought and practical ideas for managing tutorial sessions in secondary schools.

McLaughlin, C. and Holliday, C. (2014) *Therapy with Children and Young People*. London: Sage.
An excellent overview of the different approaches to therapy with children of school age, including organisational issues such as safeguarding and working with families.

Kyriacou, C. (2009) 'The five dimensions of social pedagogy within schools', *Pastoral Care in Education: An International Journal of Personal, Social and Emotional Development*, 27(2): 101–108.
This article looks at the potential role of 'social pedagogy' in UK schools based on approaches more common in other parts of Europe. It highlights the importance of care and welfare, inclusion, socialisation, academic support and social education and the potential for a new professional role as a social pedagogue in schools.

References

Bowlby, J. (1979) *The Making and Breaking of Affectional Bonds*. London: Routledge.

British Association for Counselling and Psychotherapy (BACP) (2015) *Ethical Framework for the Counselling Professions*. Lutterworth: BACP.

Centers for Disease Control and Prevention (2009) *School Connectedness: Strategies for Increasing Protective Factors Among Youth*. Atlanta, GA: US Department of Health and Human Services.

Coleman, J.C. (2011) *The Nature of Adolescence*, 4th edn. London: Routledge.

Department for Education (2015) 'Counselling in Schools: a blueprint for the future; Departmental advice for school leaders and counsellors'. Available at www.gov.uk/government/uploads/system/uploads/attachment_data/file/416326/Counselling_in_schools_-240315.pdf (accessed 4.1.16).

Erikson, E.H. (1968) *Identity: Youth and Crisis*. New York: Norton.

Fox, K.C., Nijeboer, S., Dixon, M.L., Floman, J.L., Ellamil, M., Rumak, S.P., Sedlmeier, P. and Christoff, K. (2014) 'Is meditation associated with altered brain structure? A systematic review and meta-analysis of morphometric neuroimaging in meditation practitioners', *Neuroscience and Biobehavioral Reviews*, 43:48–73.

HandsOnScotland (2016) 'Solution-focused interviewing techniques'. Available at www.handsonscotland.co.uk/topics/techniques/solution_focused%20_Techniques.htm (accessed 4.1.16).

Holliday, C. (2014) 'The therapeutic relationship', in McLaughlin, C. and Holliday, C. (eds), *Therapy with Children and Young People*. London: Sage.

Kroger, J. and Marcia, J.E. (2011) 'The identity statuses: origins, meanings and interpretations', in Schwartz, S.J., Luyckx, K. and Vignoles, V.L. (eds), *Handbook of Identity Theory and Research*, pp. 31–53. New York: Springer.

Marland, M. (1974) *Pastoral Care: Organising the Care and Guidance of the Individual*. London: Heinemann.

McLaughlin, C. and Clarke, B. (2010) 'Relational matters: a review of the impact of school experience on mental health in early adolescence', *Educational and Child Psychology*, 27(1): 91–103.

National Institute of Clinical Excellence (2004) *Depression: Management of Depression in Primary and Secondary Care*. National Clinical Practice Guidelines, No. 23. London: the Stationery Office.

Office for Standards in Education (Ofsted) (2015) 'School inspection handbook: Handbook for inspecting schools in England under section 5 of the Education Act 2005'. Available at www.gov.uk/government/uploads/system/uploads/attachment_data/file/458866/School_inspection_handbook_section_5_from_September_2015.pdf (accessed 6.1.15).

PSHE Association (2015) 'Preparing to teach about mental health and emotional wellbeing'. Available at https://pshe-association.org.uk/resources_search_details.aspx?ResourceId=570&Keyword=&SubjectID=0&LevelID=0&ResourceTypeID=3&SuggestedUseID=0 (accessed 24.1.16).

Stewart, D., Sun, J., Patterson, C., Lemerle, K. and Hardie, M. (2004) 'Promoting and building resilience in primary school communities: evidence from a comprehensive 'health promoting school' approach', *International Journal of Mental Health Promotion*, 6(3): 26–33.

Stewart-Brown, S. (2006) 'What is the evidence on school health promotion in improving health or preventing disease and, specifically, what is the effectiveness of the health promoting schools approach?' Copenhagen, WHO Regional Office for Europe (Health Evidence Network Report). Available at www.euro.who.int/document/e88185.pdf (accessed 4.1.16).

Taren, A.A., Creswell, J.D. and Gianaros, P.J. (2013) 'Dispositional mindfulness co-varies with smaller amygdala and caudate volumes in community adults', *PLOS-ONE*, 8(5).

Taylor, S., Hart, A. and Hove Park School (no date) *The Resilient Classroom: A Resource Pack for Tutor Groups and Pastoral School Staff*. Brighton: BOND and Young Minds. Available at www.youngminds.org.uk/assets/0001/1548/The_resilient_classroom.pdf (accessed 4.1.16).

UNICEF Office of Research (2013) *Child Well-being in Rich Countries: A Comparative Overview, Innocenti Report Card 11*. Florence: UNICEF.

Werner, E.E. (1995) 'Resilience in development', *Current Directions in Psychological Science*, 4: 81–5.

14

Selecting PSHE Education Teaching Material and Resources and the Effective Use of Visitors to the Classroom

Aim

This chapter aims to clarify how you can evaluate teaching materials in terms of suitability and quality.

Learning objectives

Through reading and reflecting on the content of this chapter you will:

- be familiar with a comprehensive set of criteria to apply to any teaching materials or resource you are considering using in PSHE education lessons
- be aware of the possibilities offered by bringing visitors into the classroom and some key professional considerations.

Before we start

Consider

What are all the elements you would look for in a high-quality resource to support the teaching of PSHE education? what might encourage you to use a particular resource? What might put you off using a particular resource?

Introduction

Some teaching resources are available commercially, some are produced by local authorities, faith groups, charities, single interest groups or 'not for profit' organisations, and others may be produced by PSHE education leads and teachers for use in their own schools. Before we consider the range of teaching resources for PSHE education, it is worth pausing. One of the most powerful resources for teaching PSHE education will always be the existing knowledge, understanding and experiences of young people in your class. By exciting their curiosity and by helping them explore their existing experiences, expectations, values, beliefs, understanding and skills, the whole class can benefit from the contributions they make in response to good classroom questioning and dialogue.

Powerful learning can be undertaken with little more than large sheets of paper, pens and a well structured dialogue that encourages young people to reflect, question and discuss. A single well chosen photograph, artefact or even a single sentence or question written on the board can act as a powerful stimulus for learning. However, there will be times when we need external resources to enrich or provide structure to our teaching and to take young people beyond their existing experience.

Choosing resources for PSHE education can be a daunting task. They range from paper, DVD, online and even to people in the form of 'theatre in education' or 'visiting speakers'.

Print or electronic teaching resources tend to come in two broad categories: those that offer teachers an entire 'programme' and those that focus on a single issue or element. Some will have been field trialled in classrooms whilst others will not. Some will be based on sound educational theory whilst others will not. Some will be based on research gathered from young people to ensure that the authors really understand their starting point and learning needs, and some are not. Some will be free whilst others can cost a significant amount of money. Some will promote a specific message, such as abstinence, or be backed by an organisation that has a broader social, charitable or spiritual basis or come from sources with vested or commercial interests. You need to be aware of all these possible sources and how their message may be influenced by a particular point of view. Sifting evidence based approaches from all these possible starting points can be challenging.

If you are unfamiliar with teaching a particular theme within PSHE education, especially a more sensitive area, it can feel reassuring to use a published resource. However, this needs caution, as no author will understand the needs of a particular group of pupils or the context within which they live as well as experienced teachers do.

It is important to recognise that some teaching resources for PSHE education may have sponsorship or endorsement from nationally recognised figures or organisations. Sadly this does not always equate to sound educational practice. The PSHE Association quality assures material that meets standards of good practice and this can offer a starting point for selecting material (see https://www.pshe-association.org.uk/). Never be frightened to adapt any resource if you feel it will better address your group's needs. Never be frightened to reject any resource if you feel it is inappropriate or fails to meet the needs of your young people.

'Human teaching resources'

Visitors to classrooms bring different qualities, which are explored in greater depth below. Whilst there are experts in the knowledge or 'facts' associated with many of the sensitive issues that teachers of PSHE education will address, this expertise does not necessarily translate into an expertise in teaching and learning. Visitors skilled in their own field do not automatically have the experience and understanding to explore the values or develop the skills pupils will need to first process and then make use of new knowledge. Many will be driven by a genuine passion for prevention, having seen for themselves, for example, the devastating effects of road traffic incidents, bullying or knife crime. However, they might not be aware that attempts to shock or frighten are counterproductive in PSHE education (UNODC, 2004:Ch.3). Always consider how to get the best out of these 'human resources' for the young people you are teaching, plan the lesson together, ensure the visitor is prepared and able to meet *your* learning objectives rather than expecting you to provide a platform for them to meet objectives of their own, and never expect a stand-alone or one-off input to be enough.

Bear in mind that any programme should be led by the needs of young people, not the sequence or structure of a resource. Therefore first establish your students' learning needs and then your learning objectives and intended learning outcomes; only then look through resources for materials that will help you to meet them, not the other way round. When starting out as a teacher of PSHE education you may be given a scheme of work that lists the resources available in school for each medium-term plan and from that you are required to plan your own lesson. Tempting though it is to look through all the resources and select materials or activities that you feel you could or would like to use in a lesson and then plan a lesson that allows you to use them, this may not be the best course of action. Think about what it is you want the young people to be able to do, say, understand, feel by the end of the lesson that they couldn't before (i.e. your intended learning outcomes) and then assess each activity or resource's potential to help you achieve those outcomes with your group.

In the real world, effective, comprehensive resources will often give you teaching ideas that you might not have thought of yourself so there is a balance to be struck. You need to know what your young people will need and how to judge the quality and relevance of teaching resources before investing in new ones.

The majority of teachers will naturally want to adapt any resource to either meet their students' particular needs or their own personal teaching style. In the hands of a good teacher, many resources end up more as a stimulus for the lessons that are taught than as a 'script' that they follow.

Practical criteria

Whilst it may not be your decision, a personal log, exercise book or folder (either in hard copy or electronic) is a must. Whilst the onus in a PSHE education lesson is not primarily on written work, it is important that young people have somewhere to reflect and record their own learning, for them to keep all their work together and for you and them to measure their progress.

If a resource is accessible online do you have sufficient access to computers? Will all young people be able to interact equally with the material? Do you have the technical ability and confidence to use the resource effectively in the lesson? Will using the online resource enhance the PSHE education learning or will the lesson become 'about' using the resource?

Resources that offer worksheets also need careful scrutiny. Poor PSHE education frequently consists of 'death by worksheets' – an unhelpful preponderance of non-interactive written work on individual sheets. Worksheets should not be wholly dismissed as a teaching and learning tool, however. There is a world of difference between one that offers only closed questions requiring responses limited to answers that have already been determined by the author, and one that asks open-ended questions that demand independent enquiry, locating and evaluating sources of information and presenting and evidencing findings, whilst valuing young peoples' differing opinions and experiences.

The critical question when looking at worksheets, whether paper or electronic, is to see each as an individual resource within a wider programme and apply the criteria we have outlined below.

Educational criteria

Now consider the educational criteria that should be applied to any potential PSHE education resource. Some will be 'deal breakers' (e.g. if the values promoted by the resource are not congruent with the school's, you will probably wish to reject it), whilst others such as failure to offer ideas or material for assessment could be overcome but will require you to do more work.

Some questions to consider when determining whether a resource meets best practice principles

First things first:

- *Are the underpinning values and beliefs stated and are they consistent with those of our school?* Some resources are produced by organisations that promote, either overtly or more subtly through the material offered, a set of values or beliefs. Are these values congruent with your school's overarching values? Are the values promoted by the resource congruent with relevant school policies?
- *Is it inclusive?* Will all young people be able to interact with it? Will some be left behind? Does it allow you to differentiate the learning outcomes and activities for individual young people?
- *Are the materials free from stereotypes?* Look at images and case studies in particular. Do the images of young people send any 'hidden messages'? For example, do they all look like fashion models (all slim, all 'good looking', no one with a single spot or wearing glasses)? Ask yourself, 'Will my pupils be able to see themselves in this resource?' or

would they say, 'These people are nothing like me, my friends or my family'. Does the material offer images or scenarios that are stereotyped or focus on the 'extremes of behaviour', for example are all images of young people who are portrayed as bullies scruffy in appearance or obviously look aggressive? Do all drug users portrayed use 'class A' drugs such as heroin and look like they are about to drop dead at any minute? Ask yourself, 'Is this relevant to my students?'

- *Do the materials take account of religious, cultural, physical, sexual and gender diversity and special educational needs? Are they inclusive?* Whilst overtly addressing this full range in each individual lesson might be difficult, what about the overall resource? Each learning experience should enable every young person to 'recognise themselves' in the learning and be able to create their own personal meaning.
- *Might the resource inadvertently encourage or assist young people in being more committed or more competent in risky behaviours?* (See Chapter 3.)
- *Has the material been developed in consultation with young people and teachers and has its effectiveness been evaluated?* It is important to separate the trivial from the significant. Strong resources are based on research into how young people of the target age are making sense of their world and provide flexible learning that provides an initial direction and structure that teachers can 'fine tune' for their groups. There is a world of difference between a research evidenced resource that has been evaluated in the classroom and one that can only claim 'pupils really enjoyed these lessons'. 'Enjoying lessons' is great, but it doesn't mean that any meaningful, relevant learning took place. Having said that…
- *Will the material be engaging and interesting for young people?* It is unlikely that a resource will have been shown to be effective if what it's most effective at is sending young people to sleep, or frustrating them but try to put yourself in the young people's shoes and ask yourself 'will this grab and keep their interest as well as fulfilling my needs for the lesson?
- *Is there guidance on how to identify students' existing levels of knowledge and understanding, skills, beliefs and attitudes and how to incorporate these into planning?* (See Chapter 5.) Does the resource offer techniques that will enable you to establish your young people's existing knowledge, understanding, values or beliefs (e.g. 'brainstorm', 'first thoughts', or 'draw and write' activities) or does it assume their prior learning?
- *Does the resource allow you and/or the young people to assess their learning and measure their progress from their starting point in terms*

of their knowledge, understanding, skills and attributes? Will it help you determine whether young people have achieved the stated learning outcomes? (See Chapter 6.)

- *Do activities incorporate a range of teaching and learning styles?* Does the resource provide a rich variety of teaching styles or is it restricted to a few? This can be less critical in a smaller resource that may provide one or two lessons but is essential in a larger, more comprehensive programme.
- *Is there guidance on evaluating activities?* This is not the same as assessment (which we address fully in Chapter 6). Does the resource provide opportunities and techniques to enable young people to feed back how useful they found the learning offered by the resource?
- *Does the material include guidance on the knowledge and skills needed by the teacher to ensure effective delivery and to help build teacher confidence?*

All these questions need to be used flexibly and to encourage reflection. Some may be less applicable than others for individual resources.

Teaching and learning

Now let us consider the teaching and learning the resource offers:

- Does the material outline processes for establishing a positive and supportive learning environment (e.g. developing ground rules)?
- Is active learning promoted?
- Are discussion and reflection encouraged?
- Do the activities cover the development of knowledge, skills and attitudes? Does it encourage pupils to share how they feel but not invite them to make personal disclosures?
- Is the content differentiated, and can it be adapted for use with particular groups of pupils?
- Is guidance given on assessing learning outcomes?

Content

Now consider the content:

- Does the content covered meet your young people's needs?
- Is the content factually accurate, balanced, objective and up to date?
- Are learning outcomes clearly stated?
- Are learning outcomes sufficiently challenging?

- Is the content appropriate to young people's needs in terms of language, images, attitude, maturity, understanding, and is prior knowledge required?
- Is the content 'inclusive'? Will all young people recognise it as relevant to them?
- Does it include positive images of a range of people, and will the imagery and language appeal to pupils?
- Do the activities encourage young people to think about their attitudes and values and take account of a range of perspectives?
- Do the activities encourage young people to reflect on their learning and apply it to situations in their own lives?
- Does the content encourage young people to obey or conform, or does it help them develop their own sense of responsibility to make safe or healthy choices?

Broader curriculum issues

If you are considering a comprehensive resource that offers a complete programme rather than a single issue resource, ask yourself;

- Does it contribute to broad and balanced PSHE education provision?
- Does the material say how it covers statutory and non-statutory learning outcomes?
- Does the resource support continuity and progression across all ages?

Activity

Consider one resource used in a school's PSHE education programme and using these criteria, work with a colleague to critically review either the whole resource or just one lesson. Where does it address the questions above, where does it not?

Now think about the young people in your school. How might you adapt it to make it more relevant for their needs? Think about their age, their ability and the locality within which the school operates.

Using visitors in the classroom

Now consider a different type of resource, the 'visitor to the classroom' and how they can support and enrich PSHE education. Visitors can make a powerful contribution to any PSHE education programme. As part of a well planned developmental programme they can add real value to young people's learning. Any visit should enrich a planned PSHE education programme and never be treated as a 'one-off' (there is one exception – see the end of this chapter).

Always check with your school leadership team the necessity for any visitor to have disclosure and barring service (DBS) checks undertaken before working with your class.

A visitor to your classroom should never be left unattended by you. This is no reflection on them, but is simply for mutual professional safety. There may be discipline problems and as the teacher you always have overall responsibility for any work a visitor does in the classroom. You should know what happens in the session, and if the visitor is an expert you can always learn something.

Why use 'visitors' at all?

Teachers cannot be expected to have a complete and current knowledge of every element of a comprehensive PSHE education programme and therefore the use of visitors is an important adjunct to many schools' programmes.

With any piece of learning the first question is always 'What am I trying to achieve?' (What are my learning objectives, the learning outcomes I expect to see demonstrated by the young people, and how will I assess these?) followed by 'Is inviting a visitor the best way to achieve these learning outcomes?', then ask 'Can this visitor provide something worthwhile that I cannot?'.

It is important to think about a visitor as a classroom resource and not as a substitute teacher. Some professional organisations provide comprehensive training for personnel expected to work with secondary school students whilst others will have little or no training or experience. An expert in a particular subject or issue may not have the skill to adjust their input and especially their language for the age and ability of your class. For this reason we have used the term 'visitor' instead of 'speaker'.

What can a visitor bring to the classroom?

- If they are competent in their own field, they can bring expertise in a particular relevant issue or topic that a teacher may not have (nor should be expected to have).

- They can act as an expert witness, recounting events in their lives from a personal or professional perspective. In this way they can help make learning 'real' (e.g. a mother with a new baby; an older person reflecting on how the community has changed; a local professional sharing their working practice; a local councillor discussing their democratic responsibility).
- Visitors to the classroom may also be older students who have perhaps undertaken research which they present to younger students or young people who have recently left the school and can talk about their new experiences in the workplace, further or higher education. This is sometimes called 'peer education', although it is more often the case that the students are older than the group they are working with. Peer education is especially valuable for the peer educators.
- All visitors have a 'novelty' value and we know that the brain finds it easier to recall novelty.

Consider

Can you recall a visitor coming into your own classroom to provide an input to a lesson or a 'talk'?

Perhaps you can recall them and have an impression of what type of person they were. The chances are also quite strong that you can't remember much, if any, of what they actually said, perhaps just one or two key points, and much of what they said is probably out of date by the time you are reading this.

Now try to recall the lesson before and after it. The chances are that you can't.

What does that tell you?

- Visitors can also establish a valuable 'first contact' to a support agency. For example, it can be really hard for a young person to approach any source of support 'cold'. Establishing a relationship in a classroom session can help to overcome this (e.g. establishing a relationship with a school nurse or a member of a national or local support agency such as your local sexual health service).

Bringing a visitor into the classroom should be an active rather than passive learning experience. Skills of interacting with a visitor are transferable, whilst the actual information they impart may swiftly date or be forgotten.

Consider

Find out how visitors are used in PSHE education programme in a school with which you are familiar.

- Why have they been chosen?
- What is it that the school believes they bring to the learning?
- How is this learning assessed?
- How is their input evaluated?

Why is it so important to consider these sessions carefully?

As the session facilitator, regardless of who is working with your class, you, their teacher, are responsible for managing the learning.

Young people are always learning at a variety of levels both consciously and unconsciously. For example, a visitor will not only be providing their input, they will also be transmitting and modelling messages about who they are as well as the values they represent officially or by association. When you invite a visitor to work with young people you get the whole package, not just the content of their input.

Consider

Imagine this scenario. A school has decided to bring in a person who has recovered from drug dependency who now offers drug education sessions through a local agency. You are told that this is a 'hard hitting' session and will discourage young people from experimenting with drugs. The person describes how dreadful life was for them and how difficult it has been to recover from their dependency. They are highly charismatic and provide a graphic description of living with serious drug dependence and their relationship to their suppliers. They talk about the steps they took to hide their behaviour from their family and friends and the effect their drug use had on them. They tell the group that most young people will try illegal drugs and so need to be warned about the dangers. Their story is genuinely harrowing. Some young people are moved to tears and they give the presenter a spontaneous round of applause at the end. After the session the young people tell you this was a really good session.

Why might you question this input? (See also Chapters 3, 8 and 9.)

Whilst there is a genuine risk of dependence in any substance misuse, young people who experiment with an illegal drug are at more immediate risk of accidental overdose, accidents or poor decisionmaking whilst intoxicated and difficulties with family and the legal system. They are far more likely to get any illicit or illegal substance from a friend rather than a 'dealer'. However, in this session they may be learning that recovered drug dependants are charismatic and have status – after all, their teacher has invited them to talk with their class. They will certainly be learning that 'most young people use illegal drugs', which is untrue. While this sort of session might be part of a former user's recovery, it is not an effective approach to drug education (see Chapter 9).

Contrary to common sense, attempting to 'shock' pupils into healthy choices (sometimes called 'fear arousal') seldom, if ever, works and can seriously backfire, neither does being moved to tears mean the session was effective. For example, some pupils may feel a sense of excitement rather than anxiety whilst others may see it as so disconnected from their reality that they make no connection with it at all.

'Interesting and enjoyable' is not the same as 'relevant and useful'.

Look back at the health action model in Chapter 3, Figure 3.1. To what extent was the emotional arousal generated by the session balanced by sound cognitive input?

Some essential considerations

- Who is/are the people you are inviting into your lesson?
- What skills, needs, expectations, experiences or knowledge do they bring?
- How do you know?

These questions are absolutely essential to consider. Never confuse a leaflet, a professional looking website or the written testimonials of other teachers or head teachers (unless you can contact them in person) with the expertise needed to work with the young people in your class. If they bring a body of knowledge, does it come with a personal message or set of attached values? Do you know what these are, and are they in harmony with your school policies?

It is important not to confuse 'passionate and well intentioned' with 'appropriate and skilled'.

Consider

Many issues within PSHE education generate strong views in different parts of society. Many of these issues have organisations for people who hold a particular position, often with great conviction, and who are keen to promote this position in schools.

In the context of a school or community, what issues do you think might need careful consideration when planning for balance?

Do we have a responsibility to consider the legitimacy of any organisation's position prior to any invitation to work with our young people?

Does the fact that we have invited a visitor imply to our pupils that we (or our school) have sympathy with their position on an issue?

Is the visitor happy to act as a 'resource' with you managing the learning, or do they expect to 'run the whole session'? If they do expect to take the lead role, are you confident that they have the teaching and classroom management skills to achieve your learning objectives and outcomes with this particular age group, in your community, with young people they have never met before?

If they have been endorsed or recommended by another organisation, ask yourself whether you have confidence in that organisation to assess the visitor's ability to work with your young people. Does that organisation have the expertise to really make a valid assessment?

In an ideal world we should try to watch any visitor work in a similar learning environment before confirming their visit to our session, but more realistically we could ask what other local schools or settings they have worked in, and talk to professional colleagues there.

There may be times when you know the visitor is expert in their field, sympathetic and friendly to young people, but hasn't the skills to work interactively with pupils. The follow-up work that you do can extend and crystallise the learning the visitor promoted. You can ask what they remember being told, how useful they think it will be, whether they still have questions in their minds about it. You can help widen and deepen their understanding. This is another reason why you need to be present when a visitor is working with your class.

It is sometimes argued that it is acceptable to offer young people a visitor with an extreme position provided you have a second speaker with an alternative point of view. For example, exploring termination of a pregnancy could involve speakers advocating both 'pro-life' and 'pro-choice' and encourage pupils to draw their own conclusions. Unfortunately it is not always that simple. If one is a more powerful or better prepared speaker than the other, there is a danger that force of personality can unbalance the rationality of the argument. Such an approach needs a strong chairperson to ensure that young people hear a genuinely balanced argument and should only be attempted with great care.

Negotiation

If you think there might be any professional role conflict (e.g. a member of an organisation or agency has a policy or protocol for confidentiality that differs from the school's), this needs addressing before any session takes place and groundrules renegotiated if necessary with the young people attending the session. Always ask:

- Does this visit fit within my scheme of work?
- Is the input relevant?
- Does it build on, extend or enrich previous work?
- Does it offer a stimulus for future work and if so, do my team or I have the skills and knowledge to capitalise on it?

What do you plan to do after the visit? Following any input it is very possible that issues have been opened but left unexplored. If young people raise questions or express anxieties after the visit, perhaps days or even weeks later, do you have a means to answer their questions or address their concerns?

Confidentiality and school policies

Consider the following questions:

- Might any young person be upset by a visitor's input?
- What if a young person becomes upset or reveals something disturbing about their own or another's personal experience?

It is wise to have a protocol in place to support any young person who becomes distressed (e.g. a member of the school's pastoral team who is aware the lesson is taking place can offer support or escalate to the designated safeguarding lead if required).

No matter what policies the visitor (or any organisation they might represent) has with regard to confidentiality, your own school's policies will always take priority. It is essential that safeguarding protocols and policies are clearly shared with any visitor to the classroom, including the boundaries about what can and cannot be kept confidential, and that these protocols and policies are fully adhered to.

Involving pupils

For a 'visitor experience' to be at its most valuable, young people need to be fully involved from an early stage. Consider the following questions in your planning and consider how your pupils can be involved at each stage:

- How has this visitor been selected? Who selected them? What were the criteria:
  - for deciding a visitor was needed?
  - for deciding who should visit?

- Were young people involved in the selection? Practically this might only be realistic if the visitor has been before and the pupils are old enough to be involved, but offering a range of possibilities, considering the pros and cons of each, is often possible if the actual visit is sometime ahead.
- What do or will the pupils know about the visitor prior to their session? Who do they work for? What do they do? What is their role? What might they look like?
- How big will the audience be? If large, what opportunity will there be to ask questions or break into smaller discussion groups?
- If you have selected the visitor, have you explained to the young people your criteria for their selection? Can you explain why you feel they can trust the visitor as a source of information or advice? What gives you confidence they are a reliable source of support?
- Do pupils already have a relationship with, knowledge of or experience with this visitor?
- How will the visitor be invited? By letter? By email? By telephone?
- Who will make the arrangements? Will they need a map? Where will you arrange for them to be met and by whom?

- How will the visitor be briefed and by whom?
- Will the visitor be provided with questions in advance? How will you balance the input of their information with young people's questions?
- If questions are to be provided, how will they be generated?
- If there are lots of questions, how will the young people prioritise them?
- Who will 'chair' the session?
- Who will escort the visitor off the premises? Who will thank the visitor, and how?
- Will the visitor receive any feedback? Will they be informed about what young people feel they learnt?
- How will you find out what the pupils found interesting or surprising? What did the visit make them think for the first time about, think more about or think differently about the issue or role? What did they enjoy?
- Will there be an opportunity for follow-up questions? Will the young people be able to forward recordings of their subsequent work, for example emailing photographs of displays?

Sometimes it will be better if a visitor interacts with one or more small groups of pupils. In the real world this may not be possible and you may be compelled to have them work with larger groups or the whole class. Again this needs careful consideration.

Consider the difference between:

- a class of mixed ability and life experience, well prepared, and arranged in groups of six, experiencing a combination of expert input and question-and-answer session, with a carefully briefed, selected visitor building on the young people's previous PSHE education learning

and

- the same class of mixed ability and life experience (or even the same class with the rest of their year group) being addressed by a speaker talking from a script about the dangers of a particular behaviour. This may be better than nothing – but not by much! The time and effort involved in the follow-up that will be needed to ensure the young people gained usefully from this would have been better spent setting up the first scenario.

Where possible, visitors need to work interactively with small audiences where young people can not only receive the benefit of their input, but can also practise the skills of gathering information from someone they haven't met before and begin to form a relationship with them and, if appropriate, their organisation.

Turn the experience 'upside down'

The best 'visitor sessions' are always collaboration between you, the visitor and the young people. For example, consider turning the session 'upside down' and making the visitor the learner, though this will need time to set up.

Ask the young people to create questions that they have about the visitor's subject matter, perhaps supplemented by your own questions. These become lines of enquiry that the class investigates. The pupils are now ready to present their findings to the 'expert visitor' who assesses each presentation with regard to its depth, breadth and accuracy and then adds anything they feel has been missed.

For example, pupils are asked to investigate how to keep safe in different situations. Now they might create a presentation to show all their key findings and messages, perhaps aimed at helping a younger class. Now picture them presenting to a visiting expert, perhaps a police officer, a nurse or a road safety officer.

You can extend this idea. What if the results of the young people's enquiry could be presented to a relevant decision maker? Could they present the information they have gathered and their recommendations to the school leadership team, the school's governing body, a local councillor or the local MP?

The 'one-off' rule exception

The only exception to the no 'one-off' rule is a response to a local, sudden and perhaps unexpected incident. Pragmatically you might realise that an immediate local danger will not be covered in your programme for some time and that young people need to quickly have their attention drawn to this particular issue or threat.

Any 'one-off', however, can only raise awareness and perhaps offer or (better) remind young people of some quick strategies. If young people need to act on these, they will still be drawing on the range of decisionmaking, problem solving and communication skills they have developed through their previous PSHE education programme.

A 'one-off' can't possibly teach all these but can connect them to an immediate threat or issue. It is highly likely that an emergency response such as this will still need follow-up work.

For example, imagine someone locally has been trying to entice or force young people into a car. In order to manage this safely, young people might require situational awareness, risk assessment and management, clear communication skills, assertiveness, controlled aggression and the ability to summon help. They will need strategies to protect not only themselves but also others if they feel they are at risk. These cannot all be taught in a 'one-off' input.

Chapter overview

This chapter set out the things to be considered when choosing teaching material and resources for PSHE education in your classroom. In particular, it warned about materials that, despite their appearance, might contain unsuitable content or represent dubious quality. We offered a set of criteria to enable you to identify good teaching material confidently. The second half of the chapter considered the use of visitors to the classroom to help enrich and extend learning.

Further reading

PSHE Association (2013) Criteria for resources: good practice principles. Available at www.pshe-association.org.uk/content.aspx?CategoryID=1048 (accessed 25.1.16).
This document summarises much of this chapter and offers a useful checklist for practitioners.

References

United Nations Office on Drugs and Crime (2004) 'Schools: school-based education for drug abuse prevention', p. 30. Available at www.unodc.org/pdf/youthnet/handbook_school_english.pdf (accessed 21.1.16).

Part Four

Appendices

In this final part we offer further material to support the guidance in previous chapters. Appendix I suggests a broad set of questions to help young people deconstruct a case study or scenario as described in Chapter 3. Appendix II summarises the different delivery models used in schools for the organisation of PSHE education discussed in Chapter 4. Appendix III comprises a sample of classroom action research tools that will provide you with the insights you need to plan relevant learning for your young people. Appendix IV provides an overview of some of the key health data for young people living in the UK in 2015.

Appendix I

Using Story, Case Studies and Timeline in PSHE Education

We encourage the use of 'Timelines' to explore stories and case studies. They are a way of relating what is happening in the present to what happened in the past and might or probably will happen in the future. Look for stories where characters are facing challenging decisions and think about these as 'the present': perhaps it is a 'crunch moment' – the moment when they need all their skills, beliefs about themselves and knowledge because a difficult decision has to be made and actioned.

If this was a DVD we have just pressed the pause button, literally putting the world on hold while we think about what to do next. The fun of 'Timeline' is that you can fast forward to try things out, rewind and try something new, fast forward months again to see how things turn out in the more distant future or rewind months to change things to make crunch moments less likely to occur or to be more easily managed.

These are only suggested questions and would need to be adapted for the ability of the pupils.

We can explore the present through questions such as:

- What do you think they are thinking right now?
- What questions might they have? (This could lead to a line of enquiry, such as imagine they ask us these questions, how would we answer them and convince them that our answers are accurate/valid.')
- How do you think they are feeling right now? Could they be having lots of different feelings at the same time?
- Do you think what they are feeling and thinking is different from what they are saying and doing? Why?

- What do you think their feelings might be pushing them to do?
- Which part of them is in charge right now? Their 'adult' or thinking self, their 'child' or feeling self or their 'parent' ought-to self? (Or do their thinking selves and feeling selves want to do the same thing or different things?)
- If you were invisible and watching from a really safe place, what would you be feeling?
- If someone who really cared for them was watching them now, what would they be feeling? Is it different? Why?
- If someone in authority was watching, what would they be thinking?
- Imagine that suddenly they can see you, but the rest of the world is still on pause. They ask your advice. What would you tell them to do? They think for a minute and then ask you 'why?' Could you convince them? What more would you like to know/need to know to really convince them?

If we could go from when this decision is being made into the future (the next day, a week, a month), what might you see? What might you hear being said? How do the people feel? How do you know? We can explore the future through questions such as:

- What do you think will happen next? Is that good or not so good?
- Is anyone 'at risk', could someone get hurt? Their body? Their feelings?
- Could anyone not actually in this present situation still end up getting hurt later? Who? Why? How? In what way?
- What could be going really well?
- What specifically could be good or not so good about the likely outcome?
- What do you think might happen tomorrow, next week, in the future if this decision is made?
- Who else might become involved in the future?
- What might others feel and say now, soon, in the future? Is that good or not so good? Are things getting better or worse? If they are getting better will it stay better?
- Can you think of better/healthier/safer ways this situation could develop?
- If you can, what has to be said or done differently? Who has to do it? What might push them forward? What might hold them back?

We can explore the past through questions such as:

- If we could turn the clock back, what do you think might have happened before this situation?
- What might they have been feeling? Were their feelings helpful or not so helpful?

- Could there have been a critical moment when someone could have said or done something different that could have stopped this situation from happening?
- Would it have been easier to have said or done something then rather than now?
- If we could have spoken to these people a week, a day, an hour, 5 minutes before this happened, what would have said to them?
- What if they asked us 'why?', could we convince them?

If we feel it is appropriate we can then take the group into the situation.

What if it were you?

- Could we ever imagine this happening to us?
- Where might we be? Who might we be with?
- What would we be feeling? Saying? Doing?
- Can we have more than one feeling in a situation like this?
- Might our feelings conflict with one another? Could they be encouraging us to do different things or even opposite things?
- What questions might we have? (How could we answer them?)
- What would be the risks for us, now, tomorrow, soon? How do we feel about this? (This could lead to a line of enquiry such as 'Who is going to research this for us and report back?', 'How will you convince us that your findings are "valid"?')
- Do we think we know enough to make a good/healthy/safe choice? One we would be happy to live with tomorrow, next week, the future? If not, what would we like to know?
- Could we have made decisions earlier that would have stopped us getting into this sort of situation? What would they have been?
- Suppose things didn't go according to what we intended and we realise we have made a bad choice, who could we talk to about it?
- Imagine we could see into the future and change it. If we could see ourselves in this situation, what would we say and do differently now?
- Imagine we could split ourselves into two and take an 'invisible us' with us. What advice would we give ourselves?
- Imagine we could take anyone we want with us invisibly – someone you know would be really good in a situation like this. Who would it be? You don't have to say – but you know who it is. Your best friend? A member of your family? A character you admire from a book/film/soap (they don't have to be real)? A favourite musician or singer or sports person? (Perhaps even your pet!) What is it about

that person that gives you confidence in them? What are they like? How do they see things? What can they do? What advice would they give you to say and do?

- Could we be held responsible/accountable for anything? Who might hold us responsible/accountable? What might be the consequences of that responsibility?

If we do take young people into a future, especially if it is sensitive, it is important to bring them back into the present. Try:

- 'Of course, right here and now in the classroom that isn't really happening. However, you may find it helpful to keep with you some of what you learned in that imaginary situation we have been exploring. It may be helpful in real life in the future.'

If you want use this opportunity to increase or reconnect young people with factual information it is important to use an appropriate language. Each of these is subtly different.

'Let's stop the story at this point and let's add something…'

1. You now know, or perhaps you already knew…
2. Imagine you have just discovered… and now you say to yourself 'I know…'.
3. Imagine telling yourself 'I know…'.
4. Imagine I told you…
5. Imagine someone you trusted told you…
6. Imagine you read…

In 4, 5 and 6 some the emphasis is on the credibility of the source of the information. In 1, 2 and 3 the language is 'clean', and encouraging thinking that begins 'I know…' can be very powerful. Ethically we should consider using this type of language very carefully.

If you are confident that all young people in a group are making unwise or dangerous choices it would be appropriate to ask:

- Now you know…, how will this change what you are going to say or do?

If you are not certain, then a softer

- Now you know…, does this change what you might say or do?

This is much safer since it allows young people with safe or healthy strategies to retain them.

You could also use stories and case studies to explore young people's perceptions about the behaviour of their peers. Young people's perceptions of their peers' behaviour or beliefs can be highly inaccurate yet may act as powerful influences on their thinking and subsequent behaviour. It is therefore really important to challenge any incorrect assumptions you discover.

Do you think this type of situation happens often?

- What do you think most young people would want do in a situation like this?
- What do you think most young people would actually do in a situation like this? (Is there a difference and if so why?)

You could open up the issue more widely:

- Do you think that many of young people of your age (a little older than you) are making these choices?
- What decision do you believe most young people make?
- How common do you think [this type of behaviour] is among young people who are[specify age]?
- What made you think this? [Peers stories? Overheard conversations? Media?]

Now, if appropriate, offer information or data that may support, clarify or challenge their perceptions.

- Do you think there might be a difference between what people say and what is really happening? Why?
- Consider this information/data from [xyz] source. Are we confident it is a credible source? Why?
- If you now know … is the real situation (e.g. only X per cent of young people your age use/do/have ever done/have ever tried 'xyz'), how do you feel now? Are you surprised? Reassured? Is this encouraging you to rethink your own choices?
- Knowing most young people actually choose …, why do you think they make this choice? Are there reasons that you would agree with/support? Are there some you would challenge?

Source: Taken with authors' permission from N. Boddington and A. King (2009) *Health for Life 15–16*. Cheltenham: Nelson Thorne.

Appendix II

Summary of Organisational Models for the Teaching of PSHE Education

Organisational model	Advantages	Disadvantages
Regular weekly timetabled lessons, plus additional opportunities across the curriculum and enrichment activities	• Allows for continuity and progression. It allows teachers and young people to assess progress and measure the impact of the programme • Works well as part of a whole school approach • Greater 'ownership' of PSHE education by whole staff team • The subject has status and profile • More likely to be valued by teachers and young people • Time available to ensure comprehensive coverage and rigorous assessment • Possible to deliver PSHE education to the same standard and with the same rigour as other subjects	• Other subjects 'lose' curriculum time for additional off-timetable 'drop down' days and other enrichment activities • Hard to monitor and assess the effectiveness and impact of the elements of PSHE education delivered through other subjects
Regular timetabled lessons for PSHE	• Allows for continuity and progression. It allows teachers and young people to assess progress and measure the impact of the programme • Time available to ensure comprehensive coverage and rigorous assessment • Possible to deliver PSHE education to the same standard and with the same rigour as other subjects. Same status as other 'non-core' lessons	• Pressure on other subjects for curriculum time, as PSHE education lessons are timetabled • May cause timetabling difficulties depending on the staffing model

Organisational model	Advantages	Disadvantages
'Rolling' PSHE education lessons: i.e. a different lesson each week is replaced by PSHE education for the whole school, usually delivered by form tutors, e.g. Week 1, PSHE education is Monday period 1, week 2 it's Monday period 2 etc.	• Can provide adequate time to deliver a comprehensive programme • Tends to involve all staff, so potential for greater 'ownership' as part of a whole school approach • Most time slots on the timetable will only be replaced by PSHE education once a year (e.g. with a five-period day, there will be 25 different time slots before the same period is 'hit' again), so more acceptable to other subject teachers as they don't feel they are giving up a regular amount of their subject time to allow PSHE education to be timetabled	• Gives a message that PSHE education does not warrant its own timetabled lesson • Can be unpopular with teachers who may still see this as 'losing a lesson', however infrequently • Cumbersome to manage for the PSHE education lead • Can feel disjointed and confusing for teachers and young people
Programme taught in form/ registration time	• May avoid some timetabling difficulties as form time is already in place and staffed	• Form time is primarily for administration and pastoral care, so it is difficult to create the learning environment that is necessary to deliver a curriculum subject to the same standard as any other • Form time is rarely longer than 20–30 minutes and often as short as 15 minutes, which is insufficient to deliver a curriculum subject • Less likely to be viewed as a 'lesson' or taken seriously by teachers and young people • Too easy to avoid teaching PSHE education at all if the teacher lacks confidence or motivation – the time can be filled with form administration, discussion etc. • Very hard for the PSHE lead and school leadership team to monitor delivery
Programme taught through off-timetable 'dropdown' days only	• No necessity to timetable PSHE lessons • Some or all of the day can be delivered by external providers • Can provide a memorable experience for young people and an opportunity to explore an issue or concept in more depth	• These days tend to have higher rates of absenteeism and those absent might miss their entire provision for sex and relationships or drug education, e.g. by missing that one day • One-off events can be memorable but the learning is very short-lived unless it is prepared for in lessons in the run-up to the event and embedded through subsequent lessons • It is almost impossible to assess progress over time and ensure continuity and progression with this model

(Continued)

(Continued)

Organisational model	Advantages	Disadvantages
Occasional one-off lessons or talks from 'speakers' but no planned programme	• 'Something's better than nothing'	• This model provides little continuity and progression • Almost impossible to assess learning and evidence impact • Inadequate time to cover more than the most basic course content • More likely to be repetitive year on year than developmental, or lead to a series of one-offs • Listening passively to a speaker does not allow pupils to develop the crucial skills, strategies and attributes that PSHE education aims to develop
PSHE education taught across the curriculum through other subjects	• Discrete curriculum time does not need to be found for PSHE lessons • May increase 'ownership' of PSHE education by all staff and sense of responsibility for it as part of a whole school approach	• Requires absolute commitment and 'buy-in' on the part of the school leadership team and all staff to make this model work • Difficult to ensure that PSHE education learning objectives are achieved as they tend to take second place to those of the other subject • Tends to be tokenistic without any real sense that there is an equal focus on the PSHE education objectives and intended learning outcomes • Difficult to ensure continuity and progression and very difficult to assess progress in PSHE education as opposed to the other subjects • Young people find it very hard to draw the PSHE education learning together in a way that allows them to make sense of it in relation to their own lives • Theoretically we could teach English (especially literacy) purely through other subjects, but without a developmental programme of English lessons the learning would be disjointed, each pupil's progress would be very hard to assess over time and across subjects and there would be no context through which to teach the theory, grammatical principles, rules of punctuation etc. in a way that allowed young people to really process and master them. The most effective way to teach English is with a coherent programme taught through discrete English lessons, enhanced by a whole school focus on developing literacy skills through all subjects. The same applies to PSHE education!

Appendix III

Baseline Assessment Tools[1]

Bus stop people

A group of people from our school have met at the bus stop on the way home. They are talking and thinking about . . .

---

[1] These tools have been taken from: Wetton, N. and Boddington, N. (2006) *Health for Life 11–14*. Gloucester: Nelson Thorne.

Bus stop people is a simple research tool but is one of the most important. Ask pupils to imagine they meet a group of young people on the way home from school. You can vary this by making them a little older, younger or the same age. They are all talking and thinking about some aspect of PSHE education, for example they might be talking and thinking about future employment prospects (but it could be almost anything). What do your students imagine they are thinking and saying? You could also add some more clouds and ask 'How do you think they are feeling?'.

This can give both you and your young people insights into the opinions they believe their peers may hold about a topic or issue. We know these beliefs about their peers' opinions can have a strong influence on their own choices or behaviour.

You can extend this by inviting young people to draw themselves into the picture and add what they would be thinking and saying.

'Looking back – looking forward'

Looking back, looking forward is a useful research tool to help young people reflect on their past and speculate about their future. It can be particularly insightful at transitions. For example, looking back over a year at their achievements and looking forward to the opportunities in the coming year. You can add structure this by specifying some 'clouds', for example 'One thing you are really looking forward to doing' or 'One achievement of which you are really proud'.

Park bench

The park bench research tool is incredibly simple but can generate a wealth of data. Young people imagine two people sitting on a bench. One has a difficult decision to make or problem to solve, for example 'I think I am/my girlfriend might be pregnant' or 'I seem to be worried all the time'. Simply place this dilemma into one of the speech bubbles and then invite young people to consider:

- What might this individual be thinking and feeling?
- What might the person listening [perhaps them] be thinking and feeling?
- What would the person listening now say?

This can provide you with useful insight into how your young people consider the best way to manage such a dilemma.

Storyboards

Storyboards offer young people an opportunity to construct what they believe is the best strategy to help an imaginary person solve a problem and share it with you. It provides you with data concerning their current thinking about how to solve a problem, which you might want to agree with and reinforce or to challenge – perhaps urgently!

This can also offer a useful assessment tool since it can be revisited following new learning to see if young people still think it would work or if they now have new or better ideas for a strategy.

Simply put the dilemma or problem into the speech bubble of the right-hand character in box 1. Ask what they might be thinking and feeling, what the other person (perhaps your students) would be thinking, feeling and saying.

Now ask them to draw the steps they would take to reach the final square where one person is saying 'Problem solved'!

Appendix IV

Key Data on Adolescence in 2015

Adolescence is a critical time for laying the foundation for health and well-being in adulthood. Collating age specific data about this age group can lead to a better understanding of their health needs, and can help us to provide more appropriate, youth friendly health services.

In this 10th anniversary edition of the biennial *Key Data on Adolescence* we draw on publically available data relating to young people aged 10–24 years, looking at the social determinants of health, information about health behaviour and lifestyle, sexual health, mental health, physical health and long-term conditions, and use of health care services.

Demographics: There are 11.7 million young people aged 10–24 in the UK; one in five of the population. More than 20 per cent is from an ethnic minority. The majority of young people are living with their parents. Adolescence is generally a healthy life stage but those aged 10–24 do die (2,349 in 2014), often from preventable causes. Young men die more frequently than young women and the major cause of death in this age group is road traffic accidents, particularly in the years 15–24. Death from suicide is also a significant contributor, as is cancer.

Social determinants of health: Adolescence is a key period for establishing life-long health behaviours and these develop in the context of the family, school and community. These contexts can be structural, such as national wealth, income inequality and educational opportunities, or proximal, including family factors, availability of social support, and quality of the neighbourhood and school environment. Without equal access to resources and support across all these contexts, some young people are put at a disadvantage.

More than one-tenth of those under 19 are living in situations of low income and material deprivation. One in eight young people under 15 live in workless households in the UK, and 14.6 per cent of secondary school children are eligible for free school meals. Nearly two million young people aged 10–19 live in the most deprived areas of England. Nearly one in five of the 19–24 age group is not in education, employment or training. Deprivation is linked to a range of health outcomes including obesity.

Other indices of disadvantage include the numbers living in temporary accommodation, being looked after by the local authority, arriving as unaccompanied asylum seekers or being held in youth custody. Some trends are encouraging – youth custody, for example, has fallen considerably over the last 10 years. However, the needs of these groups of young people for extra support are particularly high if their long-term outcomes are to be good. Supporting good educational outcomes is key, but while 55.4 per cent of the age group achieve 5+ GCSEs graded A*–C at age 16, only 14 per cent of those in local authority care do so.

Health behaviour and lifestyle: Many life-long health behaviours are set in place during the second decade of life. Physical activity declines across adolescence, particularly for young women, and nutrition often falls short of national recommendations. Around one in five school pupils aged 11–15 are obese. Rates of smoking, drinking and drug use in this age group have all fallen over recent years, which is good news. One in ten say they have drunk alcohol in the last week, and even fewer say they are regular smokers – the lowest rates since the 1980s. Concern remains over a small group who do get drunk regularly, and data are just emerging on e-cigarettes and legal highs, new to the scene; it is not clear what part they will play in the overall picture in coming years. One-quarter of secondary school pupils say they do not get enough sleep and managing media and communications activities may be part of the problem. Use of smartphones has opened up a new world of swift, flexible communications and access to media, bringing both challenges and opportunities.

Sexual health: The average age of first heterosexual intercourse is 16. In 2013, rates of conceptions in the under-18 age group were at their lowest level since 1969, but the UK still has a relatively high rate of births among

15–19 year olds compared with other countries. The highest rates of sexually transmitted infections are among those aged 15–24 (particularly chlamydia), and continued testing is vital for this age. Primary care and community contraceptive services are important sources of information for young people aged 15–24, as is good quality sex and relationships education at school.

Mental health and wellbeing: Half of all lifetime cases of psychiatric disorders start by age 14 and three-quarters by age 24. Some estimates suggest the majority start before age 18. Yet we lack up-todate, representative data on recent trends in mental health for this age group. Older data suggest that around 13 per cent of boys and 10 per cent of girls aged 11–15 have mental health problems including anxiety and depression, eating disorders and hyperactivity and attention deficit disorders. Suicide rates have fallen since the early 2000s for this age group but there were 41,921 hospitalisations for self-harm by poisoning or other methods among 10–24 year olds in England in 2014, representing a slight rise since 2007/8. However the majority of young people rate their wellbeing as good.

Physical health, long-term conditions and disability: Although the years 10–24 tend to be a time of good physical health, young people do experience a range of short-term physical health problems and around 15 per cent of those aged 11–15 have long-term chronic conditions or some kind of disability. Approximately 800,000 teenagers in the UK suffer from asthma, 63,000 young people under 19 have epilepsy, 35,000 under-19s suffer from diabetes, 2,500 under-17s develop arthritis every year and 2,200 young people aged 15–24 are diagnosed with cancer every year.

Healthcare: Young people are regular users of healthcare, particularly primary care and community contraceptive clinics but also child and adolescent mental health services (CAMHS) and hospital admissions. Although many are satisfied with their experiences, many are not, and the proportions saying they are not tend to be higher than for other age groups. There is a particular shortage of CAMHS provision; despite at least 10 per cent of the age group having mental health problems, only 1,400 young people are referred to CAMHS per 100,000 of the population aged 0–18.

Source: Hagell, A., Coleman, J. and Brooks, F. (2015) *Key Data on Adolescence 2015*. London: Association for Young People's Health. To access the full, free online interactive PDF of *Key Data on Adolescence 2015*, go to www.ayph.org.uk/key-data-on-adolescence © AYPH 2015. This summary is the property of the Association for Young People's Health and may only be reproduced where there is explicit reference to AYPH.

Index